A Teacher's Guide to Assessment

A Teacher's Guide to Assessment

D S Frith

H G Macintosh MA

Stanley Thornes (Publishers) Ltd

First published 1984 by
Stanley Thornes (Publishers) Ltd
Old Station Drive
Leckhampton
CHELTENHAM GL53 0DN, UK

Reprinted 1985
Reprinted 1986
Reprinted 1987 (twice)
Reprinted 1988
Reprinted 1990
Reprinted 1991

British Library Cataloguing in Publication Data

Frith, D.
    A teacher's guide to assessment.
    1. Grading and marking (Students)   2. Education,
    Secondary
    I. Title   II. Macintosh, H.G.
    373.12'64   LB3051

    ISBN 0-85950-111-6 (hard covers)
    ISBN 0-85950-517-0 (paperback)

Typeset by Tech-Set, Gateshead, Tyne & Wear.
Printed by Bell and Bain Ltd, Glasgow.

Introduction

A Teacher's Guide to Assessment first appeared as a project of the International Association for Educational Assessment. It was compiled as a resource for its members who, amongst other activities, were concerned with in-service training of teachers in the construction and uses of assessment.

Discussions during and after its compilation suggested a wide range of possible applications. It could, for example, provide a reference book for senior teachers, teacher trainers, local authority advisers and course organisers. It could also be used as a self-teaching manual for teachers working on their own or for students under training.

Assessment is, of course, a very comprehensive term and the compilers of the guide are only too well aware that they have by no means covered every aspect of the subject. There have had to be a number of deliberate omissions in order to keep the guide within manageable proportions; for example, it is only concerned with the cognitive domain and there is a bias in the coverage towards the secondary level of education.

It is felt, nevertheless, that the guide presents a basic framework within which can be found sufficient theoretical and practical information, simply presented and comprehensively cross-referenced to meet most of the demands of the contemporary teaching situation.

Contents

The Contents and Possible Uses

The first three chapters introduce the reader who is interested in the 'nuts and bolts' to the main factors which need to be taken into account when preparing and using assessment.

The material provides both explanations and practical assistance through the use of examples. An extensive reading list which needs to be kept up to date is also provided at the conclusion of each chapter. The guide is, nevertheless, the product of selection, and readers, if they are to gain the maximum value, must add to and reinforce this selection from their own practical experience.

Self-teaching exercises are also to be found at the end of each chapter. These exercises are intended to help those who wish to reinforce their reading. They are aimed particularly at practising teachers, who can base their responses upon their own classroom experiences. There are, of course, no absolutely correct nor incorrect answers and the compilers regret that they cannot undertake to provide solutions on request!

Where a self-teaching exercise has been provided, the number of the exercise, for example '5.17', is shown at the end of the relevant paragraph(s). All exercise numbers have the prefix '5' and a complete index of exercises is provided at the end of the third chapter. It should also be noted that Chapter 5 has been given over to a number of longer duration self-teaching exercises which relate to the whole guide.

During the compilation of the guide, members of IAEA and others who had been asked to comment suggested the following uses:

initial training of teachers at colleges of education,
modules within a degree or diploma programme,
refresher courses for senior staff,
in-service training of teachers under tutorial guidance,
a basis for the design of programmed instructional material,
a general work of reference.

There are, of course, other possibilities.

The guide concludes with a case study designed to provide an example of how some of the issues referred to in the text might actually be applied in practice. In the view of the compilers, the case study approach has considerable potential. References to the imaginary school, Plowden Comprehensive, created for the case study, are also to be found within the text in order to illustrate particular points and a brief description of the school and its staff is given at the commencement of the case study.

Most references in the text to source material are in the form of the author's name and the date of its publication. Further details can be gleaned by perusal of the 'Reference' section at the end of each chapter.

Finally, an extensive Index and Glossary is provided with a considerable number of cross-references.

Acknowledgements

The compilers would like to express their gratitude to the officers and the members of the International Association for Educational Assessment for their help and encouragement in the provision of material and for their comments upon the original drafts of the guide. They are also grateful to those organisations and individuals referred to in the text who have given permission for some of their products to be used as examples.

The following bodies have been particularly helpful in an advisory capacity and in the provision of material:

Associated Examining Board, Aldershot, UK

Canberra College of Advanced Education, Australia

Center for the Study of Evaluation, University of California, USA

Joint Matriculation Board, Manchester, UK

National Foundation for Educational Research, Slough, UK

Schools Council for the Curriculum and Examinations, London

Southern Regional Examinations Board, Southampton, UK

Tile Hill Wood School, Coventry, UK

In conclusion, the compilers are most grateful to Mrs Gillian Kilmartin for her typing of the main drafts of the manuscript.

1

Purposes and Objectives

Chapter Contents

Purposes and Objectives

'Education is a complex process involving the selection of ideas (concepts, values and skills) and the planning of experience designed to foster mastery of those ideas in the people subject to the educational system programme. Choices must be made in the planning of the educational programme and the effectiveness of the programme must also be studied. Evaluation is, therefore, inevitable in education.'

'Evaluation in Higher Education', P.L. Dressel (1961)

WHY DO WE ASSESS?

1.1 When trying to establish the worth of anything, and hence to evaluate it, we need information and we need yardsticks against which to judge not only the information we require, but the information we receive. In education, where we are concerned with the worth of such things as curricula, teaching methods and course materials, one major significant source of information, although not the only one, is the performance of those being taught — the pupils. We, therefore, need to look for methods both formal and informal of assessing their performance. It is with these that *A Teacher's Guide to Assessment* is primarily concerned. The chosen methods must, however, match our needs as closely as possible. We have, therefore, to concern ourselves at the outset with the question 'Why assess?' and hence with purposes and objectives.

1.2 (a) Many writers have defined purposes and although the viewpoints may be different there is common thread of agreement in all of them.

    (b) Rowntree (1977) defines assessment as occurring whenever one person, in some kind of interaction, direct or indirect, with another, is conscious of obtaining and interpreting information about the knowledge and understanding, or the abilities and attitudes, of that other person. Assessment is seen as a human encounter.

1.3 (a) Harlen (1978) identifies the following reasons for assessment of pupils as part of the evaluative process: namely to:
        (i) gather information about a wide range of pupil characteristics as feedback for making decisions;
        (ii) accumulate records of progress;

    (iii) provide information from which teachers can obtain insights into their own effectiveness;

    (iv) inform other teachers who have to make decisions about the pupils.

(b) Deale (1975) provides other reasons which supplement those of Harlen and are relevant both to course evaluation and to the assessment of individuals. Namely to:

    (i) allocate pupils to sets;

    (ii) compare progress of pupils under different teachers;

    (iii) compare new teaching materials with old;

    (iv) give incentive to learning and an aid to remembering;

    (v) inform parents about progress;

    (vi) inform employers or establishments of higher education about attainment;

    (vii) decide upon entering pupils for external examinations.

(c) The reasons provided by Deale suggest a more predictive use of information gained from assessment of individual pupils. The decisions which these varied usages involve are less concerned with 'improving the pupils' learning and the teachers' effectiveness' than are those put forward by Harlen. They are, nevertheless, decisions which can have potentially far-reaching effects upon a pupil's future outside school.

(d) From these views it is possible to distinguish two groups of purposes. The first is concerned with helping the pupil and the second with improving the teaching. It is also apparent that both aspects are dynamic and involve continuous interaction between pupil assessment and evaluation of the curriculum.

(Exercise 5.1)

THE PURPOSES OF ASSESSMENT

1.4 In Pidgeon and Yates (1969) can be found a succinct statement of purposes:

(a) Diagnosis — of pupils' strengths and weaknesses.

(b) Assessment — of the extent to which pupils have benefitted from a course of instruction.

(c) Evaluation — of the effectiveness of methods of teaching.

(d) Prediction — of pupils' future performance.

(e) Placement — of pupils in the most beneficial educational situation.

1.5 Macintosh and Hale (1976) introduce Guidance as another purpose and provide some useful definitions of six purposes which seem to be a synthesis of those contained in paragraphs 1.3 and 1.4:

(a) Diagnosis — to monitor progress and to find out how the pupil is assimilating what is being taught. Specific action may be instituted as a result of diagnostic assessment.

(b) Evaluation — to evaluate the effectiveness of the teaching which again can lead to specific action.

(c) Guidance — to assist pupils in making decisions about the future, whether it concerns choice of a subject or a course, or whether it is to help in choosing a suitable career.

(d) Prediction — to discover potential abilities and aptitudes and to predict probable future successes whether in school or outside.

(e) Selection — to determine which are the most suitable candidates for a course, a class or university.

(f) Grading — to assign pupils to a particular group, to discriminate between the individuals in a group.

It is true that these purposes could be expressed in many different ways, but the meaning would not be very different. As noted earlier, diagnosis, evaluation and guidance appear to be pupil-centred, and prediction, selection and placement more teacher-centred, but feedback is a possible outcome in all cases.

1.6 The six purposes, therefore, provide a useful summary and should not be regarded as being separate. They are interdependent and there is considerable overlap when translated into practice, for example prediction and selection: in discovering potential abilities (prediction) we can obtain valuable indicators as to possible future courses for a pupil (selection).

(Exercise 5.2)

SOME ISSUES FOR CONSIDERATION

1.7 The translation of the purposes into appropriate teaching and learning situations will involve the selection of suitable techniques, but before tackling this requirement there are a number of broader issues which need to be considered:

(a) **The Different Bases for the Comparison of Performance**

(i) There is a tendency to assume that comparisons must of necessity be made between individuals. This is known as norm referencing. It has one major disadvantage in that by differentiating between individuals one is liable to reinforce failure and does not establish *per se* any externalised concept of standards. Comparisons may, however, also be made against external criteria. This polarisation between norm referencing and criterion referencing, as the latter form is called, is, as Rowntree (1977) reminds us, rather misleading in that it is too narrow. He points out that we can assess the performance of individuals by comparison, with some predetermined criterion (criterion referencing), or a norm established by colleagues (norm referencing), but it is also possible to judge them against their own previous performance.

However, assessment tends in practice to involve elements of both norm and criterion referencing. A swimming test demands certain levels of performance and is ostensibly criterion referenced and yet the criteria can change with improvements in levels of performance, for example the qualifying times for the Olympic games are governed by the norm.

A driving test demands a knowledge of the Highway Code and an ability to stop, to turn the vehicle around and to signal correctly when about to change direction or speed. All these are criteria, but the application of the criteria could be governed by norms. In this case the norm might be decided by the examiner or imposed by the Government as a measure to reduce the number of drivers on the road.

(ii) Of the three bases the third is the more dynamic since criteria will change in conformity with the student's level of performance. In practice the dividing line between norm or criterion referencing is blurred, and it is not always clear whether any distinction between them arises from the design of a particular test (and therefore reflects purpose) or whether it emerges from an interpretation of test results (which relates to usage).

(iii) Norm and criterion referenced tests have very different characteristics. The norm referenced test is a discriminating test which aims to discover how much each pupil has benefitted from the course. It spreads out the pupils as widely as possible in terms of their ability. The criterion referenced test is a mastery test, designed to establish how many pupils have achieved a certain standard, or whether an individual pupil has performed a given task.

(iv) Criterion referenced assessment uses predetermined levels of performance, assessment being made in relation to objectives (which are discussed later in this chapter). This has the obvious advantage that the criteria can be pitched at any level, the primary concern being to ensure that as many pupils as possible reach the requisite level. Typically, it is used for guidance and diagnosis. Comparison can be made against external criteria which can be adjusted to take account of a wide range of differences.

(v) The following histograms illustrate the different characteristics of the score distribution in norm and criterion referenced assessment. The norm referenced assessment has distributed the candidates over the range of marks or grades available while the criterion referenced assessment has provided a measure of the level of mastery attained by the group:

Hypothetical Score Distributions

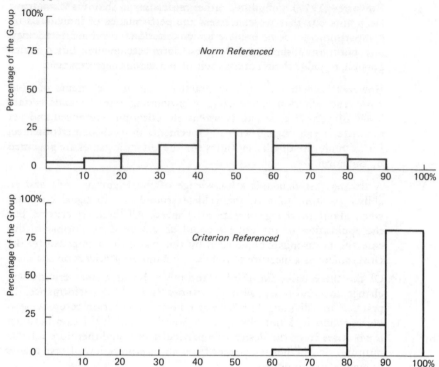

(vi) The criterion referenced assessor would be reasonably pleased with the distribution of the scores because his intention was to show whether pupils had learned well enough to attain the objectives. The norm referenced assessor prefers to set his test to ensure a wider spread of scores over a broader band of objectives, such as is necessary for grading results in public examinations. He will be able to tell whether one student is either more or less expert than another, but cannot in the end say what aspect of the subject matter has been mastered or expertise acquired. In other words, he will not be able to say whether this or that objective has been attained. In this respect it could be said that norm referencing was less helpful to the teacher. Both, however, can be said to be suitable for particular purposes.

(vii) Macintosh and Hale (1976) point out that norm and criterion referenced testing can be combined to provide a series of in course hurdles which have to be mastered before a terminal test can be taken; for example, in a course on educational measurement at MacQuarie University in Sydney, Australia, all students have to take a series of tests which are related to sections of the course. An 80% mastery is required, and the test can be taken at any time chosen by the student within the course period up to a maximum of three times. For this purpose three forms of the test, each equivalent in their demands, are used. In such a situation, the students, in addition to obtaining a result which will count towards their final degree, obtain an immediate feedback on their strengths and weaknesses in relation to specific sections of the course. This information is also available to the instructors and can be used by them to review the course material and methods of instruction. From it they can identify and remedy individual student weaknesses. Furst's paradigm (1958) illustrates the dependent elements of this process:

Furst's Paradigm

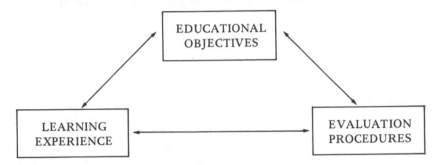

(b) The Role of Assessment in Relation to National Policy Making

It is a short step from its quite legitimate role of maintaining standards to the creation of national criteria for curriculum in schools, when objectives of assessment can become national goals. Examples can be seen in the American National Assessment of Educational Progress (NAEP) and the British Assessment of Performance Unit (APU).

(c) The Necessity for the Assessment to be Directly Relevant to the Course

Mismatches can occur when assessment is constructed by an agency other than those who are to use it. The results of an examination may be used for quite a different purpose than that for which it was designed. As a result totally wrong conclusions could be drawn which might have far-reaching effects on a candidate's future or could mean that unnecessary changes may be made to a course syllabus and to teaching methods, or that opportunities for remedial action could be missed.

(d) The Desirability of Trying to Assess the Whole Individual

Canberra College of Advanced Education (1977) suggest that the process of assessment of the individual pupil can be seen to operate at three levels:

  (i) In the classroom.

 (ii) Within a section or department of the school.

(iii) As part of the school, in its wider role as a corporate entity serving the community.

A Teacher's Guide to Assessment is primarily concerned with the cognitive aspects which can be assessed within the first two levels, but affective aspects cannot be neglected if personal development is seen as the most significant outcome of the school curriculum. Two very valuable studies upon assessment in the affective domain have been developed by members of the International Association for Educational Assessment. The first is that of de Block (1972) who has explored and formulated general cultural attitudes and developed criteria for their assessment, and the second is the project undertalen by the Scottish Council for Research in Education for the 'School based Assessment in the Affective Domain'. Another very interesting scheme is the 'Record of Personal Achievement' of the Swindon Education Authority in the United Kingdom. (Swales, T., 1979)

(Exercise 5.3)

APPROACHES TO ASSESSMENT

1.8   For translating into action the six purposes of assessment as put forward by Macintosh and Hale (paragraph 1.5) there are two possible approaches. There is the pragmatic approach which would be concerned with the actuality of the teaching–learning situation or the predetermined approach which relies upon the initial imposition of a plan. The two approaches are, of course, not self-contained and overlap considerably in practice.

The principal characteristics of the two approaches are:

1.9   (a)   **The Pragmatic Approach**

   (i)   Assessment of what is actually 'going on' in the classroom.

   (ii)   Analysis of the results of assessment to discriminate between pupils and to ensure that the assessment is well balanced.

   (iii)   The adaptation of techniques of assessment to meet opportunities presented by unexpected outcomes.

   (iv)   The postponement of final grading until all outcomes of assessment can be properly balanced and adjusted.

   (b)   **The Predetermined Approach**

   (i)   The establishment of satisfactory aims.

   (ii)   The setting of objectives by which these aims can be achieved.

   (iii)   The determination of criteria by which the progress or level of mastery of the pupils can be measured.

   (iv)   Pre-testing and post-testing of assessment material. First to establish that it is appropriate for the age and ability range of the pupils. Secondly, to ensure that it is relevant to the subject being taught. Thirdly, to ensure that the results obtained are taken into account.

   (v)   The determination of ultimate levels for mastery, i.e. pass grades.

1.10 In recent years the predetermined approach has tended to dominate assessment practices, particularly in large-scale examinations. Its influence is now, however, probably on the wane. Nevertheless, the stages which characterise this approach and which are referred to in 1.9 (b) continue to be of importance for the development of any assessment and are, therefore, considered in turn in paragraphs 1.11 to 1.18.

AIMS AND OBJECTIVES

1.11 (a) Purposes are inevitably broad ranging in scope and consequently need to be stated in more specific terms if they are to be implemented in practice. The first step in any such translation is to relate the purpose to particular courses of study and to those taking the courses. From this, aims for specific courses should emerge, stated in terms of desired outcomes. This, in turn, should lead to the selection of the measures necessary to realise these outcomes. The whole process is thus one of increasing specificity and practicality whereby broad ranging and imprecise aims turn into realisable objectives.

(b) An aim should be the product of considerable thought and discussion. It should be stated simply and concisely and should sum up what is the intended outcome in terms of benefit to the pupil, and should lead to the selection of relevant objectives.

(c) Shipman (1979) points out that the effectiveness of schooling can be judged by the degree to which the aims and objectives of a school have been attained. He suggests that a teacher can arrive at the objective of a course by asking 'What will my pupils know and be able to do at the end of their course, which at present they do not know, or cannot do?'

(d) A practical example of the problems associated with the translation of a single aim into a related set of practical course objectives can be provided by reference to the experience of the History Department of Plowden School (our imaginary school) which follows.

Claude Chippendale had produced the following aims and objectives for a Local History course for the Head of History.

Title of Course: 'History is With Us'

Aim: To make pupils better informed about their surroundings.

Objectives:

   (i) Pupils should be aware of the origins of their town.

  (ii) Pupils should have some understanding of the reasons for the town being as it is.

 (iii) The names of the famous people who lived in the area.

 (iv) The development of transport systems.

  (v) The closing of Peppermans Salt Mine.

 (vi) The reasons for Petty Poland.

(e) The Head of Department felt that the aim was vague and did not state in sufficiently concise terms what were the intended outcomes. The objectives were in consequence very vague and could in most cases be applied to other aims. Bruce Bennett, a teacher with some experience, produced the following alternative. The reader is invited to consider to what extent, and in what respects, this might be considered to be more acceptable.

Title of Course: 'Local History'

Aim: To help pupils acquire a thorough understanding of the historical background of Hadowton.

Objectives: The pupil should be able to:

(i) Describe in the correct sequence the historical events by which Little Tufton became renamed as Hadowton.

(ii) Describe how early industries (sheep rearing, weaving of tweeds and salt mining) first began, and account since then for their growth and final decline.

(iii) Explain the historical causes for the existence of a Polish minority in the area.

(iv) Explain the reasons for the success and final collapse of Peppermans Salt Enterprises.

(v) Explain how Tufton became an important part of the British armaments industry.

(vi) Describe the stage-by-stage rejuvenation of Tufton, both economically and socially, in the 1930s.

(vii) Place in historical perspective the contributions made by influential local personalities, in particular:
Elias Catchpenny
Mrs Oliphant
Sir Giles Rushton
Stefan Radezck
Lord Bligh
Stella Rothschild, M.P.
Fred Roberts, M.B.E.

(viii) Outline the fifteen points of the 1969 Hadowton Industrial Redevelopment Plan.

(ix) Account for the present pattern of road and rail communications.

(x) Plan a conducted tour of Hadowton for a group with special interests.

THE PREPARATION OF OBJECTIVES

1.12 Objectives can arouse feelings of apprehension in the minds of many teachers, for the term has a mechanistic and rigid ring. Objectives, nevertheless, are an important link in the chain between statements of purpose and the realisation of that same purpose. It is true that some teachers do not regard the need to define objectives as self-evident. What then is claimed to be their particular virtue? Macintosh and Hale (1976) liken them to pieces of lifting equipment which can 'get thought off the ground'. They urge a balanced approach to the topic and suggest that teachers can with advantage be more specific without placing themselves in a straitjacket of rigid acceptance of *the objective* as an essential factor in assessment. They suggest that the taxonomies, such as those put forward by Bloom, Ebel and Gagné, have values as stimuli. Taxonomies in the field of educational measurement provide classified lists of essential objectives. They are discussed in greater detail later, see paragraphs 1.14 and 1.15.

1.13 (a) The virtues of objectives have been very succinctly expressed in the statement that if people do not know where they are going or what they are doing, they will be unable to find out whether they have arrived or what they have achieved. At some stage in every educational activity, someone has to stand back and ask questions such as: 'What are we doing?', 'How successful or unsuccessful are we being?', 'In what ways could we do better?'

(b) This can only be done if two things have happened:

First, that statements have been made of what it is proposed should happen (the aim) and, second, that the objectives which it is hoped to achieve have been developed from that aim.

(c) These statements need to be set out, preferably in writing, so that others can read and discuss them.

It is not sufficient for individuals to say that they know what they are doing. They must be willing, and must be in a position, to discuss every stage of a proposed assessment plan.

(d) The objectives which in particular need to be exhaustively discussed should have three basic characteristics. They must state the actions to be performed by the student, the conditions under which the performance is to occur and the minimum level of acceptable performance.

Since these outcomes relate to the behaviour of the pupils, they are usually known as Behavioural Objectives.

(e) The following general rules, published by the Center for the Study of Evaluation (1978), may be applied in the construction of behavioural objectives:

(i) Objectives are used for stating ends intended by the syllabus and not means.

(ii) The objectives should indicate the level of skill attainment which it is intended should be produced.

(iii) Concrete verbs should be used so that the desired response should be observable, for example 'Write', 'List' and 'Describe', rather than 'Know', 'Appreciate' and 'Understand'.

(iv) The use of Indicators is to be encouraged where practical skills are the

subject of the objective. These can specify particular levels of proficiency, for example the ability to set up (an experiment) within
20 minutes.

This approach, of course, is based upon the premise that it is desirable to
use behavioural objectives. This is not necessarily accepted by everyone
to be the case (see paragraphs 1.17 and 1.18).

(f) The Center for Vocational Education, USA, illustrates through the following
flow diagram the whole process of preparing assessment objectives, so that
they meet the desired purposes.

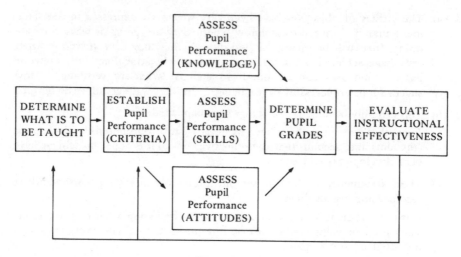

(Exercise 5.4)

(g) Examples of objectives and some notes upon weighting will be found at
Appendix B.

TAXONOMIES

1.14 (a) Since Bloom and Ebel have been referred to in 1.12, it may be helpful,
briefly, to reiterate the main items of those two well-known taxonomies.
The first, by Bloom (1956), lists six cognitive objectives in ascending order
of complexity:

1. Knowledge

2. Comprehension

3. Application

4. Analysis

5. Synthesis

6. Evaluation

(b) Each class of objective can then be broken down and expanded into sub-categories. A somewhat more informative taxonomy has been produced by Ebel (1979) which is based upon categories of examination questions and is reprinted here by permission of Prentice Hall Inc., Englewood Cliffs, New Jersey:

1. Understanding of terminology (or vocabulary).
2. Understanding of fact and principle (or generalisation).
3. Ability to explain or illustrate (understanding of relationships).
4. Ability to calculate (numerical problems).
5. Ability to predict (what is likely to happen under specified conditions).
6. Ability to recommend appropriate action (in some specific practical problem situation).
7. Ability to make an evaluative judgement.

1.15 (a) There are of course many taxonomies, for example that of Coltham and Fines (1971), based on Bloom, who suggest the following cognitive skills and abilities as being appropriate to History:

1. Vocabulary acquisition.
2. Reference skills.
3. Memorisation.
4. Comprehension.
5. Translation.
6. Analysis.
7. Extrapolation.
8. Synthesis.
9. Judgement and evaluation.
10. Communication skills.

(b) Gagne (1970), who has also been mentioned in paragraph 1.12, produced a hierarchical taxonomy based upon types of learning rather than outcomes.

(c) Gerlach and Sullivan (1969) base their system upon overt learner behaviour.

These all have their merits, but they all suffer from the inherent danger of objectives — that of restriction.

ADAPTATION OF TAXONOMIES

1.16 Taxonomies are in essence frameworks upon which to build. They need to be expanded to meet the needs of the subject being studied. An example of such an expansion, taken from Coltham and Fines, using comprehension, translation, analysis and synthesis in relation to a History Course, will be found at Appendix A. The product is four lists of related behavioural objectives.

POSSIBLE DISADVANTAGES OF OBJECTIVES

1.17 (a) Behavioural objectives have advantages in their emphasis upon the student rather than the teacher. Assessment seems at times to be conducted with the teacher in mind rather than the student. Quite often too, assessment seems to be designed to show what students cannot do rather than provide opportunity for them to show what they can achieve. The need to define objectives has been enthusiastically (and uncritically) accepted by some, and equally unenthusiastically and uncritically rejected by others. We need to find middle ground.

   (b) Hogben (1973), has offered five suggestions as pertinent guidelines for those who seek this middle ground. He does not argue for acceptance nor for rejection of classification systems such as those put forward by Bloom, but argues that a search should be made for more flexible systems which will embrace the diversity of pupils and utilise the advantages that can result from greater definition and precision. He suggests that:

   (i) Course objectives should be stated, by all means, but it is not necessary that they are all stated in highly specific behavioural terms.

   (ii) We should not be afraid to state long-term objectives.

   (iii) We should be continually on the alert for unexpected and unintended outcomes.

   (iv) In translating broad curricular goals or aims into more specific language, we should make sure that the sum of objectives faithfully reflects the full intention of the original goals which gave them birth.

   (v) We should not allow measurement considerations alone to dictate the formulation of objectives and teaching strategies.

1.18 (a) It is important that we should be aware of the possibly harmful effects of defining objectives — particularly in the context of curriculum development. Eisner (1967) is well worth reading upon this aspect, as is Stenhouse's paper (1969) on 'Behavioural Objectives in Curriculum Development — their Limitations'.

   (b) Having considered the two approaches, some thought should be devoted to the nature, or what Rowntree (1977) calls the modes, of assessment.

(Exercise 5.5)

VARIETY IN MODES OF ASSESSMENT

1.19 Rowntree (1977) answers the question about how to assess not in terms of describing a variety of techniques, but through consideration of a series of conflicting modes of assessment. These in their turn require the use of differing techniques. He identifies eight of these modes as follows:

> Formal vs Informal
>
> Formative vs Summative
>
> Continuous vs Terminal
>
> Coursework vs Examination
>
> Process vs Product
>
> Internal vs External
>
> Convergent vs Divergent
>
> Idiographic vs Nomothetic

Although the distinctions made are on occasions too fine, and there is very considerable overlap between the modes, Rowntree's contrasting presentation highlights a number of points of significance for the construction of assessment. A number of these are summarised in the following paragraphs, 1.20 (a) to 1.20 (h).

1.20 (a) Formal assessment, which aims solely at obtaining knowledge about the student, is obtrusive but has no direct instructional function. Education, as most people conceive it, cannot be measured solely by formal assessment. Informal assessment which is often used diagnostically, must be unobtrusive if the teacher is to obtain reliable insights about the pupils' abilities and state of development. The former can be said to be a 'publicly satisfied purpose for public use' and the latter as a 'privately specific purpose for private use'.

(b) Formative versus summative should not be seen as conflicting forms of assessment so much as indications of the intentions and interpretations of the assessor. The criterion is whether the teacher sees himself as getting to know the students in order to teach them better (formative) or to help others to feel better informed about them (summative).

(c) Continuous assessment should not be exclusively identified with formative assessment, nor terminal with summative. Continuous assessment may be used formatively at the time it is taking place, but may contribute subsequently to summative assessment. A teacher could dispense with terminal assessment if a satisfactory summative assessment could be compiled from a series of continuous assessments.

(d) The use of examinations cannot be justified merely on the grounds that summative assessment is necessary. A student can be assessed at the end of a course in the light of what has been done during the course and if some terminal task was required it could be something very different from what is traditionally considered as an examination.

(e) A 'product' may fail to reveal all about the 'processes' which produced it, although these may be recoverable through discussion with the student about the product. Recalling and talking about processes is not the same as demonstrating them. Processes leave their mark on the students. They help to determine not only what students do and what the students know, but also what they are.

(f) If too much reliance is put upon convergent assessment, with its rigid structure, in pursuit of comparability, measurability and fairness, more may be learnt about the similarities among students (and may help to create them), than about the ways in which they diverge. Convergers excel when rationally focusing upon a clearly defined task. The archetypal convergent form of assessment is the objective test. There is a danger that creative and perhaps idiosyncratic qualities, which are encouraged by divergent assessment will be lost, unless the task is open-ended and there is no single correct answer.

(g) Idiographic assessment aims to find out about the uniqueness of individuals, what they do, know and what they are. Formative assessment must be idiographic, but must to an extent be nomothetic as well.

(h) Nomothetic assessment collects data about individuals with a view to comparing one with another and using generalisations made from those assessed for the assessment of others. Idiographic assessment could be said to be concerned with differences and nomothetic with similarities between people.

(Exercise 5.6)

EDUCATIONAL RELEVANCE, RESPECTABILITY AND COST

1.21 (a) Further considerations in the preparation of an assessment plan, Rowntree (1977) suggests, are the criteria of Educational Relevance, Respectability and Cost. Educational relevance is perhaps the most important. We must be satisfied that a particular technique would be appropriate to the content and style of the teaching and learning experienced by the pupil.

(b) If the techniques selected are appropriate, they should also be relevant to the educational objectives and assessment constructs or goals, in so far as the content and style relate to those objectives and constructs. However, this relationship may be distorted. For example, it is only too easy to encourage History pupils to memorise facts, when in reality the intention is to help them to think historically.

(c) It is, therefore, necessary that the techniques selected must relate to the aims and objectives, and must be those most likely to produce reliable indications of the abilities or qualities looked for in the pupil. Assessment techniques should relate also to significant objectives.

(d) Rowntree (1977) points out that there are also the criteria of respectability (outsiders may only favour certain techniques, for example employers' predilection for the three-hour written examination) and cost (some techniques involve more time, materials and numbers of assessors). There are no ground rules for the manipulation of these criteria in any selection of assessment techniques, but any innovation that will challenge traditionally held views or will cost more, can only be justified by establishing its greater educational relevance.

CHARACTERISTICS – VALIDITY AND RELIABILITY

1.22 Whatever the approach there are certain rules which need to be observed in constructing an assessment plan. Assessment, if it is to adequately fulfil its purpose(s), should satisfy the requirements of Validity and Reliability.

1.23 Deale (1975) defines validity as the quality which a test should have if it is to achieve the outcome(s) that is/are intended. He suggests that there are several forms of validity:

(a) Face Validity – The test should look as if it is testing what it is intended to test. This, however, Deale warns is only the starting point.

(b) Criterion Related Validity – The relationship between scores on the test and some other criterion such as estimates or results of an external examination. These could be either:

(i) Concurrent – test results compared with another measure of the same abilities at the same time; or

(ii) Predictive – test results compared later with another criterion, such as success in a particular job or in higher education.

Criterion related validity can be important where the test is to be used to decide entries for a public examination.

(c) Content Validity – Almost certainly the most important for the practising teacher, being the extent to which a test adequately covers the syllabus to be tested. To have good content validity a test must reflect both the content of the course and the balance in the teaching which led up to it. Consideration must be given to the:

(i) Length of test. A short test could not adequately cover a year's work. A syllabus needs to be sampled and a representative selection made of the most important topics to be tested.

(ii) Selection of topics. The selection must be made and the test questions prepared in such a way that they reflect the way the topic was treated during the course. It is necessary to be quite clear as to the objectives, so that by their careful analysis and by analysis of the course content, a valid framework for the design of a test can be created.

B

(iii) Test blueprint or specification grid. Deale suggests that better content validity can be achieved by the use of a specification grid. He warns nevertheless, that content validity is very much a matter of individual judgement and can only relate to what the teacher setting the test is trying to do. An example follows of such a grid for a test in Physics (magnetism and electricity) for a group of pupils aged 13+. The teacher wishes to test recall, understanding and knowledge of certain laws and principles as applicable to:

the magnetic effect of the current

the effect of force on a conductor

electromagnetic induction

The teacher has to decide on the weighting (percentage of the total marks) to be attached to each ability and the most suitable number of questions. It is in this phase that the subjective nature of the operation is perhaps most apparent.

ABILITY TO BE TESTED	Magnetic Effect of a Current	Effect of Force on a Conductor	Electromagnetic Induction	Number of Questions
Factual Recall	4	3	3	10
Understanding	5	6	4	15
Knowledge of Laws and Principles	1	2	2	5
TOTAL MARKS	10	11	9	30

Summary — It is not an easy task to ensure that a test is valid, but since the information derived from an invalid test is not only useless but could be dangerously misleading, it pays to take a great deal of time and trouble over this aspect. The degree of validity achieved by a test can be judged through the subsequent analysis of the test results. This can provide information upon what actually happened and the results can be compared with the intended outcomes.

(d) In an interesting paper, Harte (1981) concludes that it is possible to quantify content validity in a meaningful manner by the calculation of a content validity coefficient. This would permit:

(i) Comparison of two or more examinations with each other.

(ii) Comparison of alternative combinations of questions in an examination where a choice is given.

(iii) Examination boards to set limits of tolerance within which an examination should conform to the specification matrix, and then to ascertain whether it was within the set limits.

(iv) The search for sources of content validity, either in terms of broad classifications, such as subject areas or educational objectives, or by narrowing it down to particular areas or objectives within certain questions.

RELIABILITY

1.24 (a) Deale (1975) defines reliability as consistency, meaning how far the test would give the same results if it could be done again by the same children under the same conditions. He points out that this is, of course, a theoretical definition since such conditions would be almost impossible to impose, and, therefore, a perfectly reliable test would be equally impossible to produce. The factor of variability, even if it is inevitable, needs to be reduced to an acceptable minimum, and to do this it is necessary to identify the principal sources of variability; these would seem to be:

(i) Variations in performance of the pupil taking the test. These may stem from extraneous influences such as physical or mental or nervous conditions and anxiety and stress related to taking the test. Not much can be done to prevent these factors, but the teacher can take them into account when interpreting the results.

(ii) Variations in the test. The test can only measure a small sample of a pupil's ability and a different sample could give a different result.

(iii) Variations in the marking. Except for objective tests, the marker's judgement can be as variable as the pupil's performance. The problem can be most troublesome in marking essays and is least likely to create difficulties in short-answer tests. Variations can occur for a variety of reasons: for example, as a consequence of an interruption during the marking of a batch of scripts, resulting in different standards being applied after the break; or the marker's standards being affected after marking a set of either very good or very bad scripts; or the teacher subconsciously being influenced by knowledge of the pupil whose work is being marked.

(b) The effects of the first two sources of variability can be lessened by giving a series of several tests at intervals. The third source can be neutralised by the use of several markers where judgements are aggregated, or by the establishment beforehand of firm criteria governing the award of marks.

(c) The Head of History, at our imaginary Plowden Comprehensive School, took steps to guard against variability in marking within the Department by the use of Agreement Trials. He very wisely delegated responsibility to Bruce Bennett, his most senior and well-respected colleague.

(d)   (i) At a departmental meetting Bruce explained to his five colleagues that each of their teaching groups should be set a common question. He suggested that the following, taken from the fourth year (internal) examination set in November last year, should be used:

'The Enclosure Movement took place at a time when great improvements occurred in Agriculture. Could the same improvements have been introduced during the time of the Open Field System? Explain your answer.'

(ii) Marking was to be based upon ten criteria, and these criteria were discussed in some detail and agreed. Three related to the basic skills and the remaining seven were subject based, for example understanding of the characteristics of the Open Field System. He then invited his colleagues to submit two unmarked scripts from each of their five teaching groups with the spread of abilities made up as follows:

Teaching group 4M one high one low ability

Teaching group 4N two medium ability

Teaching group 4O one medium one low ability

Teaching group 4P one high one low ability

Teaching group 4Q one high one medium ability

(iii) On an agreed date the teachers handed in their scripts and Bruce, having obliterated any indications of the pupils' identity on their scripts, gave them each an identifying number (from 1 to 10) and reproduced five complete sets. One set to be issued to each teacher with two copies of a marking record sheet which is reproduced on page 23.

(iv) When the complete record sheets had been handed in by his five colleagues and he had also marked the set of originals, perhaps as a point of honour, but maybe also as a control, he had six record sheets, these he then collated and produced an analysis, with the maximum marks reduced from 100 to 10, for distribution to the teachers. Being not only well-versed in assessment but discreet in his dealings with his colleagues, each teacher had been allocated a code letter by Bruce which only he and the teacher concerned knew. The analysis sheet gave the following information shown in the table at the top of page 24.

(v) The most valuable part of the exercise then followed. Bruce suggested that the spread of marks for each script was too large and that this probably indicated that the criteria needed to be more closely defined. The Head of Department then encouraged teachers to 'talk through' their marking of particular scripts and their application of the criteria. This was somewhat reluctantly undertaken, but Bruce was pleased to be told later by teachers C and F that they were alarmed at the difference between their marks and the norm, and found the discussion of the ten criteria very helpful, when from their copies of their marking sheet they could compare their marks with those of their colleagues.

	PLOWDEN SCHOOL — HISTORY DEPARTMENT										
	Agreement Trial (Date)										
	Marks Awarded — Out of 10 for each Criterion										
SCRIPT NO.	CRITERION										TOTAL
	1	2	3	4	5	6	7	8	9	10	
1											
2											
3											
4											
5											
6											
7											
8											
9											
10											

List of Criteria

1
2
3
4
5   (As agreed at Department Meeting)
6
7
8
9
10

Signature of Teacher . . . .

SCRIPT NO.	1	2	3	4	5	6	7	8	9	10	TOTAL MARKS	TEACHER'S MEAN MARK
	SCORES MARKED OUT OF TEN											
Teacher A	8	3	5	4	5	2	8	3	8	4	50	5.0
B	7	4	5	5	4	2	9	3	8	5	52	5.2
C	9	5	6	6	7	4	9	4	8	5	63	6.3
D	8	3	4	5	5	3	8	3	7	5	51	5.1
E	7	4	5	5	5	3	8	3	7	4	51	5.1
F	6	2	3	4	4	1	6	2	6	3	37	3.7

	1	2	3	4	5	6	7	8	9	10	
Totals (Scripts)	45	21	28	29	30	15	48	18	44	26	304
Means (Scripts)	7.5	3.5	4.6	4.8	5.0	2.5	8.0	3.0	7.3	4.3	5.06
Spread of Marks	4	4	4	3	4	4	4	3	3	3	

Conversion Graph

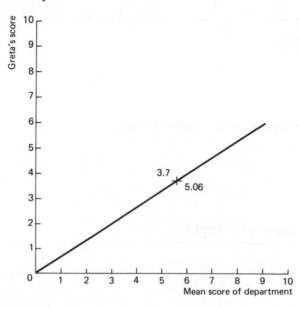

MARK CONVERSION GRAPH

(e) Greta Glover asked Bruce for some help in adjusting her marking to that of the consensus. He suggested that she construct a straight line graph (shown at the bottom of the opposite page) using her score and the mean consensus score from the agreement trial as the two bases. She could then reconsider the copies of the trial agreement scrips and adjust her scores, bearing in mind the agreed criteria. Greta was teacher F. It was, of course, very rough and ready, but if used as a check against gross discrepancy and backed up by a careful analysis of the reasons why the consensus differed (the discussion upon criteria should have been particularly helpful for this) it could check her tendency to be too severe.

FACTORS AFFECTING VALIDITY AND RELIABILITY

1.25 Deale (1975) suggests that if a teacher is to prepare tests which are acceptably valid and reliable, there are five factors which should be taken into account:

(a) Length of test. This has already been discussed in paragraph 1.23 (c) (i). A short test is likely to be less valid and less reliable than a long test (although lengthening an invalid and unreliable test is unlikely to improve it).

(b) Choice of test technique. This is dealt with at length in Chapter 2. Each technique has certain tendencies, for example, essay questions tend to be less reliable than short-answer questions. Structured essays are usually more reliable than open titles, such as those which merely state a subject title and require the candidate to 'Discuss . . .'. Improved reliability should, however, never be used as a justification for the use of an invalid test technique.

(c) Techniques of writing questions. This also is dealt with more fully in Chapter 2. Vaguely worded or ambiguous questions, trick questions or questions using obscure vocabulary or complicated syntax wil adversely affect both validity and reliability.

(d) Method of test administration. Adequate time must be allowed for the majority of the candidates to finish the test. This provision should prevent wild guessing, or slick and facile answering. Instructions need to be clear, otherwise confusion may reign and both validity and reliability will suffer. The physical conditions under which the test is undertaken must be favourable for the pupil. There must be adequate space, lighting and heating, and provision must be made for pens, pencils, rubbers, etc. Pupils must be able to work independently and the possibility of distractions in the form of movement and noise must be guarded against.

(e) Method of marking. The marking should be as objective as possible. The Appendices to Chapter 2 provide some guidelines which may be useful. Marking which depends upon the exercise of human judgement cannot be other than subject to all the variations of human fallibility. It is, for example, quite easy to mark objective items quickly, but it is also surprisingly easy to make careless errors. This is especially true where large numbers of scripts are being marked. A system of checks is strongly advised, one of the most effective being through the comments of the pupils themselves when their marked papers are returned to them. Marking is dealt with at greater length in Chapter 2, paragraphs 2.28 to 2.36.

INTERACTION BETWEEN VALIDITY AND RELIABILITY

1.26 **(a)** The concepts are considered to be 'twin', in that they are interdependent. Reliability, as Nuttall and Willmott (1972) have pointed out, is a necessary but not sufficient condition for validity. They cite as an example the golfer who, if his drive is both valid and reliable, will hole in one on each and every green. If his play is invalid but reliable, the ball will always land in the rough or in a bunker, and never in the hole. If his drives are unreliable, the ball will be as likely to go into the rough, or into a bunker, as on the green, hence his drives cannot hope to be valid. It follows that one must always take care that validity does not suffer when trying to improve reliability — reliability always comes second to validity.

(b) If, therefore, a question is believed to be valid, there is some point in working to increase its reliability. But it is important that in the process the validity does not suffer.

(Exercise 5.7)

THE ASSESSMENT PLAN

1.27 **(a)** Macintosh (1976) suggests that the first stage in the preparation of an assessment plan is to relate the purposes to the area to be studied, taking into account the age and ability range of the pupils being taught. This will provide a very general overall programme for the entire course and should indicate where particular purposes are best met; for example, diagnosis would be helpful early in the course and at perhaps termly intervals, whilst assessment of the benefits derived would be more useful at the conclusion of the course. Evaluation might have to be based upon a comparison of the results of diagnosis and the concluding assessment. Assessment, nevertheless, may be undertaken at any time if it is suspected that some anomalous situation has arisen, for example, when an individual student or a group does not appear to respond as expected.

(b) Shipman (1979) feels that the realisation of each purpose requires different kinds of information and this will be obtained in response to a variety of assessment techniques, and the kind of measurement instruments we use will be determined by the purposes we have in mind.

For outsiders, assessment can be a more meaningful process if made against external criteria rather than by making comparisons with a norm. It is a common practice for teachers to use for predictive purposes, norm referenced assessment, comparing pupils' performances against that of a group or class, school or even a nation.

1.28 Jackson and Hayter (1978) state that in framing a plan, there are some general requirements which should be met:

(a) Pupils should be made aware of the assessment procedures which are to be used and must understand the system by which final results, whatever their form, are to be arrived at. They need to be reassured of the relevance of the whole plan.

(b) The plan and the methods of assessment need to be congruent with the aims of the school, i.e. the curriculum, whether 'open' or 'hidden', the curriculum, being defined by Jackson and Hayter, as all the educational provision activity and influence of the whole school.

(c) Schools' records should be sufficiently comprehensive for the production of adequate profiles of the pupils. This is the subject of the case study in Chapter 4.

(d) A wide range of different techniques should be considered, but the basis would probably be:

Written Examinations,

Practical Examinations,

Oral Tests.

(e) Informal observation should be used to supplement the results of formal testing.

(f) The scope of any assessment plan depends upon the purposes. It is impossible to take account of everything. A selection must be made and that which is chosen must be as representative of the whole as possible. The preparation of an assessment plan is a complex process and it is advisable to tackle it in an orderly sequence.

SEQUENCE OF THE PLAN

1.29 Shipman (1979) suggests that the following five stages can be helpful to the planners:

(a) State the objectives of the exercise in such a form that it will enable their achievement to be verified (i.e. What is being aimed at and over what period of time?).

(b) Spell out the actions that are seen to be necessary for the objectives to be attained (i.e. Equivalent to the establishment of indicators in quantitative evaluation).

(c) Spell out the criteria by which the attainment of the objectives is to be assessed (i.e. How will the assessor know when the objective has been achieved?).

(d) Spell out whose judgements are involved for each component of the plan.

(e) State the arrangements for any standardisation procedure and the forms of reports and records which are to be maintained.

WHEN TO ASSESS – TIMING

1.30 (a) Macintosh and Hale (1976) point out that assessment can be introduced at different stages of a course of study, for example:

    (i) Continuous assessment – a continuous updating of judgements about a pupil's performance.

    (ii) Periodic assessment – measures levels of attainment reached at pre-determined intervals throughout the course.

    (iii) Terminal assessment – measures the attainment of pupils at the end of the course.

(b) Techniques can benefit some but can be also disadvantageous, hence there is a need for balance.

(c) This whole topic is treated in greater detail in Chapter 2, paragraphs 2.3–2.4 but the following table, which is based upon a table by Ward (1980), summarises the most common methods of assessment and their likely incidence within a course of instruction.

(d) Methods – timing of assessment.

ABILITIES TESTED	TIMING OF ASSESSMENT		
	Terminal	*Periodic*	*Continuous*
Theory[*] (Cognitive domain)	Written examination	Tests, projects and assignments	Coursework
Psychomotor skills	Practical test	Practical tests, projects and assignments	Practical coursework
Oral communication	Oral test	Discussions, lectures, question and answer sessions	Oral coursework
Affective domain		Projects and assignments	Observation of coursework

[*]'Theory' includes abilities in the cognitive domain as well as the basic communication skills of reading, writing, calculation and graphics.

BALANCE

1.31 (a) The assessment plan has to attempt to establish a state of equilibrium between the nature of its demands and the kind of responses which it aims to provoke. It is not a simple concept, involving as it does a whole series of elements, some of which are in potential conflict, in a complicated balancing act.

(b) Feedback is a constant requirement, and a balanced plan is very unlikely to be achieved by one individual working alone. It must emerge as a result of collaborative effort by all those involved.

1.32 (a) The categories of purposes inevitably overlap and equally inevitably teachers will, therefore, have to thread their way through potentially conflicting purposes in their search for and development of balanced programmes of work. Whilst teachers' use of assessment will be influenced by the expectations of the system within which they work, their attitudes to assessment are bound to reflect their own ideas of what education is about. Thus one teacher, seeing assessment as an objective and accurate means of determining present achievement and future potential, may employ it as a legitimate device for selection, and by stressing its relevance to pupils' future needs uses it to reinforce classroom control. Another teacher may see it as a means of providing useful advice and guidance and hence as a means of developing relationships with those being taught. Some balance has inevitably to be struck between what are, at times, seemingly conflicting but important requirements.

(b) The virtues of an assessment plan as a means of discovering the state of development of a pupil's abilities can be said to be self-evident. Nevertheless, the assessor needs to guard against some pitfalls in an apparently straight and level path to educational progress.

LIMITATIONS OF ASSESSMENT

1.33 (a) According to Harlen (1978) there are limitations to the value of assessment.

   (i) the result may adversely influence the teacher's subsequent judgements;

   (ii) teachers may allow their knowledge of a child's ability in one area to affect their judgement in another (the 'halo' effect);

   (iii) the teacher's knowledge of a child's ability may affect the achievement of the pupil; the child who is expected to be bright makes more progress than those of whom there are lower expectations.

(b) Ingenkamp (1977), in a review of assessment, says:

'Educational criticism is aimed chiefly against the direction of assessment towards selective practices and its educationally undesirable side effects and also against adverse effects on the pupil's personality due to stress, examination anxiety, the notion of competition, cheating, frustration and the falsifying of educational objectives, through orientation towards competitiveness and efficiency. It is argued that the only assessment which is educationally justifiable is that which promotes the individual learning process. Measurement for this purpose is objective- or criterion-referenced and is formative not summative.'

Variations in a teacher's approach can help to overcome some of these limitations, allowing the teacher an opportunity to observe pupils under different conditions.

STRUCTURE

1.34 Structure may be defined as the room for manoeuvre to be allowed to those responding to a set task. Broadly stated, a learning situation can be launched from two extreme standpoints:

(a) The formal, didactic approach, which allows the pupil little room for manoeuvre or freedom of thought. The outcomes of this can be relatively easily assessed.

(b) The informal approach in which the pupils are introduced to a limited subject area and are instructed to find out all they can about it. This is much less easily assessed.

1.35 Most teaching situations rest somewhere between the two extremes. The extent to which structure is introduced is decided on the basis of the demands of the subject and the needs of the pupils.

This produces variations in a teacher's methods in order to maintain a lively and ongoing learning situation. The assessment plan, for the same reason, needs to involve equally varied methods of assessment. There is a considerable range of techniques available from which to select the most appropriate and in Chapter 2 these techniques are presented and discussed.

(Exercise 5.40)

CAUTIONARY NOTES

1.36 (a) Pidgeon and Yates (1969) warn that there is a danger in implicit belief in measuring instruments. It must be recognised that however carefully educational tests are devised or selected an element of error is invariably associated with the results that they yield. Marks and scores can never be accepted at their face value. They provide only an estimate of the qualities or characteristics under review.

(b) Morrison (1980), writing on 'Measurement in Education', claims that the value of assessment cannot be decided until one has a reasonable appreciation of its nature, scope, strengths and weaknesses. He sees measurement as a comparative process, in that it is not possible without some clearly defined or appreciated standard which can be used as a basis for comparison. It cannot be regarded purely as a quantitative process involving the manipulation of numbers according to strict rules of logic. Educational measurement involves more than the concept of numbers and numerical calculation; it involves human error and variability. The probability of the existence of error requires knowledge of its possible magnitude before any interpretation of measurement can properly be made. Variability is a major consideration in any attempt to define an acceptable standard and the successful application of measurement techniques is dependent upon the ability to define what is to be measured in specific and unambiguous terms.

1.37 (a) Hoffmann (1962) says, 'A pupil does not really know what he has learned until he has organised it and explained it to someone else. The mere recognition of what is right in someone else's wording is only the beginning of the awareness of truth . . .'.
Macintosh and Hale (1976) suggest that assessment is therefore essentially an exercise in communication. Instructions or stimuli are given to those being assessed in a variety of forms. They can be used on their own or together in a variety of combinations. They may require facts to be given or arguments to be propounded. Opinions may be sought, attitudes may be explored or the solutions to problems may be required.

(b) There are equally as many forms of possible response to instructions or stimuli. But are these forms of response relevant to human conditions? Rarely, if ever, can a single human behaviour be said solely to be the result just of thinking or of unrelated feeling or of doing. It will consist of elements of all three outcomes and always with a different mix or emphasis. If the aims of curriculum developers are not to be distorted, assessment should be carefully integrated into curriculum planning.

(c) The techniques used to assess affective behaviour or physical skills will be different from those required for the assessment of cognitive skills and attainment. The general principles of assessment nevertheless remain the same. The object of the exercise should be stated in precise terms, and the procedures to be followed to attain the object must be prepared with care and in as much detail as is possible. In general, most testing, both in the classroom and in external examinations, has failed in the past to use the variety needed to match the actual complexity of human responses. All assessment is limited and must never be regarded as the means by which a definitive statement can be made of an individual.

(d) Limitations in approaches to assessment are manifested in several ways, for example:

   (i) The acceptance as a principle that responses should be provided in the same medium as the instructions (an oral question has to be answered orally).

  (ii) The separation of different forms of question from each other within tests (oral questions and written questions in separate sections).

 (iii) The separation within tests of objective items from open-ended questions (multiple choice and essays).

1.38 (a) Such conventions ought not to go unchallenged; assessment involves communication in at least two directions. Human beings employ many combinations of types of responses to match a current situation and will quickly change the type of response when necessary. If asked for directions by a stranger, an individual may respond in words, by gestures, by the drawing of diagrams, and even by demonstration if necessary, using one or several responses in turn, as may seem most appropriate.

(b) Instructions, stimuli and responses can be divided into three broad categories: written, spoken and practical, and the next chapter will be devoted to describing a selection of some of the many varieties of techniques which can be utilised in order to obtain the responses required.

1.39 This chapter has been concerned with the basic structure upon which an assessment plan can be developed. Unless such a foundation is sound and well-defined, the course may lack a sense of purpose, and assessment may create uncertainty in the minds of the pupils when ill-defined objectives perhaps lead to questions on subject areas not definitely covered in the course.

The pitfalls have also been touched upon; in particular a too rigid an adherence to concrete objectives, which can lead to sterile teaching situations where no benefit can be derived from unexpected outcomes or individual interests.

(Exercises 5.8 to 5.12)

Self-teaching Exercises

Number	Exercise
Number	*Exercise*

5.1   State in your own words what you consider to be the distinction between assessment and evaluation. In your school, college or organisation, list those activities which you consider would fall under the two headings.

5.2 (a)   Consider the system of assessment in operation in your school, college or organisation and make a list of those activities which have the same purposes as the six listed in paragraph 1.5.

5.2 (b)   Is there any activity where the purposes overlap? If so, indicate them.

5.2 (c)   Are there any purposes which are not included in the six, or any purposes for which there would seem to be no provision made in your school, college or organisation for assessment or evaluation?

5.2 (d)   What use is made in your school, college or organisation of the information gained from assessment for the purposes of evaluation?

5.3   Having regard to the definition of norm and criterion referencing given in paragraph 1.7, provide three examples of norm referenced and three examples of criterion referenced tests.

5.4 (a)   Consider any external public examination. What purpose(s) does this fulfil for each of the following?

   (i) The pupils taking the examination.

   (ii) The teachers of the course being examined.

   (iii) The school or college attended by the pupils.

   (iv) The parents of the pupils being examined.

   (v) Employing agencies likely to employ the pupils on their leaving school or college.

   (vi) The community which the school or college serves.

5.4 (b)   If the course in 5.4 (a) had no external examination but was instead assessed by you as the teacher, would this change your answers in any way to the questions in exercise 5.4 (a)? Give details.

Could meeting the requirements for this same externally set examination conflict in any way with the aims of the school or college? If so, give details.

5.4 (c)   Has preparing pupils for an external examination had any positive or negative results upon the manner of your teaching? Give instances.

5.5 (a)   Make a plan for a course in your subject, which you feel would meet the current needs of your pupils and at the same time would:

    (i) conform with the aims of your school or college,

    (ii) fulfil the expectations of:
        parents of pupils,
        the school management and teaching staff,
        would-be employers.

5.5 (b)   Draft the aims of the course (do not exceed 50 words).

5.5 (c)   Develop from the aims, a list of objectives by which the aims could be achieved.

Note: In order to complete this list, in addition to the subject, you should state the age and sex of your students and give an indication of their ability range.

5.5 (d)   Place each objective in order of its importance and indicate against each the most suitable method of assessment.

5.5 (e)   Are there any objectives which you would have liked to have assessed, but did not include because you could not see how they might be assessed? Is there a real distinction between course and assessment objectives?

5.6   By reference to the modes of assessment described in paragraphs 1.19 and 1.20, identify examples of the various types of assessment currently in use in your school or college by listing them under each method.

5.7 (a)   Define, in your own words, what is meant by validity and reliability in relation to assessment.

5.7 (b)   Take a particular plan of assessment with which you are familiar and consider it with regard to its validity and reliability. How could it be improved in those two respects?

5.7 (c)   Describe the procedures in force in your school, college or organisation whereby the outcomes of assessment are reviewed and acted upon in order to improve its quality. Are there any further steps that you would recommend?

5.8 (a)   Using your own experience as well as the information contained in paragraphs 1.19 and 1.20, define what is meant by:
    Periodic assessment,
    Continuous assessment,
    Terminal assessment.

5.8 (b)   What do you consider to be the advantages and disadvantages of the three types of assessment you have defined for exercise 5.8 (a)?

5.9   Define informal assessment. What provision would you make for including the results of informal assessment within the overall assessment of pupils?

5.10 (a)   Take an example known to you of a written test recently used in your school, college or organisation and supply the following information about it:

(i) State how the test was constructed.

(ii) Indicate its purpose.

(iii) Assess whether it achieved its purpose.

(iv) List any useful information gained as a result of using the test.

(v) Describe how you feel the test could be improved and discuss any practical difficulties likely to prevent such improvements being implemented.

5.10 (b)   Did you find it easy or difficult to obtain this information?

In what ways could your task have been made easier?

5.11   Take as another example a recent test constructed by some external agency for use in your school, college or organisation and answer the same questions contained in exercises 5.10 (a) and 5.10 (b).

5.12   What do you understand by the term 'educational measurement'?

Appendix A — Examples of an Adaptation of a Taxonomy — Cognitive Domain

These, taken from that of Coltham and Fines (1971) (see paragraph 1.15), are in respect of:

Comprehension

Translation

Analysis

Synthesis

and the subject area is History. The expansion produces lists of related cognitive behavioural objectives.

COMPREHENSION

A.1 The behaviour referred to here is that required in the first stages of an encounter with any new material. It is the result of examination at the surface or literal level — attention to the immediately observed features without any depth of cognitive treatment — resulting in an understanding of the general nature of the material. Such deciphering heralds the beginning of an enquiry.

(a) Describes or portrays salient feature(s) of a piece of evidence.

(b) Gives the gist of material read.

(c) Uses own experience to explain described behaviour of a character.

(d) Formulates what is interesting, puzzling, etc., about a piece of evidence or secondary source material.

(e) Formulates question(s) to be asked about and of evidence.

TRANSLATION

A.2 The material of History is available in a variety of forms and the ability to turn information received in one form into some other form has two aspects:

(a) Translation can aid deeper comprehension than was described in the previous category since closer and more detailed examination is necessary if the translation is to be valid; this is a cognitive behaviour acting as a means of extending comprehension before other procedures are undertaken.

(b) If the material evokes responding and imagining, then translation can lead directly to the creation of a product. The actual translation is still a cognitive behaviour but is here infused with a personal element. Examples of objectives for both aspects are given.

(c) **Example Objectives**

   (i) Describes accurately in words, features of a picture or object or map.

   (ii) Can present verbal material in diagrammatic form, mathematical form (table or graph from report), as a model or as a map.

   (iii) Can turn information received in factual form into narrative.

   (iv) Can make a precis of verbal material.

   (v) Uses year numbers and period names as alternatives.

ANALYSIS

A.3 As the heading of the category indicates, the cognitive behaviour intended here is that of separating a whole into its elements or component parts; this enables the learner to attain a still deeper level of comprehension than those described in the two previous sections. It is a means both to apprehension of the particularity of the material and to critical appraisal of it. The learner has to build up a repertoire of possibilities which guide analytical behaviour — the possible nature(s) of component parts — and it is knowledge of these, as well as the cognitive behaviour of 'pulling apart', which is indicated in the examples of objectives given below:

(a) Can name separate parts of an object orally.

(b) Shows by drawing, description, etc., what component parts are.

(c) Can design proformas for translating material (preparation of statistics for tabular presentation).

(d) Identifies inconsistencies within one piece or between two or more pieces of evidence or of secondary source material.

(e) Identifies $\begin{cases} \text{bias} \\ \text{point of view} \\ \text{value judgement} \end{cases}$ in a piece of evidence or secondary source material.

(f) Can state criterion (criteria) being used in analysis.

(g) States similarities and differences between two pieces of evidence or secondary source material.

(h) Identifies nature of connecting links between elements.

(i) Recognises lack of connection (a gap) in evidence or argument.

SYNTHESIS

A.4 The 'putting together' signified by the heading to this category is a skill which may be needed at all or several stages of study, from the formulation of plans for an enquiry up to the creation of a product. It can appear in a physical form — assembly of separate creations into a model or as a 'scissors and paste' procedure — which requires decision-making (cognitive and connative behaviours) about arrangements, or may occur only as an unseen mental behaviour. It is important to recognise that the skill is something more than the ability to juxtapose elements; there must be some form or organisation for which decisions have to be made. The examples of objectives include the various aspects of the synthesising skill.

(a) Uses connecting links between elements.

(b) Uses an organising principle (temporal, behavioural, causal) to hold material together.

(c) Can combine time indicators with sequence of events.

(d) Constructs an accurate and vivid picture of conditions of life at a particular point in time.

(e) Can assimilate new (to learner) element into an organised body of knowledge.

(f) Uses entirety of relevant material of all types.

(g) Discards what is irrelevant to immediate purpose.

(h) Can formulate plans by bringing together what is known and what is not, but might be, known.

(i) Creates a product with 'no cracks showing'.

(j) Brings own fund of knowledge and experience to bear on material derived from primary and/or secondary sources.

It should be noted that while all these objectives require the pupil to do something specific, there is no reference to the detailed content which questions testing these abilities or skills would use.

Appendix B — Examples of Objectives and Notes upon Weighting and Principles of Learning

SOURCES

B.1 The following three examples may be of interest. The first two syllabuses are taken from the General Certificate of Education. The English Language syllabus was set by the examiners of the Associated Examining Board (AEB). The Physical Science is a Mode 3 syllabus, i.e. it was prepared by the teachers of a school or a group of schools, and was subsequently approved and validated by the AEB. The third syllabus, Parentcraft, for the Certificate of Secondary Education, is another Mode 3 prepared by the teachers of a school and approved by a panel of teachers appointed by, and acting for, the Southern Regional Examinations Board (SREB).

LANGUAGE — OBJECTIVES

B.2 **(a)**
1. The effective use of the language as a means of communication and expression spoken or written.
2. The ability to understand passages of prose of different kinds, for example: descriptive, factual, expository, controversial, with a firm grasp of salient points and an understanding of the relationship of the parts to the whole.
3. Discrimination in the use of language so that it is appropriate to the circumstances and to the purposes of the writer and the needs of the reader.
4. Clarity and economy of expression.
5. The orderly arrangement and development of relevant ideas.
6. Practice in uses of the language appropriate to business and the professions, for example dictation to a machine.
7. The development of confidence and flexibility in the use of language appropriate to the needs of business and the professions.

(b) It is interesting to see how few of these objectives apply only to the subject of this particular syllabus, and how many have a much wider application, for example, objectives 1, 3, 4 and 5 could apply equally well to other subjects. It is only 2, 6 and 7 which are strictly relevant to the syllabus which is of a specialised nature.

(c) A criticism of objectives 6 and 7 could be that they are too diffuse and would need considerable expansion before they would be of any direct assistance to the teacher responsible for assessment. On the other hand, this vagueness would equally well prove to be an advantage, and would allow the teacher more scope to match the syllabus to the pupils, their abilities and aspirations.

PHYSICAL SCIENCE – OBJECTIVES

B.3 (a)   1. The ability to perform practical skills, such as the use of apparatus, taking measurements and observation.

2. The ability to understand the principles of Physical Science likely to be encountered at home and at work.

3. The ability to apply such principles in unforeseen circumstances.

4. The ability to comprehend scientific work of a suitable difficulty.

5. The ability to identify relevant information and to express this succinctly.

6. The ability to produce project work of sufficient depth and length and to show an ability to work independently.

(b) It is only objectives 5 and 6 which could have a much wider application, the remaining objectives are relevant and actionable by an assessing teacher. Some expansion would, of course, be necessary to breathe life into the assessment plan.

PARENTCRAFT – OBJECTIVES

B.4 (a)   1. A knowledge of the anatomy and physiology of the human body in relation to:

   (i) the development of both partners through adolescence to adulthood;

   (ii) the process of procreation;

   (iii) child development and growth.

2. A knowledge of and an ability to evaluate the importance of the rules of health.

3. A knowledge of the causes of accidents in the home, methods of prevention and the practical ability to deal with them.

4. Practical ability in craft-work to enable the child to produce equipment for the nursery and also toys and garments.

5. A knowledge of the stages of a child's intellectual development and the modes of learning appropriate to each stage.

6. A knowledge of the psychological development of the child and the ability to select the appropriate solution for behavioural problems in the context of family life.

7. An understanding of the contribution which an inadequate family life can make towards social problems, for example drug-taking, delinquency.

8. A knowledge of the tensions created by the interaction of personalities within a family, their possible consequences and the contribution which the supportive services can make.

9. A knowledge of decisions which might have to be made leading up to marriage. in marriage and in family life, for example, the choice of a partner, size of family, division of responsibilities, etc., and an ability to establish priorities in decision-making.

10. The ability to evaluate the moral and social issues basic to the existence of a family (for example, the sanctity of life, population explosion, etc.).

(b) The ten objectives are all relevant to this particular syllabus. Both the teacher and assessor are given clear targets, the only imponderable being the level at which the objectives are to be pitched, for example, 'A knowledge of the anatomy and physiology of the human body . . .' would have to be in relation to age experience and ability level of the pupils who are to be taught.

(c) A criticism which could be levelled is the absence of concrete words. 'A *knowledge* of . . .' could be taken to mean 'slight' on the one hand and 'encyclopaedic' on the other. Standards of mastery or criteria of assessment would need to be prepared, discussed at length and agreed.

(d) At this stage in the preparation of objectives it is useful to refer to the aims of the course. In this case they are hardly concise!

(i) To prepare students of both sexes for aspects of family life.

(ii) To encourage them to be aware of and to be sympathetic to the responsibilities which come with marriage, the birth of children and the establishment of a family unit.

(iii) To realise the value of a happy, healthy and stable family background in the physical, mental and moral development of the individual.

The aims are virtually a summary of the objectives rather than their mainspring.

(e) From a consideration of the aims and the objectives it is possible to draw up a plan of assessment. The next problem, and it is probably one of the most difficult to solve, is to decide the relative importance of each objective. If, for example, it is decided to allocate 100 marks for all ten objectives, should they each be allocated an equal number of marks? Does objective 9 merit more marks than objective 4? Should there be a reserve of marks for un-expectedly good outcomes?

THE WEIGHTING OF OBJECTIVES

B.5 Having arrived at lists of objectives for particular subject areas, consideration can be given next to the relative importance (or weighting) of each component of the assessment plan. For this operation a grid may be useful. The example below, taken from Pidgeon and Yates (1967), refers to part of a Geography syllabus devoted to a regional study, and to four objectives. (All elements have been much simplified.)

SUBJECT AREA	OBJECTIVES				TOTALS
	Recall of facts	*Formation of Concepts*	*Understanding Relationships, Principles and Laws*	*Applying Knowledge to New Problems*	
Physical Features	10%		10%	5%	25%
Climate	5%	10%	5%		20%
Communications	5%	10%		5%	20%
Agriculture and Industry	10%	10%	5%	10%	35%
TOTALS	30%	30%	20%	20%	100%

(Weighting can be defined as the value to be placed upon a particular aspect or skill. It is a subjective judgement which should take into account not only the relative importance of what is to be done but also the time taken to do it.)

B.6 (a) From the table above it can be seen that the objective summarised as 'Recall of Facts' has a weighting of 10% for the subject area of Physical Features. It is now necessary to consider the most appropriate techniques of assessment, which are discussed at length in Chapter 2. From these, the overall weighting for each objective can be broken down to each technique.

(b) The table on page 43 gives an example of the grid prepared for the Parent-craft syllabus set out in B.4, which has ten objectives and uses seven tech-niques (almost certainly too many).

OBJECTIVE	TECHNIQUES OF ASSESSMENT							WEIGHTING
	THEORY		PRACTICE					
	Written Exam	Oral Test	Discussion	Practical Test	Course Work	Observations	Project	
1	5				5		5	15%
2		5					5	10%
3	5				10			15%
4	5			5				10%
5						5		5%
6	5			10				15%
7		5		5				10%
8	5							5%
9	5							5%
10			5				5	10%
WEIGHTING	30%	10%	5%	20%	15%	5%	15%	100%

SOME BASIC PRINCIPLES

B.7 When framing objectives, Dressel (1961) suggests that principles of learning, such as those evolved by Saupe, could profitably be borne in mind:

(a) Learning is a process by which experience develops new, and reorganises old, responses.

(b) Without appropriate readiness on the part of the pupil, a learning experience will be inefficient. Learning will not occur.

(c) Learning proceeds more rapidly, and is retained much longer, when that which has to be learned possesses meaning, organisation and structure.

(d) Learners learn only from what they themselves do.

(e) Only those responses which are learned are confirmed.

(f) Transfer can occur only when there is a recognised similarity between the learning situation and the transfer situation.

(g) Transfer will occur to the extent that students expect it to occur.

(h) Knowledge of a model(s) of problem-solving or aspects of critical thinking can contribute to its improvement.

References

de Block, A. (1972), *Evaluatie van Attitudes via Observatie van Gedragingen* (Seminarie en Laboratorium voor Didactiek)

Bloom, B.S. (1956), *Taxonomy of Educational Objectives* (Longman Group, London)

Canberra College of Advanced Education (1977), The Curriculum Evaluation, *Report on Annual Conference* (CCAE)

Coltham, J.B. and Fines J. (1971), Educational Objectives for the Study of History, *Historical Association Pamphlet, TH 35*

Deale, R.N. (1975), Assessment and Testing in the Secondary School, *Schools Council Examinations Bulletin 32* (Evans/Methuen Educational, London)

Dressel, P.L. (1961), *Evaluation in Higher Education* (Houghton Mifflin, Boston)

Ebel, E.L. (1979), *Essentials of Educational Measurement*, 3rd Edition (Prentice Hall, Englewood Cliffs, NJ)

Eisner, E. (1967), Educational Objectives — Help or Hindrance?, *School Review*, 75

Gagnè, R.M. (1970), *The Conditions of Learning* (Holt, Rinehart & Winston, New York)

Gerlach, V.S. and Sullivan, H.J. (1969), Objectives, Evaluation and Improved Learner Achievement, in *Instructional Objectives*, ed. W.J. Popham, E.W. Eisner, M.J. Sullivan and L.L. Tyler (Rand McNally, Chicago)

Hamilton, J.B., Norton, R.E., Fardig, G.E., Harrington, L.G. and Quinn, K.M. (1977), *Establish Student Performance Criteria*, Module D1, Category D, Instructional Evaluation Professional Teacher Education Series (The Center for Vocational Education, American Association for Vocational Instructional Material, University of Georgia)

Harlen, W. (1978), *Evaluation and the Teacher's Role*, Schools Council Research Study (MacMillan Education, London)

Harte, R. (1981), How Valid are School Examinations? An Exploration into Content Validity, *British Journal of Educational Psychology*, 51, 10–22

Hoffmann, B. (1962), *The Tyranny of Testing* (Collier Macmillan, New York)

Hogben, D. (1973), The Behavioural Objective Approach — Some Problems, Some Dangers, *Journal of Curriculum Studies*, IV, No 1

Ingenkamp, K. (1977), *Educational Assessment*, Council for Europe (National Foundation for Educational Research, Slough)

Jackson, R. and Hayter, J. (1978), *Evaluation and the Teacher's Role*, Schools Council Research Studies (Macmillan Education, London)

Macintosh, H.G. (1976), *Assessing Attainment in the Classroom*, Canterbury Study Books (Hodder & Stoughton, London)

Macintosh, H.G. and Hale, D.E. (1976), *Assessment and the Secondary School Teacher* (Routledge & Kegan Paul, London)

Morris, L.L. and Fitzgibbon, C.T. (1978), *How to Measure Achievement* and

How to Calculate Statistics, Program Evaluation Kit (Center for the Study of Evaluation, Sage Publications, University of California)

Morrison, R.B. (1980), *Values and Evaluation in Education* (Harper & Row, London)

Nuttall, D.L. and Willmott, A.S. (1972), *British Examinations — Techniques of Analysis* (National Foundation for Educational Research, Slough)

Pidgeon, D. and Yates, A. (1969), *An Introduction to Educational Measurement* (Routledge & Kegan Paul, London)

Rowntree, D. (1977), *Assessing Students — How Shall We Know Them?* (Harper & Row, London)

Shipman, M. (1979), *In-School Evaluation* (Heinemann Educational Books, London)

Stenhouse, L. (1969), *Behavioural Objectives in Curriculum Development — their Limitations*, A Paper to the British Psychological Society

Swales, T. (1979), *Record of Personal Achievement*, Schools Council Pamphlet 16 (Schools Council, London)

2

Techniques of Assessment

Chapter Contents

Techniques of Assessment

ASSESSMENT METHODS

2.1 (a) There is a considerable range of techniques by which the abilities and acquired skills of pupils can be tested and the process of selecting the most appropriate must be governed by a number of important considerations, in particular the:

    (i) *purpose* for which the assessment is to be undertaken;

    (ii) *time and resources* available;

    (iii) *age and ability* of the pupils.

(b) Each technique has advantages and disadvantages, and similarly there are both advantages and disadvantages in using a variety of techniques. If a variety is used, this can, of course, avoid or reduce the disadvantages embodied in a single technique. The combining of information obtained from the use of several techniques is, however, a complex exercise and can often lead in the process to a loss of information rather than a gain. As always in assessment, a balance must be struck and therein lies the art of planning.

2.2 (a) This chapter is simply concerned with a description of a range of the techniques available. It makes no judgements as to their appropriateness in any given situation — that is for the reader to make.

(b) The techniques are presented within the framework of six types of assessment, in the following order:

    Written Assessment

    Practical Assessment

    Oral Assessment

    Aural Assessment

    Pupil Questionnaires

    Coursework (including projects and field work)

The chapter concludes with four Appendices as follows:

    Appendix A — Criteria of Assessment

    Appendix B — Some Notes on Oral Testing

    Appendix C — Extract from SREB's Integrated Studies Handbook 'Project Work'

    Appendix D — The New Coursework System — History 13–16 1982

    Appendix E — History of Multiple Choice Items

(Exercise 5.13)

THE TIMING OF ASSESSMENT – WHEN TO ASSESS

2.3 It is as important to determine when to assess as it is to determine how or what to assess. When talking of timing in relation to assessment the three words 'terminal', 'periodic' and 'continuous' are often used. What exactly do these three words mean and what are their relative merits and demerits?

Terminal is much the easiest of the three words to define. It simply means assessment that takes place at the end of a predetermined set period or unit, as, for example, a school year, a course or a unit of instruction. It ought, therefore, if it is to be valid, to concern itself with the whole of what is being assessed. As a consequence of this requirement, one of the major problems with terminal assessment which is extensively used, particularly in large-scale public examinations, is that of selection. What should be included and what should be excluded? Terminal assessment can, of course, involve more than one measure, but however extensive its nature, selection will always remain a key issue.

2.4 (a) Periodic assessment is designed to permit a series of intermittent probes to be taken over a course or a given period of time. These probes will, however, take place at set periods, and it is this point that ought primarily to distinguish periodic from continuous assessment. Unfortunately, the term 'continuous assessment' is often wrongly used. What it ought to mean is a continuous updating of judgements about performance in relation to specific criteria which will allow, at any time, a cumulative judgement to be made about performance upon these same criteria. Rogers, in Macintosh (1974) likens continuous assessment to the progress of a missile. As the missile homes on to its target it rarely follows the path originally planned for it. Its course is constantly monitored and modified by feedback provided from its previous path. A similar process of modification ought to take place in education and a well-designed flexible programme of continuous assessment is one means of enabling this to happen.

(b) If the above definition of continuous assessment is accepted then there are important implications. Any resulting programme must involve those actually teaching the students being assessed in the process of assessment, and this raises questions about teacher will, teacher skill and resources. A second important consideration is that of the pressure upon those being assessed. Programmes involving continuous assessment can easily generate an 'if it moves assess it' attitude amongst those involved and this will eventually result in much greater burdens being placed upon the students than is justified by the information gained. Finally, the nature of what is being assessed may not lend itself to continuous assessment. Take, for example, subjects within the school curriculum. Continuous updating in relation to a linear subject, such as Physics or Geography, would be impracticable, indeed unworkable, whereas it would be perfectly appropriate for a cyclical subject such as English or French. In the former case, the assessment process cannot be a smooth-flowing stream, but has to consist instead of a series of cataracts.

(c) Fitness for purpose must apply to the timing of assessment as well as to the methods used. Although theoretically the full range of methods can be used whatever the timing, it is likely, in practice, that genuine programmes of continuous assessment will make use of less formal approaches and place a greater premium upon observation (see in particular paragraph 2.43 on the continuous assessment of practical skills).

WRITTEN ASSESSMENT

2.5 (a) There is a tendency to use a wide range of terms when describing written questions, for example Free Response, Short-answer. It is probably simpler, however, to consider them in relation to the room for manoeuvre they give to the person responding to them. Against this criterion, written questions run the gamut from 'open' to 'closed', from almost limitless room for manoeuvre (Physics is Fun – Discuss) to very little room indeed (Paris is the capital of France – True/False). A question at the open end of the spectrum is likely to ask the respondent to supply material and require more writing than reading. Such questions are, moreover, likely to be easier to set than to mark and to provide a relatively limited coverage of the content being assessed. Questions at the closed end have these character-istics reversed, for example the respondent selects from given material and has more reading to do than writing. They are easier to mark than to set and permit a wide content coverage. Incidentally, this system of classification can be applied equally well to oral questioning, except, of course, that reading becomes listening and writing becomes speaking.

(b) Questioning, whether orally or on paper, is, of course, a crucial technique for all who teach. Teachers constantly ask questions of their students, and the form these questions take has a significant effect not only upon student achievement, but also upon the teaching/learning environment in the class-room. Some useful guidance upon basic and advanced questioning techniques has been produced by the University of Sydney in their Microskills Series 1 and 2 (Turney et al., 1978).

2.6 When considering the construction of written questions as here, it is more con-venient to use the three broadly based headings of Objective Items, Structured Questions and Open-ended or Essay Questions.

(a) **Objective Items**

An objective item (item is the term more commonly used than question) is one which is asked in such a way that there is only one predetermined correct answer. This definition rules out any question which requires an answer to be supplied, however short, since judgement is needed in the marking of such answers, even if only to determine acceptable degrees of incorrect spelling. It needs emphasising at this point that the only thing that is objective about an objective item or test is its marking; everything else about it involves the taking of subjective decisions, for example, what to include and what to exclude in the options. (Paragraphs 2.7 to 2.17 provide examples.)

Short-answer questions will, on this occasion, however, be considered as a separate category (paragraphs 2.18 and 2.19) under Objective Testing, since they often appear thus in the literature. They, moreover, play a very important part in much classroom testing.

(b) Structured Questions

Structure is a far from simple concept and is currently used in at least three different contexts when referring to written questions. First and most common, there is the structure of the format of the question itself in order to break it down into manageable elements for the purpose in hand (even to the provision of potential paragraph headings on occasion). Secondly, there is the structure of the material used in the question, for example the editing of a document or a quotation; the simplification of a drawing or a diagram. Thirdly, there is the structure of the problem posed; the framing of questions in the form of problems and dilemmas rather than simply asking the respondent to describe or discuss.

A potential disadvantage of structured questions, which may well come in sets related to common material, is their length; they can, ironically, all too easily become extremely wordy in their efforts to clarify. The illustrations of structured questions provided in paragraphs 2.20 to 2.22 are inevitably extremely limited and only scratch the surface of what is probably the most stimulating area for future development in written questions (see particularly the work being currently undertaken on the History 13–16 Curriculum Project which is based at Trinity and All Saints' Colleges, Brownberrie Lane, Horsforth, Leeds LS18 5MB, England).

(c) Open-ended or Essay Questions

The use of the words 'open-ended' implies two things: first, that those answering the questions decide what to include and what not to include in their answers and, secondly, that no precise limits are normally set in the questions themselves as to length or style of answer. They thus deliberately provide little in the way of guidance to the respondent. Both in the classroom and in public secondary examinations, the half-hour essay has been the most frequently used open-ended question, although more often than not it has in reality been partially structured. When, as happens on occasions, longer or shorter answers are asked for, then the time allowance is adjusted accordingly. The essay and extended written responses in general provide the most appropriate vehicle for assessing command of language and for demonstrating ability to analyse, to argue, to synthesise and to reflect.

(Exercise 5.14)

OBJECTIVE ITEMS

2.7 (a) The philosophy behind tests composed of objective items, we are told by Schofield (1972), is that marks are awarded only on relevant grounds, and are awarded in such a way that they cannot be influenced by the personal preferences and prejudices of the marker.

(b) As with all questions, considerable skill is needed in writing objective items. The main requirements for producing a good item are:

(i) Sound knowledge and understanding of the subject matter to be tested.

(ii) Appreciation of the abilities and attainment which the test is designed to measure.

(iii) Experience of teaching pupils at the same level as that for which the test is designed.

(iv) Collaboration with colleagues who may be able to point out errors, ambiguities and omissions in drafts of items.

(c) The History Department of Plowden School worked well together in improving multiple choice and short-answer questions. The need for action had been precipitated by some rather acid comments from their indomitable Headmistress, Serena Williams, regarding the low level of passes obtained by the History candidates who had taken public examinations in the previous year.

Bruce Bennett reported to a department meeting on his 'post mortem' session with candidates just after they had taken the examination. Amongst other criticisms, the multiple choice items were felt to have been very difficult. Harry Davenport, the Head of Department, expressed surprise since to him they seemed reasonably straightforward, and Bruce agreed, but stressed that the candidates were unanimous in their judgement.

(d) After some discussion it was conceded that there were two areas which could be given special attention. The first concerned multiple choice:

(i) Pupils should be given more opportunities to tackle multiple choice items and to become more familiar with the technique. This could be achieved by using pre-tested items in homework assignments, and giving pupils the opportunity to draft multiple choice items themselves on current work.

(ii) The quality of items written for internal examinations should be looked at. Bruce Bennett was requested to provide all members of the Department with some direction upon the compilation of multiple choice items and to include some examples of good and bad items with some element of explanation.

(e) The second area of concern related to pre-testing. The Head of Department announced that the short-answer questions and the multiple choice items for the coming fourth year terminal assessment had been pre-tested very roughly under arrangements made by Bruce Bennett, using the current fifth year groups. The results had been most surprising in respect of the multiple choice items where eleven out of twenty needed to be redrafted. Only four of the ten short-answer questions needed revision.

He had revised the short-answer and multiple choice questions and the paper was now ready. Bruce was asked to hand round copies of the pre-test results, which he then did.

(i) *Short-answer Questions* (each for a maximum of two marks)

QUESTION	CANDIDATE										TOTALS
	A	B	C	D	E	F	G	H	J	K	
1	2	2	2	2	0	2	1	2	2	2	17
2*	0	1	0	0	1	1	2	0	0	1	6
3	1	1	2	2	2	1	2	1	2	2	16
4*	1	0	0	1	0	0	0	1	0	1	4
5	1	2	2	2	2	2	1	1	2	1	16
6*	?	0	1	1	1	0	2	2	2	0	11
7	1	2	2	2	1	1	2	2	1	1	15
8	1	2	2	2	1	0	2	2	2	2	16
9	2	2	2	2	2	2	2	2	1	2	19
10*	1	1	0	1	0	0	0	1	2	1	7
TOTALS	12	13	13	15	10	9	14	14	14	13	127

Overall Mean $\dfrac{127}{200} \times 100 = 63.5\%$

(ii) Bruce had decided that the minimum acceptable mean, bearing in mind that this was a fourth year test, being attempted by fifth year pupils in their first year, should be 75%. The following questions which produced low scores were reviewed and redrafted for the stated reasons:

Question 2 – found to be ambiguous

Question 4 – an error in the date quoted

Question 6 – phraseology rather complicated

Question 10 – question not at all clear

QUESTION	OPTIONS					ACTION TAKEN
	A	B	C	D	E	
1	26				4	Accepted but only as a reassuringly easy opener
2	23		4		3	Stem & Options A & B Redrafted
3		24	3		3	Accepted
4		18	9	3		Stem Redrafted
5		1		1	28	Distractors Revised
6	1		2	25	2	Accepted
7		21		3	6	Accepted
8	1	1	26	2		Stem Redrafted
9	14		1		15	Option A Redrafted
10		3		25	2	Stem & Option D Redrafted
11		15	12	3		Stem Redrafted
12	3	5			22	Accepted
13		6	23		1	Accepted
14	6		24			Stem & Option D Redrafted
15	22		2	2	4	Accepted
16		27		3		Stem Redrafted
17	1	25	3	1		Accepted
18				24	6	Distractors Revised
19	15	12	3			Stem & Options A & B Redrafted
20	2	1	3	2	22	Accepted

(iii) *Multiple Choice Items*

The Head of Department pointed out at this point that Bruce had been unhappy about the smallness of the numbers in the sample. However, in view of time being short and since it was convenient to use one class, a sample of only thirty had to be accepted. The full fifth year of nearly 200 candidates would have ensured a more reliable test. The results of the pre-test are shown in the table on page 58. The figures indicate the number of candidates who selected the option. The box indicates the answer deemed to be correct. To an outsider the figures would suggest that the test has not discriminated particularly well.

The minimum acceptable number of correct options chosen by candidates was set at 12. It will be seen that out of 20 questions only 9 were considered acceptable and 11 were accordingly redrafted and pre-tested again.

After some discussion, the redraft of both components of the paper was accepted.

MULTIPLE CHOICE

2.8 (a) SREB (1978) suggest that these items can be of two kinds. In order to follow a description of their format, it is necessary to be familiar with the terminology used, namely:

(i) Discrete Item — a single complete item.

(ii) Stem — the initial part of the item in which the task is stated; it may be in the form of a question, directions or an incomplete statement.

(iii) Options — all the alternative choices/answers (usually four or five) available to the respondent.

(iv) Key — the correct answer.

(v) Distractors — the incorrect alternative choices.

(vi) Item Sets — two or more items based upon common material, for example a passage of text, problem, graph, experiment or chart.

(b) An illustrated example of the component parts of a discrete item is given below:

'Which of the following was the primary purpose for which
the Craft Guilds were formed in the Middle Ages? ←——————— STEM

OPTIONS→ {
A. The regulation of production. ←——————— KEY
B. The distribution of goods.
C. The control of town governments. } ←——— DISTRACTORS
D. The training of new workmen.'

(c) The first kind of item is 'the question', for example:

'Which of the following was written as a reply to Burkes' Reflections on the French Revolution?

   A. The Wealth of Nations.

   B. The Social Contract.

   C. The Rights of Man.

   D. Thoughts on the Present Discontents.'

(d) The second kind of item is 'the single completion':

   'An example in London of the architecture during the period 1789–1815 is

   A. The House of Lords.

   B. St. Pancras Station

   C. Regent Street.

   D. St. Paul's Cathedral.'

ADVANTAGES AND DISADVANTAGES OF MULTIPLE CHOICE

2.9 (a) Advantages

   (i) Schofield (1972) suggests that items can be answered in a reasonably short space of time and can cover a good deal of the subject area in that time.

   (ii) Items are easy to mark.

   (iii) The marking is objective since the answer can only be right or wrong.

   (iv) When standardised, such tests can provide a good deal of comparative information about the pupils.

   (v) Multiple choice tests have high reliability.

   (vi) They can be set for any level of ability.

   In setting an item for higher ability pupils there is, however, a danger that a degree of subjectivity may creep in. The following example of what is sometimes known as a 'best answer item', illustrates this point. An extract from a book or letter is followed by this item:

   'Which of the following best states the author's belief about the nature of democracy?

   A. The decisions about the restrictions of individual liberties must be taken by the elected representatives of the people.

   B. In a democracy individual liberties should not be restricted in any way.

   C. Democracy is a form of government in which the rights of individuals should be protected.

   D. Democracy is government of the people, by the people, for the people.'

(b) Disadvantages

   (i) It is very easy to construct poor multiple choice items and hence a poor multiple choice test.

(ii) The construction of a thoroughly valid and reliable item takes a long time.

(iii) Only a simple act of recognition and recall is expected of the candidate. There is no demand for reasoning or explanation.

(iv) Pupils can become too familiar with the techniques and may be influenced in their learning methods, looking for facts rather than seeking a deeper understanding.

(v) Multiple choice test results can be distorted by candidates guessing the answers.

CHECK LIST FOR MULTIPLE CHOICE ITEM WRITERS

2.10 (a) The following check list, taken from one prepared by the Center for Vocational Education (1977), provides a useful set of criteria against which to prepare and judge an item:

(i) The central question or problem should be clearly stated in the stem.

(ii) All the distractors should be feasible.

(iii) There should be no ambiguities in the stem or the possible responses.

(iv) All the possible responses should be of approximately the same length.

(v) The responses should be grammatically correct.

(vi) Responses should be so constructed that no clues can be obtained from other alternatives.

(vii) None of the possible responses should be synonymous or opposite in meaning.

(viii) The stem should be constructed so as to assess the level of knowledge specified in the objective.

(ix) The stem should be written at the appropriate language level for the pupils answering the item.

(Exercises 5.15 and 5.16)

(b) At Plowden Comprehensive School, Greta Glover was working with Bruce Bennett on an analysis of the results of the fourth year terminal assessment. The multiple choice section scored rather high in her opinion, 10.79 out of 20 and she voiced her fears regarding multiple choice items providing an easy way out for unmotivated pupils. Surely, she reasoned they could achieve a score by guessing.

(c) Bruce agreed that they could gain marks purely by guessing, but there was a formula which could be applied called the Number Right Formula which would correct the scores and reduce the effects. This was:

$$\text{Corrected Score} = \textit{Right} \text{ answers minus} \frac{\textit{Wrong} \text{ answers}}{\text{Number of alternatives minus one}}$$

(d) 'Let us', Bruce said, 'take the marks of a pupil who had a score of 11 right answers and 9 wrong answers out of 20 items which each had five options:

$$11 - \frac{9}{4} = 11 - 2.25 = 8.75$$

Corrected score 8.75

Greta questioned whether the results of all this mathematical labour justified the effort, but Bruce pointed out that when a lower score of right answers is achieved, the corrected score is significantly different. Take a case where there are 7 right answers and 13 wrong answers:

$$7 - \frac{13}{4} = 7 - 3.25 = 3.75$$

Corrected score 3.75

(e) 'So the lower the score the more effective will be the formula?' queried Greta. 'It's all a bit too simplistic for my liking,' said Bruce. 'It does not banish with any certainty the distorting effects of guesswork. The only way to safeguard the reliability of the results of assessment is to set the facility index at the right level for the candidates. Determining what that level should be, with groups of candidates of mixed ability, is by no means a simple task.'

OTHER OBJECTIVE ITEM TYPES

(f) There are many other types of objective items. The examples that follow in paragraphs 2.11 to 2.17 give a few of the possible approaches. (You will find a considerable variety of terminology used to describe the item types in different books.)

MULTIPLE COMPLETION

2.11 (a) This is a development of the single completion item and is designed to provide items in an objective format which can have more than one correct answer. Thyne (1974) illustrates this problem in the following item:

'A distribution's degree of scatter is indicated by its

A. Standard Deviation.

B. Maximum Possible Mark.

C. Interquartile Range.

D. Median.'

There are two correct responses (A and C) here, which complicate marking. One solution, of course, would be to redraft the question to create one correct response only. Another would be to allow a maximum of two marks for A and C and one mark for either A or C. What then is to be done if one right and one wrong response is selected, for example A and B? Should B be marked minus 1?

(b) It would also be possible to redraft the question as a true/false item, but this would convert the original single item into four questions. For example:

'A distribution's degree of scatter is indicated by its

Standard Deviation	True/False
Maximum Possible Mark	True/False
Interquartile Range	True/False
Median	True/False'

(c) Using the multiple completion approach described in some detail by Macintosh and Morrison (1969), Thyne's example would read as follows:

'Which of the following can be used to indicate the extent of a distribution's scatter?

   I Standard Deviation.

   II Maximum Possible Mark.

   III Interquartile Range.

   IV Median.

   A. I only.

   B. II only.

   C. I and III only.

   D. I, III and IV only.'

This format enables there to be more than one correct option whilst ensuring that there is still only one correct answer to the question as posed (in this case C).

PAIRED STATEMENTS

2.12 'Which of the three explanations lettered A, B and C indicates the correct relationship between the pairs of statements numbered 1 to 8? Give your answer by writing the appropriate letter in the box provided opposite each pair. Number 1 has been answered by way of illustration:

A. An increase in the first will lead to an improvement in the second.

B. An increase in the first will lead to a worsening of the second.

C. An increase in the first will have no effect on the second.

   1. The number of rats in a particular area.
       The health problems in the same area.

B

2. The number of doctors in a particular area.
   Infant mortality figures for the same area.

3. The cars in a city.
   The city's birth rate.

4. Provision for education in a country.
   The country's health standards.

5. An area's birth rate.
   The area's problems of overcrowding.

6. Strict moral views among teenagers.
   Birth rate.

7. A rise in the purchasing power of currency.
   People's ability to purchase contraceptive materials.

8. The use of contraceptive methods.
   The birth rate.'

ANALYSIS OF EVIDENCE

2.13 In this example, produced by SREB, there are eight different facts and in respect of these, four conclusions are supplied. The candidate has to select the relevant facts which support each of the four conclusions.

Facts	USA	Argentina	India
A. Cars per 1000 people	420	45	1
B. Calories per person per day	3200	2800	1800
C. Radio sets per 1000 people	800	180	15
D. Doctors per 100 000 people	120	70	20
E. Dentists per 100 000 people	50	20	2
F. Death rate per 1000 people	9.6	10	16
G. Percentage of workers who work in agriculture	13	25	75
H. Percentage of adults unable to read	3	12	80

Conclusions

1. The average family income in the USA is very high.

Facts: A, B and C

2. A relatively high death rate in India is due to lack of medical facilities and poor diets.

Facts:

3. Argentina has overcome the basic health problems of a developing nation.

> Facts:

4. India has not yet overcome the basic problems of a slowly developing country.

> Facts:

Requirement

Which of the facts A to H clearly support conclusions 1-4? Put the relevant letter(s) in the four boxes provided. The same facts may support more than one conclusion and some facts may support none of the conclusions. (Number 1 has been answered by way of illustration.)'

ALTERNATIVE RESPONSES – TRUE/FALSE ITEMS

2.14 (a) In these items, produced by Tile Hill Wood School, the pupil is asked to select one of two given responses. There are several variants, for example:

> 'Indicate by deleting the incorrect judgement whether the following statements are true or false:
>
> The surface area of a circle can be calculated if only the radius is known.
>
> TRUE/FALSE
>
> Domestic water supplies have to be treated with chlorine to remove bacteria.
>
> TRUE/FALSE'

(b) It is difficult to write statements which are unequivocally true or false. It is also difficult for an examiner to distinguish in the pupils' responses, between unfortunate guessing and misinterpretation of the question. This can be overcome by including a request for an explanation of the selection of a particular judgement, for example:

> 'Indicate by deleting the wrong alternative whether the following statements are true or false. If you decide that the statement is false, write in the space provided the word which could make the statement correct.
>
> The sun is a PLANET.
>
> TRUE/FALSE ....
>
> Margarine contains ANIMAL OILS.
>
> TRUE/FALSE ....'

(c) Another variant is as follows:

> 'Draw a circle round T if the statement is always true.
> Draw a circle round F if the statement is always false.
>
> Draw a circle round TF if the statement is true under some circumstances, but false in others.

Mountains are formed by sedimentation process.

T   F   TF

Frosts develop during cloudy nights.

T   F   TF'

(d) In order to improve the statements and to lessen the possibility of ambiguity, it is advisable to avoid vague generalisations and the use of words like: 'all', 'every', 'always', 'never', 'nothing', 'none', 'sometimes', 'often', 'may', 'frequently', and 'could'. The following statements would be unsatisfactory:

    (i) Mountains are usually formed by sedimentation process. (What does usually mean?)

   (ii) Frosts seldom develop during cloudy nights. (How often is seldom?)

MATCHING PAIRS

2.15 These in their simplest form consist of two lists with instructions as to how the matching is to be undertaken and recorded, for example:

'Match the following list of three industrial products against the appropriate industrial process by inserting the relevant product letter against each process:

Products

A. Manufacture of Sulphuric Acid.

B. Production of Steel.

C. Refining of Copper.

Processes	Product
1. Contact Process	. . . .
2. Haber Process	. . . .
3. Electric Air Furnace	. . . .
4. Electrolysis	. . . .
5. Fractional Distillation	. . . . '

Such items are well adapted to measuring the relationship between large amounts of factual information in an economical way, for example names, dates, events, places, results and terms, etc. It is very difficult to test any higher ability with this form of objective questioning.

CORRECT RESPONSE

2.16 This is, of course, another variant of multiple choice, but is sometimes classified separately in the literature.

'What is meant by the assertion that every economic system faces the problem of scarcity?

Indicate with a cross in the appropriate box the response which you consider to be correct.

There are insufficient resources to satisfy the wants of society.

Economic systems develop through an early stage where shortages are common.

There are times when some products can only be had by paying high prices.

Economic systems have cyclically recurring depressions during which scarcities occur.'

ASSERTION-REASON ITEMS

2.17 (a) These are amongst the most heavily debated of all objective items, largely because of the amount of language comprehension involved. This of itself will inevitably reduce the likelihood of correct responses from certain pupils for reasons that have little to do with the questions actually being asked.

(b) Many teachers in consequence reject this type of item although it can test higher cognitive skills. The following is an example:

'The following items contain an assertion and a possible reason for that assertion. Decide first whether each is either True or False. If both are true decide whether the reason given correctly explains the assertion.

Set	Assertion	Reason	Explanation
A	True	True	Correct
B	True	True	Incorrect
C	True	False	Not Applicable
D	False	True	Not Applicable
E	False	False	Not Applicable

Set	Assertion		Explanation
A	Alcohol can be obtained by the fractional distillation of wine.	BECAUSE	Wine contains 12% alcohol.
____	Sheep are not usually grazed on fertile pastures.	BECAUSE	Sheep are more tolerant of poor conditions than are other livestock.'

SHORT-ANSWER ITEMS

2.18 (a) Thyne (1974) points out that obviously if a question is to be given a short answer the rubric must either expressly ask for a short answer or the question be so constructed as to make a longer answer unacceptable. For example:

'Define the term correlation' clearly asks for a short reply.

'What is correlation?' implies that more than a definition is required and hence encourages, or at the least permits, a longer answer.

'What is the scaling of marks?' necessitates a longer answer than:

'When a distribution of marks is "scaled" it is legitimate to alter some but not all its characteristics. What characteristics must NOT be altered?'

It will be seen in the last example that in order to obtain a shorter answer, the question may have to be longer than one designed to produce a longer answer. This is one of the great ironies of question setting.

(b) Tile Hill Wood School demonstrates that short-answer questions can be quite simple and direct, for example:

'What are the factors for the expression $3x^2 - 10x + 3$?

( ) ( ).'

'"One of us girls went down to the shops." Cross out the grammatically incorrect word and write the correct word in this space . . . . '

ADVANTAGES AND DISADVANTAGES OF SHORT-ANSWER ITEMS

2.19 (a) On the credit side it can be said that the short-answer item can:

    (i) require more than just recognition and recall;

    (ii) demand a certain amount of coherence in the answer;

    (iii) be marked more objectively than an essay question;

    (iv) embrace a greater subject area than an essay;

    (v) be marked more quickly than an essay;

    (vi) be less time-consuming to construct than a good multiple choice item;

    (vii) not provide as much opportunity for guessing as a multiple choice item.

(b) On the debit side the short-answer item:

    (i) may penalise high ability pupils by providing insufficient scope for them, and may help the less able in not allowing them an opportunity to display their weaknesses;

    (ii) makes less demand on the pupil as regards concentration and application than does an essay;

    (iii) is not suitable for certain answers, for example answers to questions on literary appreciation.

(c) Teachers who are constructing short-answer items would be wise to observe the following major points:

    (i) Decide precisely what knowledge, ideas and skills are to be tested.

    (ii) Divide subjects to be tested into areas, for example Physics could be divided into Heat, Light and Sound.

    (iii) Decide which sections within each area are to be tested.

    (iv) Spend considerable time wording the instructions at the top of the test paper (the rubric), especially if the candidates have had no experience of this type of test before.

(Exercise 5.17)

STRUCTURE IN WRITTEN QUESTIONS

2.20 (a) There is a gap in assessment techniques between the free responses sought by an essay and the limited responses required by objective items. This can be filled to a large extent by structured questions which provide pupils with some guidance as to the lines their answer might take, i.e. a framework within which to work.

(b) In their guide to writing objective items and structured questions, SREB (1978) suggest that structure can perform two very important functions. First, it can provide pupils with very definite signposts for the writing of answers, even to the extent of providing potential, although not exclusive, paragraph headings. Secondly, it can provide them with stimuli and even on occasion some basic material with which to launch their answers — particularly important for questions designed to elicit an imaginative response. Such questions can be made to operate over a wide ability range and to encourage students to demonstrate their mastery of the defined skills at varying levels of sophistication according to the use they make of the structure, and according to its complexity.

(c) Structuring has thus encouraged the organisation and interrelationship of essentially short-answer questions into sets often based upon common material or information. It is also possible to introduce additional material part way through the set of questions, but if this is done it must be exploited by the questions which follow. All material used must, of course, be concise and comprehensible to those responding to it. If, however, it is intended to test abilities other than recall then the material should either be unfamiliar to the respondents or presented in an unfamiliar way. The overall purpose of any set of questions should always be readily discernible to those attempting to answer them.

(d) Macintosh and Hale (1976) consider that in setting such sets of questions the following guidelines are useful:

    (i) The parts of the questions should in general be open-ended but require short answers.

    (ii) The questions should in general be easy at the start and grow progressively more difficult towards the end of the set. The degree of difficulty can be associated with a requirement for longer answers but not necessarily in every case.

(iii) The questions should be self-contained and not dependent upon a correct response to an earlier one.

(iv) An appropriate space should be provided on the question paper for the length of the response expected from the pupil.

(v) The questions asked should interact as much as possible with the material used.

(vi) The mark scheme should be constructed at the same time as the questions.

(Exercise 5.18)

(e) Attention has been given recently to developing ways of inserting structure into the heart of questions themselves. In order to do this, it is necessary to ask 'What makes a question more or less difficult?' The answer to this can be summed up in three words: Format, Material and Task.

Structure can, therefore, be inserted into a question in one or more of three major ways, i.e. by altering the:

(i) Question format (phraseology and form of response).

(ii) Material supplied (closed) or the factual references demanded (open).

(iii) Task posed (concepts or skills to be used).

These three elements of a question, it needs to be said, can be altered independently of one another and the question made more or less difficult as a result.

Some interesting examples of structure taken from History follow, as paragraphs 2.20 (f) to 2.20 (i), and these are followed by some rather more traditional examples taken from Geography, as paragraphs 2.20 (j), (k) and (l).

EXAMPLES – HISTORY AND GEOGRAPHY

(f) **Example 1**
(Familiar Essay Question)

'Describe and account for the successes and failures of the Irish Home Rule Movement in the period 1912–1921.'

CONTRAST

'(i) Describe the efforts to gain Home Rule in Ireland 1912–21.

(ii) Why were the Irish Nationalists more successful in 1921 than before?

(iii) In what way was their success marred?'

(1979 SUJB Paper 1 for 'History 13–16')

This is a Stepped Question (Structured *Format*). The English has been opened up and the question has been made easier to understand without in any way affecting the task or the material. This illustration makes an important point, namely that structure can make a question both easier to understand and more difficult to answer. This is a particularly important attribute if you want to use questions to assess students over a wide ability range.

(g) **Example 2**
(Familiar Essay Question)

'Discuss the role played by Arab physicians in the history of medicine.'

CONTRAST

Source A111
An illustration showing Hippocrates examining the urine of his patient.

(From a thirteenth century copy of Hippocrates' works)

'Hippocrates was an Ancient Greek physician, but he is not shown wearing Greek clothes.

What does this suggest about the ways in which mediaeval doctors came to learn about Hippocrates' ideas?'

This is a Source Based Question (Structured *Material/Content*). Here structure limits the field of reference from Arab physicians and the history of medicine as a whole to the link between the mediaeval period and Hippocrates. The task is not affected nor is the format of the question any easier.

(h) **Example 3**

'In what way were the beliefs of the Plains Indians about land-ownership linked to their way of life?'

CONTRAST

Source 1

'"You are foolish to make them so strong. They will still be here when their owners are dead." (Comments of an Indian Chief on seeing British houses during a visit to London.)

Which one of the following features of Indian life best explains the attitude expressed in Source 1?

  Belief in Spirits   Love of Nature
  Nomadic Way of Life Warrior Society

Explain your choice.'

This is an Extended Objective Question (Structured by *Material* and *Format*).

(i) **Example 4**

'Write a letter to a newspaper from the point of view of EITHER a supporter OR an opponent of railway building in the first half of the nineteenth century.'

CONTRAST

'"What can be more ridiculous than the idea of trains travelling twice as fast as stage coaches! We should soon expect people to let themselves be fired off upon one of Congreve's ricochet rockets as to trust themselves to the mercy of such a machine going at such a speed."

Quarterly Review, March 1825

  (i) We treat as normal the fact that Concorde flies at more than twice the speed of existing airliners. Why, then, did people find it "ridiculous" for railway trains to travel "twice as fast as stage coaches"?

  (ii) Give at least two reasons why railways were built in spite of these fears.'

This question is structured by *Format*, *Material* and *Task*.

(j) Example of a Structured Set of Questions

IMMIGRATION TO BRITAIN

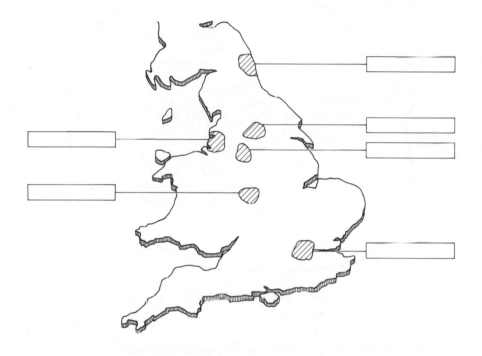

(i) Select three areas from the following list of places in Great Britain, all of which have large numbers of immigrants, and label them in the correct places on the map above:

Tyneside	West Midlands	Greater London	*Marks*
West Yorkshire	S. E. Lancashire	Midlands	3

(ii) Select from the following list a *town* which is located in each of the *areas* listed below:

Towns: LEEDS, LIVERPOOL, MANCHESTER, NOTTINGHAM

Marks

Areas: West Yorkshire   1

South East Lancashire   1

Tyneside   1

(Tile Hill Wood School)

(k) Example of a Set of Related Structured Questions

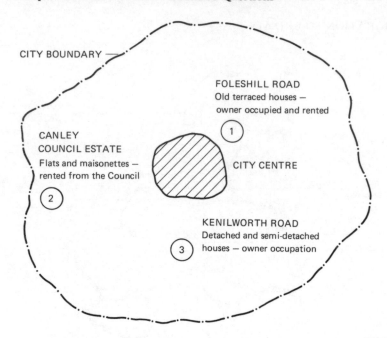

	Marks
(i) Which of the above areas in COVENTRY has a large immigrant population?	
Answer	1
(ii) Explain why you think the immigrants have come to live in COVENTRY.	
. . . .	
. . . .	2
(iii) Suggest two reasons why the immigrants have concentrated in the area you chose for question (i).	
Reason 1	
. . . .	2
Reason 2	
. . . .	2
(iv) Why do you think that the immigrants chose NOT to live in the other two areas of COVENTRY?	
Reason 1	
. . . .	2
Reason 2	
. . . .	2

(v) Do you think that it would be a good or bad idea if the immigrants were to be spread evenly throughout COVENTRY rather than concentrated in one area?

. . . .

Give two reasons for your decision.

Reason 1 . . . .

. . . . **2**

Reason 2 . . . .

. . . . **2**

(vi) Quite a lot of coloured people in COVENTRY are not immigrants. Explain how this can be.

. . . .

. . . .

. . . . **2**

(vii) Quite a lot of immigrants to COVENTRY are NOT coloured. Explain how this can be.

. . . .

. . . .

. . . . **3**

Marks

Total Marks **20**

(Tile Hill Wood School)

(l) Example of a Data Response Structured Question

The following is another example of a structured question, sometimes called, in the literature, data tests, which has been devised by Bicester School to meet the needs of an open access sixth form. The question is intended to supplement a practical test in the use of meteorological instruments.

Look at the diagram on page 76 and answer the questions that follow.

The diagram shows one alcohol-filled thermometer as it appeared on nine consecutive occasions over three days in one week. It is to be assumed that the coldest temperature for each 24-hour period occurred at 0200 hours and that the observer took readings and reset the thermometer at exactly 0900 hours each day.

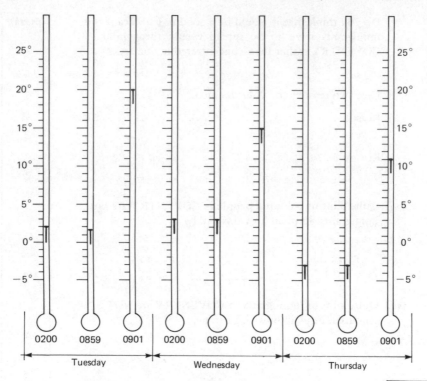

	Marks
1. What was the minimum temperature for the 24-hour period starting at 0900 hours on Monday?	1
2. What is the range of temperatures recorded as minimum values for the three-day period?	1
3. What was the air temperature at the time of the readings on Wednesday?	1
4. What was the average rate of warming up of the air on Thursday morning (express as degrees per hour)?	1
5. How much colder was the temperature at 0900 hours on Thursday compared with 0900 hours on Wednesday?	1
6. On Thursday morning the observer recorded his observation as 3 °C. What mistake did he make?	1
7. The diagram shows that the observer was careless in what he did on one morning. Explain what he did wrong.	2
8. Explain carefully why the mistake, as it turned out, did not cause any errors in the readings.	2
Total Marks	10

From *CLASSROOM GEOGRAPHER*, January 1981. P.J. PERKINS

FURTHER APPROACHES TO STRUCTURING

2.21 Another way of looking at structuring, and it needs to be stressed, incidentally, that all questions are structured to a greater or lesser degree, is to ask oneself the question 'From what sources does one obtain the structure?' There are indeed three major models of which the first is the only one that has been adequately exploited to date. All the examples given in paragraph 2.20 would come into this first category.

(a) **The Mark Scheme Model**

Questions using this model have elements of the mark scheme written into them. The primary aim is to make what is in the examiner's mind more apparent to the student.

(b) **The Classroom Model**

Questions using this model try and reflect typical classroom procedures. The primary aim is to capitalise on the fact that assessment exercises are also learning experiences.

(c) **The Psychological Model**

Questions using this model try to make use of children's ideas and misconceptions to provide the conceptual scaffolding of the question. The primary aim is to make the questions meaningful and appropriate to an 'apprentice' in the subject concerned.

QUESTION SHREDDING

2.22 Structured questions, as with any type of question, or indeed any form of assessment, benefit from being 'shredded' before use. The kinds of questions that need to be asked of questions are set out below in the complete question shredder.

(a) What sorts of response would you expect the question to elicit?

(What ideas or skills does the question address?)

(b) Can anticipated responses be ordered along a single conceptual or skill dimension?

(Will the question test one thing or many?)

(c) Of the sorts of response anticipated, how many merit reward? What is the 'lowest rewardable response'?

(Will the question discriminate in terms of the concept/skill mastery with which your course is concerned?)

(d) Is the question a 'feeder' or a 'paydirt' question?

(Is it useful for what it tells the examiner or because it serves as a signpost to the child?)

(e) How many words can be eliminated without changing the sense of the question?

(f) How many difficult words can be replaced by easier ones without changing the sense of the question?

(g) Identify the form(s) of structuring employed (if any). *Improve* the question or *replace* it with one which does the same job more effectively.

Explain in what ways your question is superior to the original.

ESSAYS – OPEN-ENDED QUESTIONS

2.23 (a) Open-ended questions have three principal characteristics:

    (i) Those answering the question must decide on the material which they will include in their response.

    (ii) Limits are not set upon the length or the style of the response, although this can be predetermined to an extent by demands made in the questions.

    (iii) Little or no structure is provided for the respondent, although the question itself should be specific and unambiguous.

(b) Such questions are a popular form of assessment, particularly for higher ability pupils. It is regarded as being an appropriate vehicle for students to demonstrate such things as:

    (i) Command of language.

    (ii) Powers of analysis.

    (iii) Discrimination in choice of evidence.

    (iv) Argumentative skills.

(c) A problem when setting open-ended questions is how best to make the meaning explicit, without discouraging at the same time a variety of open-ended responses. The directions or lead words in the question need very careful thought. If the teacher asks the pupils to 'describe the causes of the American Civil War', 'describe' is all you can expect them to do. If, however, the teacher wants them to 'account for', 'explain' or 'estimate the relative importance of the causes', then the question needs to be specific and say so by using the appropriate word or words. If this is done, then the marking can reward those who demonstrate their capacity to do what is asked.

(d) Pidgeon and Yates (1969) consider that the essay question by virtue of the relatively small number of questions which can be sensibly included in a single test is of little value as a means of securing adequate sampling of a course as a whole. It is also a form of questioning which particularly favours pupils with a facility in language, and can exclude others who have achieved perfectly adequate understanding or mastery of their subject, but cannot indicate this in prose. Marking of essays must depend very much upon subjective judgement, and for that reason accuracy and consistency of scoring (reliability) are difficult to achieve. This topic will be dealt with at some length in paragraphs 2.28 to 2.36.

(Exercise 5.18)

PREPARED ESSAY

2.24 This technique requires that the pupils are to be given in advance either the topic upon which the essay question is to be based or the actual question itself. How soon this information is supplied is best determined by the teacher responsible. Any such decision should take into account the current workload of the pupils which should be such as not to preclude adequate preparation.

ADVANTAGES AND DISADVANTAGES OF ESSAYS

2.25 (a) The essay as a technique of assessment has disadvantages:

  (i) It is time-consuming for the pupil and covers a relatively small area of the subject being studied.

  (ii) The marking is very subjective. Possible causes of variation in marking are discussed in Chapter 1, paragraph 1.24 (a) (iii).

  (iii) A single essay does not provide an acceptable measure of the ability of the writer to write at length or to sustain an argument or to analyse any views, or indeed any of the skills for which it is deemed an appropriate measure.

 (b) On the other hand, it can be said that an essay question is relatively simple to set. It is also a good measure of power of expression in a situation where the writer is not limited by a set of specific requirements and can, in consequence, develop ideas and respond to the question in any way he may wish.

OPEN-BOOK EXAMINATIONS

2.26 (a) Earnshaw (1974) suggests that Open-book examinations are perhaps best suited to English Literature, or to subjects which make use of a wider range of printed material.

  The pupil has access to the source material throughout the test. This aspect of the examination removes the temptation for the industrious or apprehensive pupil to learn the passage by heart and provide, thereby, verbatim quotations from the text.

(b) Questions for this type of examination need to be set with a view to stimulating the use of books rather than to treating them as a factual source or a
sort of licensed crib. They could take the form of a request for a comparison
of two passages, or an appreciation of the writer's style or use of poetry. It
is, of course, a form of examination which is best suited to the more able
pupils.

(c) Problems may be encountered over the use of standard works of famous
authors, such as Shakespeare, which usually contain copious notes and
appendices which could make the selection of usable questions difficult.
The use of classroom texts presents problems for the invigilators who would
have to check that the printed text had not been supplemented with useful
aides-mémoire. This can be overcome, of course, by the use of reproduced
texts either within the examination paper or as an appendix to it.

PRE-TESTING AND POST-TESTING

2.27 (a) **Pre-testing**

Pre-testing simply means trying out questions, complete tests or examinations upon those who will subsequently be taking that test or examination.
For obvious reasons pre-testing will usually be carried out on a group as
similar as possible in composition (e.g. as regards age, sex, type of school
and ability range) to the actual entry.

Pre-testing can allow evaluation of the quality of individual questions (item
analysis) and ensure that only questions of proven quality will be included
in the final form of the examination. For example, an analysis of pre-test
results such as that carried out by the History Department of Plowden
School and described in paragraph 2.7 (c) to 2.7 (e) can quite quickly
indicate where items or questions are not satisfactory. Any such analysis
needs to be treated with caution, particularly when the sample, as was the
case with Plowden School, is a small one. Large-scale pre-testing exercises,
such as those conducted by examining boards, would normally use a sample
of around 400 candidates.

(b) Pre-testing of an informal kind has always been carried out by those who set
questions either for their own use or for public examination. Questions are
tried out upon pupils as a part of normal classroom activities and some
feeling at least obtained regarding their likely difficulty and the clarity or
otherwise of their meaning for the pupils.

Nuttall and Willmott (1972) point out that it was not until the introduction of large-scale objective testing in the United Kingdom in the late
1960s, that formal and systematic analysis became a normal part of test
construction for examinations which involved their use. As well as providing
information about the ease or difficulty with which candidates answer
specific items (facility index) and the capacity of items to discriminate
between pupils (discrimination index), formal pre-testing also enables

deficiencies in the writing of items to be detected and remedied. It further provides information upon which to base the timing of the part or the whole of an examination. The value of such information has resulted in work being undertaken in recent years upon the analysis of more open-ended questions. Here question choice and marker reliability make the techniques employed for objective items inappropriate. We can almost certainly expect to see a considerable extension of this work in the future.

(c)   (i) **Post-testing**

For most teachers in the classroom, however, the systems adopted by large-scale examining bodies for pre-testing and analysis are totally impracticable. Much the same information can be obtained far less elaborately after the questions or items have been answered by the pupils in the test itself (post-testing). Teachers should moreover try to record the information, preferably as a collaborative exercise, in permanent form upon cards, and to develop a store or bank of proven questions or items for future use. Wood and Skurnik (1969) provide useful guidance upon Item Banking, although the work they describe is in relation to possible developments at national rather than school level.

(ii) **Question Banking**

Now that computer technology is becoming more familiar in schools, there is a need to devote attention to the potential for the storage and retrieval of information which this facility presents.

(iii) Post-testing can also provide very useful evaluative information. An analysis of those questions found to be most difficult will provide useful pointers, not only to the quality of the examination but also to the effectiveness of the course, the method of instruction and the materials used. It is not enough, however, simply to collect information; it must be used and whilst this involves a great deal of time the return is well worth the effort.

MARKING

2.28 (a) All assessment has two major stages, the construction of the instruments designed to elicit responses and the evaluation of those responses. When relating these two stages to secondary school internal or external assessment there is a tendency in a rather over-simplified way to use the two terms 'setting' and 'marking'. So far this chapter has concentrated on the setting process, largely, although not exclusively, in relation to written questions. The next few paragraphs will deal with marking; again this will concentrate mainly on written assessment, but the principles apply equally well to the other forms of assessment covered in this chapter.

(b) Marks in themselves have no intrinsic value. They are simply symbols, as are grades, which can be used to give an indication (very rough in reality) of a level of achievement. In the literature they are often described as tools or devices to enable comparisons to be made between individuals. The ease with which marks can be added, subtracted, multiplied and divided makes them dangerous instruments for this purpose, because they appear to be much more absolute and accurate than they are in reality. The characteristics of numerical scores and percentages will be discussed at some length in Chapter 3, see Appendix A, and their subsequent handling and interpretation in paragraphs A2 to A4 of that Appendix.

(c) True and Observed Scores

Ebel (1979) reminds us that in awarding marks one is attempting always to establish what is known as the 'true score'. A true score is an idealised error-free score for a specific person on a specific test. It may also be defined as the mean of an infinite number of independent measurements of the same trait using equivalent forms of the test. This second definition assumes that as the number of independent measurements of the same trait in that same person is increased, the average value of the errors associated with these measures approaches zero. The actual score which a person does receive (usually called the observed score) is, of course, affected by all the sources of variability discussed in the previous chapter, paragraphs 1.24 to 1.26. In terms of a formula:

$$\text{Observed Score} = \text{True Score} \pm \text{Error Score}$$

(See also Chapter 3, Appendix A, paragraph A2.2.)

(d) Any system of assessment ought to try to do two things. First, to reduce error, and, secondly to extend the information that can be squeezed out of the assessment in order to increase and improve feedback. There is a clear difference here between the needs of large-scale examining agencies, whose major concern lies with reliability, and those of teachers who are concerned primarily with feedback, although the current interest in profiling for public examinations suggests that these differences are to some extent reconcilable. For the former, marks or grades or percentages are sufficient, provided that the system reduces the error of measurement to an acceptable level or, in other words, tries to make the gap between the true score and observed score as small as possible. For the latter, marks, grades and percentages are insufficient in themselves and need to be accompanied by comment or correction indicating why they have been awarded and how they have been earned.

(e) The paragraphs which follow will, to some extent, reflect these differences and the tensions which can result from them. It is hoped, however, by looking first at different approaches to marking, and then at some general issues which arise in relation to marking, that both teachers and examination administrators will find points which are of practical value to them. In the end, of course, any marking exercise, be it large or small, must produce its own unique scheme for implementation which will reflect the nature and purpose of the exercise and take proper account of those involved. The

extent to which the marking scheme satisfactorily reflects these considerations will largely determine its success or failure. It does, however, need
stressing by way of a cautionary note, that no exercise in human judgement
can ever be wholly reliable. The most perfect mark scheme in combination
with the most carefully thought out and implemented marking arrangements will never eliminate error, they can only reduce it. Moreover, the
extent to which it can be reduced depends as much upon what and who is
being assessed as upon who is undertaking the assessment.

APPROACHES TO MARKING

2.29 (a) It is customary in the literature to illustrate differences in approaches to
marking by the terms 'analytic' and 'impression'. The analytic approach is
based upon aggregation in which the points to be rewarded and the size of
the reward in mark terms are set out in some detail. The impression approach,
on the other hand, implies an overall global judgement and those undertaking the marking are provided with relatively little detail. Such definitions
have resulted in an artificial polarisation; in reality most marking must
embody both approaches if it is to do adequate justice to the work being
marked and those responsible for it. As such, it represents another facet in
the endless struggle in assessment between, on the one hand, objectivity
and, on the other, the need to recognise and reward individual differences.
Obviously the nature of the subject or subject matter being assessed, the
extent to which skills or concepts or facts are involved, whether or not one
is concerned with specific or generalised levels of marking, the purpose(s)
for which any information gained from the assessment is to be used, the
numbers involved, and a whole host of related considerations, will affect the
approach being adopted and will deflect it in one direction or another. It
will be rare, however, for there not to be some mixture of the two approaches
in most marking and this point should be borne in mind when reading the
sections on analytic and impression marking which follow.

(b) Some recent work in England on the assessment of skills and concepts arising
out of a national secondary school curriculum project in History (History
13–16) involving a fairly wide ability range of students, has led to the
development of some rather different approaches to both marking and
weighting. One of these, called criteria related marking, is elaborated in
some detail because of its unfamiliarity, using by way of illustration a
question from the 1980 History 13–16 CSE Unseen Evidence Paper 2,
which had as its topic 'What happened to the Romanovs?' Quite apart from
its suitability or otherwise as a mark scheme for its intended purposes, it
also illustrates how feedback to teachers can be incorporated into the
marking of public examinations. (See paragraph 2.33 (h).)

ANALYTICAL MARKING

2.30 (a) Analytical marking is the system most frequently used today by large-scale
public examining agencies and probably also by teachers in the classroom.

D

Its two basic characteristics are mark allocations and mark schemes. It is, as Murphy (1979) reminds us, essential to distinguish between these two. The mark scheme provides the comprehensive statement of the explicit criteria against which the relevant work/answers are to be assessed. The mark allocation, which may or may not be indicated to the respondents, assigns specific marks to specific questions or parts of questions, and it is the marker's task to allocate these accurately and appropriately. The scheme may, of course, assist in this regard by illustrating how the mark allocation is to be broken down in relation to specific kinds of answers.

(b) In the following illustration, provided by Ward (1981), the marking schemes provide criteria which are of varying objectivity. The questions, which are linked, relate to fabrication and welding techniques.

First Question   *Marks*
'What is the function of a suppressor on a tungsten arc
gas-shielded welding set?'   (4 marks)

Marking Scheme
A suppressor is fitted to prevent inherent rectification of an
alternating current (AC) taking place.   (3 marks)
It suppresses the direct current (DC) component.   (1 mark)

Second Question
'What is the function of a contactor in a gas-shielded welding
circuit?'   (4 marks)

Marking Scheme
To ensure that the electrode is dead when not in use.   (4 marks)

Third Question
'The following gases are used for gas-shielded metal arc
welding. In each case state ONE material and the mode of
metal transfer for which each gas is most suitable.
  A. Argon
  B. Argon plus 15% nitrogen
  C. Argon plus 15% oxygen.'   (12 marks)

Marking Scheme
A. Aluminium, nickel or copper   (2 marks)
    Mode: Dip, pulse or spray   (2 marks)

B. Copper (2 marks)   (2 marks)
    Mode: Spray   (2 marks)

C. Low carbon or low alloy steels   (2 marks)
    Mode: Pulse or spray   (2 marks)

ACCEPTABLE ALTERNATIVES

(c) Marking schemes, particularly those prepared for questions where correct terminology is a factor, can be constructed to provide for acceptable or partially correct alternatives. This example of a question relates to painting and decorating.

Question
'State how the application of gloss paint at a temperature
near 0°C would affect brushing qualities of the paint.'   (2 marks)

Anticipated Correct Answer
It would increase the viscosity of the paint.   (2 marks)

Acceptable Alternative Answer
It would thicken the paint. Make it harder to brush.   (2 marks)

Partially Correct Answers
It would not drip.   (1 mark)
Brush marks would show.   (1 mark)
Undercoat would not be covered.   (1 mark)

(d) The layout and character of a marking scheme will be decided on the type
of assessment technique which is to be applied. They need not necessarily
be highly specific and the following example presents two alternative
schemes for a mathematics question.

Question
'Write down the factors of $x^2 - 9y^2$. Hence or otherwise solve the equations

$$x^2 - 9y^2 = 15$$

$$x - 3y = 5'$$ (7 marks)

(i) *First Alternative Marking Scheme (Analytical)*

	Marks	Notes
Factors are $x + 3y$ and $x - 3y$	B1	For factor (cao)
$\therefore (x + 3y)(x - 3y) = 15$		
but $x - 3y = 5$		
$\therefore (x + 3y)5 = 15$	M1	For subtracting 5 for $x - 3y$
$\therefore x + 3y = 3$	A1	For this equation
Since $x - 3y = 5$	M1	For attempting to solve the pair of linear equations properly
$2x = 8$		
$x = 4$	A1	(cao)
By substitution $4 - 3y = 5$	M1	For substituting value of x
$-3y = 1 \qquad y = -\dfrac{1}{3}$	A1	(ft)

Total   7 marks

Although this scheme may meet most requirements the second
alternative would provide greater flexibility for the marker

(ii) *Second Alternative Marking Scheme (Flexible)*

	Marks	Notes
Factors are $x + 3y$ and $x - 3y$	B1	For factors (cao)
$x = 3y + 5$ or $y = \dfrac{x-5}{3}$	M1	For trying to get $x =$ or $y =$
Substituting for x (or y) in the other equation		
e.g. $(3y + 5)^2 - 9y^2 = 15$	M1	For substituting for x
$\therefore 9y^2 + 30y + 25 - 9y^2 = 15$	A1	For expanding $(3y + 5)^2$
$\therefore \dfrac{30y}{3y} = -10$		
$\therefore y = -\dfrac{1}{3}$	A1	(cao)
Substituting $x = -1 + 5 = 4$	M1	For substituting value of y
	A1	(ft)
	Total	7 marks

Notes: (Alternative Schemes)

M = Method mark (for use of correct method).

A = Accuracy mark (for obtaining the correct answer by using the correct method).

B = Accuracy mark (for obtaining the correct answer independent of method used).

A distinction is sometimes drawn between two sets of circumstances in which marks may be awarded for accuracy.

ft = where the marks could be considered as being in the 'follow through' category. Such marks could be obtained for answers which are in fact incorrect, but are consistent with answers previously given.

cao = marks which can be awarded for the correct answer.

(e) In the next example the effect of an incorrect part answer is considered.

Question

'State which of the following vitamins are water soluble.   4 marks

Vitamin   A   B   C   D   K'

Marking Scheme
Vitamins B and C — 2 marks each
Deduct 1 mark for each incorrect answer given.

In this example the wording of the question is at fault. It could avoid negative marking and be better phrased as: 'State whether each of the following vitamins is either water soluble or fat soluble'. It would seem unjust to ignore a wrong part answer and award two marks if, for example, the pupil answered B, C and K, since the pupil who did not include K, knowing that it was fat soluble, would receive the same mark as the pupil who did not know.

(f) Marks should not be allocated for anything which is not clearly required to be answered by the phrasing of the question. The following example would be difficult to implement.

Question
'Name the teeth which make up the set of temporary (milk) teeth in a human being.'   8 marks

Marking Scheme

8 incisors	(2 marks)
4 canines	(2 marks)
8 molars	(2 marks)
Correct order	(2 marks)

Total   8 marks

The marking scheme provides for the number and type of teeth and their place in the jaw, but the question only asks that they should be named. The pupil who by chance gave the right answer would gain two marks, but those who answered the question would be penalised.

(Exercise 5.22)

IMPRESSION MARKING

2.31 (a) It will readily be seen from paragraph 2.30 that analytical marking and the preparation of mark schemes relating to this approach can be quite complex. By contrast, impression marking is simple albeit demanding. When carried out by a single marker/examiner, assessing, say, up to one hundred scripts, the following procedure is adopted.

(i) A sample of the scripts (up to about one-third) is selected at random to try to replicate the ability range involved.

(ii) These are then read rapidly by the marker to get an idea of the general standard. No marks will be given, but the papers or essays, or whatever the work may be, will be classified as good, moderate or poor. This preliminary stage can be carried through as many times as is deemed necessary in order to firmly establish the general standard.

The degree of discrimination can also be extended or reduced according to need. Five categories, very good, good, moderate, poor and very poor, probably represents the norm at which to aim, and these five categories could be assigned grades A to E or bands of marks if that was thought to be helpful.

(iii) The assessor then reads all the scripts and assigns them to the appropriate piles. It cannot be too strongly stressed that the assessor is passing a general judgement on the quality of each piece of work as the result of a quick general impression and is not required to look for points of detail.

(iv) If it is necessary to establish a rank order within categories then every piece of work within each category will have to be re-read in order to establish the end points, for example the best and the worst piece of work. All the remaining pieces of work will then need to be ranked in relation to these end points.

(b) If the exercise is a large-scale one then both the number of pieces of work and the number of assessors will be increased. The basic principles, however, remain the same, although it is possible that multiple marking will be used (see paragraph 2.32). Impression marking tends to be used for marking subjective work such as poetry or painting or English essays.

(c) Any approach to marking, as with any approach to assessment, tends to benefit some and disadvantage others. The analytical approach benefits those students who are sound on their factual knowledge and can display that knowledge in an orderly and sequential fashion without much in the way of flair or panache.

The impression approach aids those students who can express themselves fluently, but are on occasion short on information. You can conduct an interesting experiment by marking the same pieces of work first with a detailed mark scheme and then after an interval of time (say two weeks) by impression. In general you will find that the two judgements correspond for most of your students, but there are some who will do better or worse according to the approach adopted. This merely confirms the point made at the outset of the paragraphs on marking, that wherever possible you should try to use both approaches in order to provide a balanced judgement.

(Exercises 5.19 and 5.21)

MULTIPLE MARKING

2.32 (a) The descriptions given in paragraphs 2.30 and 2.31 of the two approaches have assumed that each piece of work has only been marked by one person, although, of course, it may, and probably will, have been checked by others. This need not be the case; indeed when impression marking is employed on a large scale it often involves multiple marking which makes use of two or three markers for each piece of work. There are two possible ways of using additional markers. First, simply to provide further judgements based on the same criteria whatever these may be. When this is done it is normal practice to average out the different judgements and give that average to the student This presupposes that two are inherently better than one and three are better still, which is not, of course, necessarily true. You may simply have three similar judgements. If all are sound or all are unsound then you will not have benefitted the person being assessed one iota and you will have wasted resources.

(b) Moreover, if the judgements vary as a result of the vagaries of the assessors and not as a result of the nature of the work being assessed, then again no benefit will result. The second alternative is to ask a different marker to look for and to assess something different. One common illustration of this is to ask one marker to look at the mechanics of an English essay, spelling, punctuation and the like, whilst another looks at the range of vocabulary and so on. Under such circumstances one would expect the marks to differ and one could, therefore, legitimately add them up as they stood and use them as the basis upon which to judge the assessed person. Whatever the deficiencies, multiple marking does ensure that a piece of work is judged by more than one person and this is an important principle, especially when the work involved is subjective in nature. In terms of improved reliability there is no great value, incidentally, in using more than three markers.

CRITERIA RELATED MARKING

2.33 **(a)** As already indicated in paragraph 2.29 (b), recent work on the assessment of skills and the consideration of problems of assessment in relation to a wider range of ability has brought about a reappraisal of marking approaches as well as the techniques of assessment.

The approach to marking, described here, has been developed as part of the 'CSE Examination for History 13–16', a project sponsored by the Schools Council, which has been examining candidates since 1976. A brief summary of the system follows. This gives some of the salient features of the procedures adopted, but greater detail, including examples of the question paper, answers by the pupils and marking comments, can be obtained from the report *'The 1980 Written Examination' History 13–16 CSE Examination, Schools Council Project*, pages 118–20 SREB (1980a).

(Exercise 5.42)

(b) From experience gained in previous examinations, it had become apparent that a traditionally based marking scheme was not satisfactory for an examination designed to test skills in the use of evidence. Such schemes did not:

(i) permit sufficient discrimination between different answers to a question;

(ii) encourage a sufficient variety of responses, in that the scheme implied that there was a correct answer, and markers were under an obligation to disregard some answers which merited reward;

(iii) reward adequately pupils who demonstrated that they had grasped project concepts. This was a consequence of the mark scheme being constructed around anticipated responses from pupils in respect of information.

(c) It was, therefore, decided to construct a scheme of marking based upon a hierarchically ordered set of criteria. The principle behind the 'ordering' was the establishment of a progressive series of levels of abstraction. This meant taking less for granted about the necessity for pupils to have a good grasp of supplied sources and going more for development of ideas based on, or arising out of, the information given. An example of such a set is given below:

Level 1
The ability to relate conclusions to the evidence which had been supplied in the question.

Level 2
The ability to pose specific questions in respect of the evidence supplied.

Level 3
The ability to make simple generalisations on the basis of the evidence supplied.

Level 4
The ability to extend an account by cross-referencing between sources of information.

Level 5
The ultimate level for that age range as regards their ability to consider what is to count as sufficiency of evidence.

(d) The criteria were constructed by first identifying the minimum response level which would be worthy of any reward (Level 1), and then working through the levels to Level 5, which was, for the question concerned, seen as the highest criterion likely to emerge from the answers of that age group. The set quoted in the example would, of course, be only applicable to one particular question. The actual answers might well reveal that the levels were not sufficiently discriminatory and more levels than those given in the example could be required.

(e) Prior to the examination, tentative hierarchies were constructed; these were then adjusted, after scrutiny of a sample of completed papers, by a group of teachers of the subject. The final set of criteria were thus shaped more by pupils' answers, with their conceptions and misconceptions, than by any assumptions about anticipated responses.

(f) Having established the levels, the range of marks for each level was determined on the basis of weighting, conceptual understanding, length of answer required, degree of difficulty, etc. In the example quoted later (paragraph 2.33 (h)), the allocation of marks for the question was 10, and each level was allowed a band of 2–3 marks to allow for some personal appraisal of the quality of the response by the marker.

(g) Markers were then provided with the adjusted levels of criteria plus examples of particular pupils' answers which were considered to meet specified levels. They were then required to identify the highest level of criterion met by the student in each answer and to select a mark from within the range of marks specified for that criterion.

(h) An example follows which relates to a question in which the students were invited to comment on the differences between two accounts provided for them on what might have happened to the Romanov family. The question reads as follows: 'In what ways do these two accounts of Sergeyev's investigation differ?'

Level 1 — Criteria   *Marks*
Valid superficial differences, or focus on concrete difference.   1–2

Examples of students' answers
'The dates are contradictory.'
'One is given by a Russian, one by an American.'
'Because on one he has all the information on the folder and on the other he just speaks.'
Note: One difference is sufficient to score 2 marks.

Level 2 — Criteria
Comprehension — disagreement whether all or part of the
family was murdered and, if so, where.   3–5

Example of student answer
'In evidence A it says all the Royal Family were massacred in the house — and in B it says that the Empress and her children were not shot in that house.'
Note: Reference to number: 3 marks, reference to house: 4 marks, reference to both 5 marks.

Level 3 — Criteria
Reference to attitudes, i.e. certainty, doubt, etc.   6–7

Example of student answer
'In the first account Sergeyev was quite definite. In the second account he says that the massacre was supposed to have taken place.'

Level 4 — Criteria
Recognise the different provenance of the source.   9–10

Example of student answer
'In evidence A, Judge Sergeyev strongly believes the family

was shot (and this was said to have been written by himself)
but was handed over to Judge Sokolov. But evidence B states
that only the family doctors, two servants and the maids were
shot. (This was written in the New York Tribune.) This paper
could be biased on either account.'

SUMMING UP – CRITERIA RELATED MARKING

(i) In conclusion it can be said that this approach when combined with a shift
in the timing of weighting from before to after marking ('Post hoc'), has
several general advantages. It enables markers to compensate for departures
from anticipated responses to questions. Questions may elicit higher levels
of skills of understanding than expected and require higher weighting.

Conversely, questions may have proved to be more difficult than expected.
This may be due to:

   (i) poor layout;

   (ii) ambiguities in wording;

   (iii) insufficient structure to invite more than self-evident responses;

   (iv) source material being too difficult for the ability level of the pupils.

Post hoc weighting would seem to be fairer to pupils and more rational an
application of assessment. It also has the advantage of freeing the examiner
to experiment, both with source materials and styles of questions, without
prejudice to the pupils being assessed.

In addition, the system has proved to be a considerable aid to curriculum
evaluation (as can be seen by reference to SREB (1980a and b). It may well
be asked, however, whether the approach presents markers with undue
difficulty. Experience has shown that, with training, markers can operate
this scheme as satisfactorily as any other. It has also shown that the real
difficulty lies in bringing about the change of attitude necessary if teachers
are to relate actual work to the achievement of criteria.

POSITIVE AND NEGATIVE MARKING

2.34 Regardless of the approach used, an important factor in relation to marking is
the attitude of those undertaking it. This is often expressed as the difference
between positive and negative marking. Does one reward marks for what is
correct ('correct' being defined in relation to the criteria being used and not
simply meaning accurate), or does one deduct marks for what is incorrect? In
the first case the approach is positive, whilst in the second it is negative. Quite
apart from its implications for the whole teaching/learning process, the use of
negative marking can quite markedly reduce a student's score. Try using a
positive and a negative scheme for the marking of an English or a French (or any
other language) dictation and you will soon see the differences that can result.

In general, always try to be positive and build this into your marking arrangements.

One slightly different facet of positive marking is a willingness to use the full range of available marks. Most people when marking work are extremely miserly and award 'full marks' with reluctance. This is less easy to avoid doing in a subject like Mathematics than it is in a subject like English, but even here 'perfection is seen to be out of the reach of students'! One way of trying to eliminate this negative attitude of mind lies through the use of bonus marks. This simply means giving markers an extra allocation of marks, over and above the overall total, for them to use when work of a particularly high quality is observed.

PREPARATION OF MARK SCHEMES

2.35 (a) Reference has been made frequently in paragraphs 2.28 to 2.34 to mark schemes. They obviously assume greater importance when an analytic or criteria related approach is being adopted than when using impression marking, although even here a marking framework is necessary. Whilst there are no absolute rules for the preparation of mark schemes, they can only all benefit from the application of a check list containing questions such as the following:

  (i) Are the suggested answers appropriate to the questions?

  (ii) Are the suggested answers technically and/or numerically correct?

  (iii) Does the scheme embrace every point required by the question and allocate marks for each point?

  (iv) Does the answer in the scheme include only points required by the question?

  (v) Are the marks allocated strictly according to the knowledge and abilities which the question requires the candidate to demonstrate?

  (vi) Is there adequate provision for acceptable alternative answers?

  (vii) Are the marks commensurate with the degree of difficulty of the question and the time which would be required to answer it?

  (viii) Is the time allowance appropriate for the work required?

  (ix) Is the marking scheme sufficiently broken down to allow the marking to be as objective as possible?

  (x) Is the totalling of marks correct?

  (xi) Does the marking scheme reflect undue bias towards one viewpoint at the expense of others?

It cannot be too strongly emphasised, however, that mark schemes are for use and not for decoration. Consistency of application may well, therefore, be an overriding consideration as it is for public examining boards.

(b) Consistency in the application of marking schemes was causing some concern to the Head of History at our imaginary Plowden Comprehensive School.

(c) It was now early November and Bruce Bennett was telephoned at home one evening by the Head of Department, Harry Davenport. He was concerned about the apparent difference in performance between the two fourth year forms, 4M and 4P, on Syllabus A. He had become aware of this during a routine walk around the Department. In accordance with the wishes of the Headmistress, great pains had been taken to ensure an even mixture of abilities in each form, using the third year's examination results as a basic measure of achievement. In making up groups they had also taken into account reports from the Vocational Guidance Counsellor, assessments of affective characteristics, and had tried to consider predictive aspects as well. He had every confidence in Mr. Henderson and felt sure that Miss Glover was conscientious and highly intelligent, but nevertheless he felt something was going wrong. Should he change them round, or what would Bruce, in the strictest confidence, suggest?

(d) Bruce suggested that all mark books be withdrawn by the Head of Department as a routine procedure of inspection and that Bruce should be given the opportunity to analyse those of the two teachers concerned. This was done.

(e) It was fortunate that both teachers had marked as per standing instructions. Their mark books were both up-to-date, six sets of marks each for 28 pupils. This was made possible by the following of a fairly rigid timetable, and by the issue of particular packs of resource material and work sheets at pre-determined intervals, for example 'Town and Country in the Eighteenth Century' was issued in Week 1, 'Enclosures' in Week 4.

(f)   (i) Bruce decided to produce the two sets of marks as distribution curves (see Chapter 3, Appendix A, paragraph A2.4), and to compare them. Under the standing instructions for marking at Plowden, each piece of coursework was marked out of a maximum of 10.

        The two sets of marks, the frequency with which they were awarded and the curves they produced. were as follows.

    (ii) *Dick Henderson*

Marks	Pupil/ Times Awarded	(Total Marks)	Marks	Pupil/ Times Awarded	(Total Marks)
1	3	(3)	6	43	(258)
2	5	(10)	7	39	(273)
3	6	(18)	8	20	(160)
4	11	(44)	9	6	(54)
5	30	(150)	10	0	(0)

Total Marks (28 pupils 6 Markings)   970

$$\text{Mean} = \frac{970}{28 \times 6 - 5^*} = 5.95$$

*Pupils who failed to produce work for marking.

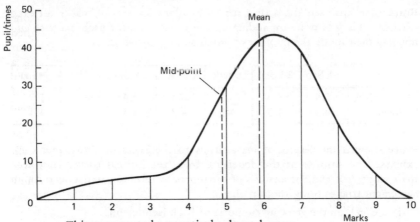

This represented a negatively skewed curve.

(iii) *Greta Glover*

Marks	Pupil/ Times Awarded	(Total Marks)	Marks	Pupil/ Times Awarded	(Total Marks)
1	5	(5)	6	24	(144)
2	17	(34)	7	10	(70)
3	29	(87)	8	3	(24)
4	34	(136)	9	0	(0)
5	41	(205)	10	0	(0)

Total Marks (28 Pupils 6 Markings) 705

$$\text{Mean} = \frac{705}{28 \times 6 - 8^*} = 4.41$$

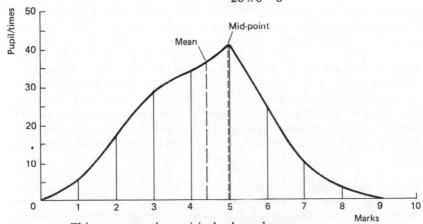

This represented a positively skewed curve.

*Pupils who failed to produce work for marking.

Bruce then analysed the scores for each of the six sets of marks for each teacher. This was done by adding up the total score for each exercise and dividing the sum by the number of pupils submitting work.

	14 Sep	28 Sep	6 Oct	14 Oct	20 Oct	1 Nov	Mean
Henderson	5.5	5.4	5.7	6.1	6.4	6.7	5.97
Glover	4.5	4.3	4.3	4.4	4.4	4.5	4.4

(g) Bruce showed the results of his analysis to the Head of Department. He expressed no surprise at the departure from the normal curve. They told their story well and the analysis of the scores he felt indicated a need for an agreement trial to bring about perhaps:

(i) a check on the growing euphoria of Dick Henderson;

(ii) a gentle nudge towards less-exacting attitudes on the part of Greta Glover.

He hoped it would help to standardise 4M and 4P without having to reveal his concern to the two teachers. He would, nevertheless, monitor very carefully the fourth year papers in the Christmas vacation.

(Exercise 5.30)

WEIGHTING

2.36 (a) One significant issue raised by the preparation of mark schemes is that of weighting. Any plan of assessment ultimately requires decisions to be taken about the relative weighting of the components that go to make up the total assessment. Put another way, decisions have to be made about the value to be placed upon this particular aspect or that particular skill. In assessment, the assigning aspect of weighting usually takes the form of allocating X or Y marks or X% or Y% to a particular question or section of the assessment. This X or Y should reflect not only relative importance, but also the time demands it places upon those being assessed. Decisions about weighting are essentially subjective decisions, but if they are to make sense they must take account of earlier decisions made about course objectives, course content and the techniques to be used for assessment. These decisions will, in their turn, have been made with specific groups and specific subjects in mind.

(b) Determining weightings and actually achieving them in practice, are, however, two different things. In practice, weighting is determined by two things. First, the selection of appropriate methods of assessment, and, secondly, the use of the full range of allocated marks. Take, for example, an assessment of English, where the weighting is as follows:

Paper 1 Comprehension	40
Paper 2 Essays on selected topics	60
Coursework	60
Oral	40

Total 200 marks

This would mean that Paper 1 and the oral are supposed to be equally weighted, as are Paper 2 and the coursework. This equal weighting will not, however, be achieved in practice if the mark range used on Paper 2 is, say, 55 (lowest mark awarded 5, highest mark awarded 60), whilst that used in coursework is, say, 20 (lowest mark awarded 25, highest mark awarded 45). In these circumstances Paper 2 will become more highly weighted in practice than the coursework. Moreover, as paragraph 2.33 on criteria related marking suggested, the predetermination of weighting may of itself make the mark scheme inflexible and hence unable to reward adequately a wide range of responses. The view that the achieved weights of examination components should be described in terms of mark loadings has, incidentally, been challenged by Adams and Murphy in a paper written in 1980. In this, they put forward the view that covariance is a more reliable alternative measurement of correlation than the correlation coefficient.

(Exercises 5.20, 5.24 and 5.41)

PRACTICAL ASSESSMENT

2.37 (a) Macintosh and Hale (1976) see practical assessment as being essentially concerned with the presentation of problems and with the provision of opportunities for students to suggest and to justify solutions to these problems. It is thus necessary for them to demonstrate mastery of relevant skills.

There are several approaches to the assessment of practical work, but they can be said to fall into one of the following three broad categories:

(i) Set piece practical exercises.

(ii) Continuous assessment in practical skills.

(iii) Project work. (This is discussed separately in paragraph 2.55.)

(b) The Center for Vocational Education (1977) suggests that assessment exercises demanding the use of psychomotor skills ought to require those preparing them to:

(i) select experiments which are relevant to the objectives being assessed;

(ii) prepare task sheets;

(iii) assemble the equipment, tools and materials required by the pupils;

　　(iv) establish the criteria for assessment, including the design of marking scales;

　　(v) develop an overall assessment strategy;

　　(vi) pre-test whenever possible.

Some examples of criteria of mastery for practical skills will be found in Appendix A, paragraphs A.10 and A.11.

SET PIECE PRACTICAL TESTS

Example – JMB Physical Science O-level

2.38 (a) The set piece practical exercise is usually presented in the form of instructions, either oral or written, to which the pupil responds in practical terms by doing something. A written question may require a written response, but such a response can, and ought to, be made to depend upon the correct completion of relevant practical work. The following example is taken from JMB's Physical Science O-level 1975:

　　　'(i) The molecular kinetic theory suggests a model to help in the understanding of the physical behaviour of materials. With respect to gases, what does the model assume about (1) the nature of a molecule, and (2) the movement of a molecule?

　　　(ii) Describe the structure at room temperature of (3) sodium chloride, and (4) methane. Give reasons why you would consider it incorrect to use the term "molecule" in describing the structure of sodium chloride, but not in describing the structure of methane.'

(b) Written answers only are required although the experiment asked for in (ii) could be illustrated by means of a diagram or diagrams. The major disadvantage of such questions is that answers to them will provide no indication of the pupil's proficiency in the practical work upon which the answers are based.

Example – SREB Home Economics

2.39 (a) Another example, cited by Macintosh and Hale (1976), of a written question, this time requiring a practical response, is taken from SREB's Home Economics 1974:

　　　'You are living in a flat with a friend, and share the domestic chores. It is your turn to cook the Sunday lunch and to clear up. Prepare, cook and serve an attractive three course lunch for two of you, costing no more than £1 (1974). Launder the table linen, set the table and arrange some flowers. Clean the stainless steel cutlery you will use.'

　　　Time allocation – Planning 2 hours
　　　　　　　　　　　　Preparation 1 hour
　　　　　　　　　　　　Examination period $2\frac{1}{4}$ hours

As a practical exercise this is not a particularly good example since the candidate is set too many different tasks whose relative importance is not made clear and which are not easy to compare.

(b) The principal disadvantage of this approach is that the realities of practical work in Home Economics are ignored; the cook may have a bad day, an ingredient may fail, or the gas pressure may be unreliable. Tests of this type often do not correlate with the teacher's estimate of practical ability (which has been observed over a much longer period). The time allocation in the example is, however, sensible and tries to compensate between the requirements of a set piece examination and the realities of the kitchen.

Example — SREB Art and Craft

2.40 (a) The allocation of time is of particular concern for examinations in Art when some set piece has to be produced. The next example is taken from SREB's Art and Craft 1974:

'Very young children are fascinated by sound, bright colours and moving shapes. Make something appealing which will include at least two of these qualities.'

The accompanying rubric states:

'The question paper will be issued to each candidate at least seven days prior to the examination. They will have a choice of questions and their response may take two or three dimensional form. Preparatory work may be brought into the examination room.

The time allowed for the examination will normally be five hours in one school day. Where a candidate requires further time, work must be completed within three weeks following the date of the examination.

Candidates may withdraw from the examination room at any time in order to get reference information, and may retire as soon as they are satisfied that their work is complete.'

(b) This approach is again different from the previous two examples, and presents special problems for the markers. Marking can only be of a most subjective nature and is best carried out by a group, assessing on an impression basis. It is probably more satisfactory to include several types of test as part of the normal activity of a year's course of study. This could ease administrative problems and ensure that all pupils are assessed over a wide range of practical activities.

Example — SREB Biology (S)

2.41 At the other end of the spectrum of structure for a set piece practical exercise is the following example, taken from SREB's Biology (S) 1974. It is a half-hour exercise.

'Tubes A, B, C, D, E and F contain colourless liquids.

(a) (i) Pipette 2–3 drops of iodine in potassium iodide solution into tube A.

(ii) Put a small piece of sample X into tube F which contains alcohol (ethanol) and shake at intervals. Then pour the liquid into tube B which contains water.

(iii) Pipette 10 drops of Benedicts solution into tube C and boil for 1 minute in the water bath.

(iv) Pipette 5 drops of standardised Bicarbonate Indicator into tube D and tube E. Invert to mix.

(b) Complete this table:

TUBE	*Change Observed*	*Substance Detected by the Test*
A		
B		
C		
D		
E		
F		

(c) What food substances should be added to those indicated in your table to provide a complete diet for a young mammal?

. . . .

. . . .

(d) Which of these tests are NOT food tests?

. . . .

. . . . ,

2.42 The setting of practical exercises as written questions which demand practical rather than written responses, can make use of every possible variety of structure, and this in its turn will condition the response and the marking. Clarity of wording and the need for the pupils to know exactly what is required of them are of paramount importance. The foregoing examples all however underline, in different ways, the major disadvantage of this set exercise for the assessment of practical work, namely its artificiality.

(Exercise 5.23)

CONTINUOUS ASSESSMENT OF PRACTICAL SKILLS – USE OF SCALES

2.43 **(a)** The general implications of continuous assessment have been discussed in paragraph 1.30, in Chapter 1, and in paragraph 2.4 of this chapter. The first tasks are, as always in assessment, to define what is to be assessed (in this case what are the practical skills) and to determine what methods to use for recording information about the results of the assessment. One means of appraisal which has been used with success, particularly in Science, involves the use of scales.

(b) Macintosh and Hale (1976) cite Duffey, who, in an unpublished paper, suggests that practical skills in Science can be assessed globally in relation to the following five-point scale:

   (i) Very neat and skilful with the hands. Attracted by any tasks involving mechanical intricacies, for example, taking a lock to pieces or repairing bicycles. Good craftsman, sensible in handling and using apparatus.

   (ii) Quite capable with apparatus. Likes practical work and is sensible in using instruments. Not averse to craft hobbies but not single-minded.

   (iii) Not outstanding in any way. Reasonably good manipulation of apparatus, handles tools and instruments competently but without skill or enthusiasm.

   (iv) Rather lacking in practical skills. Sets up apparatus insecurely. Not very interested in craft hobbies. Needs a lot of help in the laboratory.

   (v) Very clumsy and ham-fisted in using tools and instruments. No interest in practical toys or hobbies.

This scale includes some consideration of pupil attitudes to practical work, but at best it can only be used to provide a fairly wide overall judgement of a pupil's practical ability since it is inevitably lacking in detail. It nevertheless includes skills or attributes which are capable of development into scales of their own, for example, observations, or manipulative skills or qualities such as persistence. This approach is in marked contrast to the more specific criteria put forward by AEB (see Appendix A, paragraph A.10 (a)), and that of the Schools Council *Bulletin 19* (1969) (see Appendix A, paragraph A.11).

(Exercise 5.25)

ORAL ASSESSMENT

2.44 (a) Oral tests, we are reminded in Schools Council *Bulletin 21* (1971), require careful stage management, are very time-consuming and may be less reliable than any type of written examination. They may also lack face validity if they are not used throughout a course. They do nevertheless provide opportunities for some pupils, who have difficulty with written work, to demonstrate otherwise hidden qualities.

(b) The key to successful oral assessment is the avoidance of any semblance of confrontation. This is more likely to occur here than in other forms of assessment since its conduct is based upon personal interaction between the assessor and the assessed, at a particular place and at a particular time. Hard and fast rules cannot be laid down. The pupil must be put at ease, and the questions asked in an unobtrusive and friendly fashion. Some notes upon oral testing will be found in Appendix B.

ENGLISH

2.45 (a) In the oral assessment of English, SREB, for example, look for the ability to communicate ideas and sustain conversation, for clear and distinct articulation and for lively and expressive delivery. Macintosh and Hale (1976) suggest that to meet these expectations there ought to be three areas of assessment:

(i) Technical Excellence. This would include such factors as clarity of enunciation, fluency, quality of voice, extent and range of vocabulary, correct emphasis and intonation and freedom from serious grammatical error.

(ii) Ability to Communicate. This would include, for example, the ability to follow, develop and maintain an argument, and the ability to convey ideas to another person in a clear and coherent manner.

(iii) The Human Factor. This would include, for example, the natural flow of ideas, evidence of a sense of humour, signs of originality and sincerity, signs of interest in others and in the world around the pupil.

(b) It is not easy to decide under which heading a particular quality or ability should be placed, nor is it easy to avoid duplications. It is, therefore, important to secure agreement with a group of assessors for a particular test or examination as to the meaning of all the terms used in the assessment, and from that base to agree also the weighting to be given to each.

(c) There is a particular problem in the assessment of languages in general, and that is artificiality. The problem stems from the difficulty which most 16 year olds have in sustaining a free-flowing conversation. Two opposite methods have been evolved to meet this problem; the first is to adopt a highly structured approach, which at present seems to be more common in foreign languages than in English, and the other is a relatively unstructured approach. In English, the most frequently used techniques for assessment are:

(i) Reading a piece of prose, poetry or drama.

(ii) Reading from a book which the pupil has enjoyed.

Both these two techniques are now most often used as an introduction to stimulate conversation.

(iii) A short talk, based upon some recent experience of the pupil.

(iv) Answering questions asked by the assessor, or by other pupils in a group situation.

(v) An individual interview. This remains the most frequently used form of assessment in English. It has been modified to avoid the confrontation situation, by the provision of some structure in the form of selected material, or by basing the conversation upon known areas of pupil interest.

Some additional material upon the oral assessment of English will be found in Appendix A, paragraph A.9, and some notes upon oral testing will be found in Appendix B.

FOREIGN LANGUAGES

2.46 **(a)** Many of the criteria used in oral assessment of English or, of course, other native languages, can also be applied to foreign languages, but accent and pronunciation become much more significant, as well as the ability to comprehend what is being said. The problem of artificiality becomes more pressing since the difficulties of sustaining conversation in a foreign language are greater. The use of structured situations involving tapes requires competence in their use by the assessor. The skills most frequently tested in French, for example, at the secondary level are:

    (i) Comprehension — usually the most heavily weighted.

    (ii) Pronunciation, intonation and phrasing.

    (iii) Range of ideas.

    (iv) Accuracy of expression.

    (v) Extent and range of vocabulary.

(b) For testing these skills there is a wide range of techniques in current use, for example:

    (i) Reading aloud.

    (ii) Exposés, with little or no prompting from the assessor.

    (iii) List of prepared questions.

    (iv) Picture-based tests.

These four techniques constitute a formal speech situation with little interaction between the assessor and the assessed.

    (v) Free general conversation.

    (vi) Conversation based upon a prepared subject; this can follow on from an exposé.

    (vii) Role-playing or assignments in which the assessor acts a part corresponding to a role assigned to the assessed.

These latter three are reciprocal speech situations and may be more or less severely structured to meet the needs of the assessed and the assessor.

(c) As with written examinations, greater structure in oral assessment can permit a more detailed breakdown of marks and help to reduce unreliability in the marking.

OTHER SUBJECTS

2.47 **(a)** There has been relatively little use made of oral assessment in other subjects, particularly in public examinations where considerations of cost and reliability loom large. When, however, it has been used as, for example, in Chemistry, in a Schools Council study in 1971, it can take two forms: first, as a means of assessment in its own right, and, secondly, as a support or complement to another form of assessment as, for example, a project or a field work exercise, or the writing up of a practical experiment.

(b) History

Macintosh and Hale (1976) refer to a recent interesting study carried out by the University of London Schools Examination Council and the Middlesex Examinations Board (MEB), where a number of approaches to oral assessment in History were investigated. Four of these were:

    (i) An oral based on a specific topic.

    (ii) A two or three minute talk based on a specific area of the syllabus, followed by a general discussion on the course as a whole.

    (iii) A completely unstructured oral about the course in general.

    (iv) A semi-structured oral using a variety of stimulus material.

Any of the approaches used here ought to extend the potential of the course of study and should enable teachers to modify or to reinforce impressions already gained from previous performances of pupils.

A study organised jointly, between 1974 and 1976, by SREB and the Oxford Delegacy, undertook a systematic investigation into the use of oral assessment with projects in History. This resulted in the production of an assessment framework in which the oral was used to assess quite different facets of the work from that being assessed by the initial marking. This was in contrast to normal usage where the oral provides reinforcement for information already gathered by other means or provides students with a second opportunity to show their paces. A copy of this framework will be found in Appendix B, paragraph B.7.

(Exercise 5.26)

AURAL ASSESSMENT

2.48 This type of assessment is still little used in school examinations, except for foreign languages, and sometimes for music, which is surprising when one considers how much listening is done in daily life. Recently, however, there has been much greater interest shown in its use in English Language.

2.49 Foreign Languages

In foreign languages, the emphasis in school assessment tends to be upon the language of survival, for example, the ability to exist in a foreign society, and the highly structured approaches adopted have included:

    (i) Vocabulary tests based upon pictures.

    (ii) Appropriate rejoinder questions.

    (iii) True/false statements based upon pictures or dialogues.

(iv) Who? What? Where? situations presented from everyday life.

(v) More extended dialogues or narratives.

2.50 Music

(a) An interesting example here is the New Zealand School Certificate Music examination which has as its second objective the improvement of aural perception. 40% weighting is accorded to a 45 minute aural perception test, of which there are seven parts, the first three of which are:

(i) General Perception.

(ii) Dictation of Rhythm.

(iii) Dictation of Melody.

(b) Answers are recorded in special answer booklets. In test (i), the answer booklets provide a printed single or two stave unbarred score. The passage concerned is then played five times and the candidates have to complete in the booklets all or some of the following: time signatures and barlines, pace and alteration of pace, phrase marks and dynamics, and, finally, the point reached in the performance.

In test (ii), candidates have to write the rhythm only of a four-bar tune which begins at the first beat of the bar. The tune is played through once, then the first half is played through three times with 20 second pauses between playings. The candidates are also provided with the speed of the beat.

For test (iii), the candidates are required to write down a melody of not more than four bars, after being given on several occasions, as in test (ii), the rhythmic pattern and key signature.

2.51 English Language

Wilkinson *et al.* (1974) identified four elements in any communication:

(a) The person making it.

(b) The person to whom it is addressed.

(c) The topic referred to.

(d) The context.

Assessment can, of course, be directed to any of these elements, considered either on its own or in combination with all or any of the others. The authors underline the marked differences that exist between written and spoken accounts of the same topic; for example, the repetition that takes place in speech makes an oral account much longer. Such differences must be taken into account when assessing listening ability.

As part of the work described by Wilkinson *et al.* (1974), batteries of tests for several age groups have been developed, including one for 13–14 year olds which was designed to test:

Content
Contextual Constraint
Phonology
Register
Relationship

The nature of the range and techniques employed can be best illustrated by reference to the testing of contextual constraint and register. The basic principle used in testing contextual constraint was to omit a sentence from a communication and ask a pupil to supply it from a number of given alternatives (usually three), which were listed in the answer booklets. This was only possible if the words before and after the omission were supplied; an interrupted telephone conversation provided one way of presenting this item.

Register was tested by the introduction of an alien phrase into a passage otherwise spoken consistently in a single register. Many contrasts between registers can be made, for example:

Technical   — Non Technical
Formal   — Informal
Written   — Spoken
Impersonal   — Personal
Rational   — Emotional
Public   — Private

2.52 General Issues

(a) In their *Learning through Listening* (1974), the Schools Council stress that one practical implication of aural testing needs to be borne in mind and that is the need to repeat the background material used on several occasions to avoid undue emphasis on memorisation.

(b) In both oral and aural assessment, transfer is an important issue. The question of transfer is not confined to any one form of such assessment, but the more artificial the technique used, the more starkly is the question of transfer likely to be posed.

Artificiality is not only a question of technique but also one of division of function as between teaching and assessment. The more closely classroom and assessment practice can be married the more likely is the degree of artificiality in the assessment situation to be reduced.

(Exercise 5.26 (d))

PUPIL QUESTIONNAIRES

2.53 (a) Pupils' self-perceptions may influence their reactions to their teachers. Pupils who see themselves as being good at a particular activity or in a particular subject, may react quite differently to either criticism or encouragement by comparison with those less favourably placed. A wise teacher tries to be sensitive to this factor of self-esteem in pupils. The teacher who needs to obtain insights into pupil sensibilities may find that a pupil questionnaire can be of assistance.

The following example, quoted by Harlen (1978), is taken from *Man — A Course of Study* prepared by the Educational Development Center, Cambridge, Mass. in 1970. The questionnaire is based upon pupil reactions to the course and when completed is used as a basis for group discussions:

'To do well in (name of course), I have to:
(mark with a tick any three of the following statements with which you would agree most)

☐ Read well.

☐ Be able to think of many good examples.

☐ Memorise all the facts we have been given.

☐ Ask questions.

☐ Take part in class discussions.

☐ Remember everything the teacher has said.

☐ Agree with the teacher.

☐ Have my own opinion.

☐ Write well.

☐ Do extra projects.

☐ Be able to understand the films and remember them.

☐ Try to be as quiet as possible.

☐ Bring in extra information about the subject of the course.

☐ Answer a lot of teacher's questions.

☐ Do other things such as. . . . .

Although this example is perhaps slanted more towards the affective domain, the approach could be equally well applied to the cognitive domain.

(b) Rowntree (1977) provides some very interesting material upon work in the area of pupil self-assessment and concludes that self-assessment and peer assessments can take their proper place alongside teacher assessment where the outcome is a profile of the student rather than a grade or a label. Profiles are dealt with in Chapter 3.

(Exercise 5.27)

COURSEWORK

2.54 Coursework is not an easy topic to deal with, largely because it is not a technique of assessment as such, but instead makes use of any relevant technique over a period of time, which is usually determined by the length of the course to which the assessment is related. The techniques used to assess coursework ought to reflect fitness for purpose, both in relation to the subject matter being studied and to the objectives to be met. Coursework, has, however, in the United Kingdom in particular, become associated with projects and field work and these have, in consequence, come to be regarded as techniques of assessment in their own right. Coursework also raises a number of significant general issues, which are treated adequately in paragraphs 2.57 and 2.58. For convenience, therefore, projects and field work will be dealt with briefly in turn on their own and consideration will then be given to coursework in general and the issues which arise from it, some of which may well be highlighted in the paragraphs upon projects and field work. A recent system for assessing coursework is described in Appendix D.

PROJECTS

2.55 (a) A project is any set exercise from which time constraints have been largely removed. It can be tackled either as an individual task or by a group, and usually involves a significant element of work being done at home or out of school.

   (b) The selection of the subject may be teacher directed or the choice may be left to the pupils, probably with the approval of the teacher. There are certain issues which tend to become prominent when the question of assessment is considered. These are:

   (i) Is it the process or the product which is to be critical in the assessment process?

   (ii) What is to be the role of the teacher, i.e. is it that of a tutor, a continuous assessor, an ultimate judge, or a facilitator?

   (iii) What is to be the policy regarding resources? Is the teacher to supply them, or is it part of the task, and hence its assessment, for the pupil to find them? Should all pupils tackling one particular project be provided with identical packs of resources?

   (iv) Is there to be an element of structure imposed by the teacher, for example, target dates for the submission of a preliminary plan? Is there to be an agreed format for the product?

   (c) The selection of the topic will certainly profit from some discreet supervision by the teacher. Pupils and students tend to burden themselves with subjects which are too diffuse for the resources readily available. They may also need to be nudged gently on occasion into more educationally profitable areas of enquiry than their first choices, particularly in the Social Sciences.

(d) It is quite crucial to the success of project work, that pupils, in selecting their subject:

  (i) have some interest in it;

  (ii) accept it as relevant to their particular culture;

  (iii) can foresee where relevant source material may be found;

  (iv) can devise and find answers to relevant questions;

  (v) can look forward to creating a product in which they can take pride;

  (vi) will not be tied to the same old classroom routine and same old books;

  (vii) will have some hope of parental interest if not support.

An example of how structure can be applied to project work will be seen in Appendix C.

FIELD WORK

2.56 (a) An extremely useful element in any assessment programme and one which requires the exercise of many skills, both cognitive and affective, is field work. Popular with the pupils, it can often make a significant contribution to the establishment of good relations between school and community. It is by no means a simple and straightforward form of teaching or learning, calling for keen observation, mastery of concepts and skills and accurate recording.

It also requires a considerable expenditure of effort and time in planning, preparation and supervision, but the results can be very rewarding, not only educationally, but in respect of the social development of the pupils as well. Adequate staff and resources are essential, particularly time and finance.

(b) It is particularly productive to plan field studies with the principle of cost effectiveness in mind. In order to justify the cost of transport and the use of teachers' and pupils' time, a timetable and schedule of tasks should be worked out in detail and discussed well in advance of the trip itself. Pupils should not merely be taken to a starting point and released without a clear notion of the study to be carried out. They need to be brought into the preparatory planning in order to be made familiar with the area from a map. They should consider the overall aim and, if possible, take part in deciding the schedule of tasks and the priorities to be adopted.

(c) If time permits, a 'dummy run' over some nearby and not dissimilar area will help to iron out many practical difficulties. Finally, adequate time must be allowed for 'writing up' and for discussion of the findings.

GENERAL CONSIDERATIONS REGARDING COURSEWORK

2.57 As indicated in paragraph 2.54, coursework raises a number of quite important general issues in assessment which, although not unique to it, are highlighted by the use of coursework over time, and by the way it can interrelate work undertaken outside the classroom with that undertaken inside. These issues will be considered briefly in turn.

(a) Relative Weighting within Coursework

It is particularly important when planning a programme of assessment over a period, to decide upon the policies to be pursued in relation to students whose work patterns turn out to be erratic. Some of the questions that need to be carefully considered and answered here, are as follows:

(i) How much of the total weighting for the assessment should be allocated to different stages of the course, for example the first year as against the second year of a two year course?

(ii) Should there be any minimum requirements in terms of the volume or nature of the work to be produced before a result will be issued? On what basis should that minimum be determined?

(iii) Who (teacher or student or an outside agency, or some combination of all three) should select the work which is to be assessed?

(iv) What policies should be followed in the case of missing or incomplete work?

(v) What policies should be followed in regard to major inconsistencies in the quality of pieces of work submitted for assessment? Can a really good piece compensate for a really bad piece or can two medium pieces equal one good piece? (This assumes, of course, that the scheme of assessment can clearly identify good or bad pieces of work.)

(b) Support Given to Students from Outside School

With coursework (particularly when a single large-scale project is involved) there is always a likelihood that some students will have greater opportunities for success (and, of course, failure) through differences in the support they receive from their home environment. Such support will always play a part in student achievement, but it is particularly marked with coursework. However hard one tries, it is almost impossible to quantify such support in ways which would make it equitable to take it into the criteria used for assessment or into the weightings agreed for different aspects of the assessment. Teachers, in the role of facilitators, can undoubtedly help a great deal in redressing the balance, particularly in relation to the availability and extent of resources. The whole topic also raises the question of whether we should worry at all about the impact of home environment on assessment?

(c) Resources

A feature of the past decade in most countries has been the increased emphasis placed upon resource facilities in schools. At one time the library, often arbitrarily and poorly equipped, was the sole resource in many schools. Today, there are an increasing number of resource centres within schools, and developments in modern technology have increased, out of all recognition, opportunities open to schools for easy access to information. Whilst good resources of themselves do not produce good coursework, there is undoubtedly a high correlation between the two when, of course, the resources are well used.

Resource centres in schools should not be treated merely as a repository for books and documents, but should of themselves encourage the production of resources. Resources must be flexible and provide the raw material and quarrying equipment which teachers can use to pose problems and ask questions, and then attempt to find solutions and answers. As such, a resource centre should provide a permanent hard core of reference material, a range of material subject to frequent review and a substantial, but fluctuating, body of material which comes and goes according to needs. A good resource centre should always contain a wide variety of material, including pictures, newspaper cuttings, models, photographs, records, tapes, films and theatrical properties, as well as more traditional written material. All this sounds frighteningly expensive, but it is amazing what hard work and enterprise can produce in the way of resources.

(d) The Role of the Teacher

Teachers making use of schemes of coursework will have to accept that a great deal of effort, both individually and collectively, will be required of them at every stage in the work. This raises again the question of what should be the role of the teacher in relation to coursework? Is it that of a tutor, or a continuous facilitator, or an ultimate judge, or a continuous assessor? The answer is really a mixture of all four, with some aspects coming into play at one stage and others at another. If one, however, had to pick out three words which summarised the ideal role of the teacher here they would be 'continuous', 'facilitator' and 'assessor'.

PROCESS VERSUS PRODUCT

2.58 Two particular approaches, which are in reality the obverse and reverse of the same coin, have become apparent in recent years in the assessment of coursework. They both have as their basic intent the placing of greater emphasis upon the skills and thought processes stimulated by the work at the expense of the finished product. Over-emphasis upon the latter in the past has encouraged a bulk and neatness syndrome and led to far too much uncritical copying of irrelevant material to the detriment of teaching, learning and assessment. These two faults have led to, first, much greater structuring in the arrangements laid down for coursework, whether by the teacher or by an outside agency; and, secondly, the replacement of a single large-scale piece of work (or project) by a series of small-scale carefully pointed exercises, which can be evaluated against quite specific criteria which place their major emphasis upon skills and concepts.

(a) The criteria used in these exercises should evolve from an open debate involving teachers, students and examining agencies. The effect of their application has been threefold; first, to reduce quite dramatically the bulk of work produced for coursework; secondly, to improve the quality of teaching, since the criteria being used for the assessment have impacted directly upon classroom practice, and, thirdly, to make the assessment of the work easier, since the criteria are not only being more directly taught (this has dangers, of course, if they are inappropriate), but are also more easily seen within the work itself.

Examples of these two approaches, taken from public examinations, are to be found, first, within work undertaken by SREB upon project assessment in Social Studies, and, secondly, within the coursework assessment undertaken as part of the History 13–16 Project, where it carries a 40% weighting.

SREB's *Subject Panel Handbook for Integrated Studies* has recommended that the pupils should be asked to consider specific requirements relating to the subject of their project and to make proposals as to their plans for satisfying these. The work involved in developing their proposals should enable students to clarify their area of interest and to establish a framework for their enquiry. The requirements are presented to the students in the form of questionnaires or work sheets, and examples in respect of a Social Studies project can be found in Appendix C.

(b) The coursework requirements for History 13–16 involve the student in undertaking some half dozen pieces of work, each of which has to meet a specific and detailed set of criteria. These include a site plan, a biographical study, a current affairs diary, an empathy exercise and a comparative analysis of two documents. A copy of the new coursework system for History 13–16 which came into full operation for the first time in 1982, is attached as Appendix D. *Exercise 5.42* provides an example of a training exercise designed to help teachers relate criteria to specific pieces of work. Other exercises are contained in a publication entitled *Explorations*, produced jointly by the Project and SREB. Also included in Appendix A are some criteria for the assessment of coursework (paragraphs A.6 and A.12) and of projects (paragraph A.14).

(Exercise 5.28)

CONCLUSIONS

2.59 (a) The approach to assessment, in general and to external examinations in particular, has, in recent years and in most countries, undergone quite drastic revision. The ability range being assessed is much wider. It is acknowledged that ability and aptitude can manifest themselves in forms other than the written word. The whole philosophy of assessment has acquired greater breadth, and the battery of techniques available to the assessor has similarly been enlarged and developed, and the significance of the implications of the use of various techniques is better appreciated. In contrast, there is a growing awareness, as pointed out by Raven (1977), that both pupils and teachers can be diverted from major educational goals by a preoccupation with examination objectives. Teachers, moreover, particularly at the secondary level, tend to become preoccupied with those educational goals which are readily assessable and neglect others.

Increasingly, in the objectives of courses, there can be detected a greater awareness of the needs of students as they approach the threshold of the working world. There is less insistence upon recall of factual knowledge and greater opportunities are provided for the exercise of those flexible problem-solving skills which modern society needs for its survival.

(b) The preparation and conduct of assessment have dispelled a great deal of the mystique in which it was for so long shrouded. It is now more often devised as a collaborative exercise, discussed by all involved, and where possible tested before being used. The demand for accountability has encouraged the whole process to become more open, and has helped to make assessment an integral part of the teaching/learning process rather than some final and almost irrelevant culmination of a course of study. Another welcome consequence of a more liberal interpretation of assessment, is a greater understanding of its psychological impact on those taking part. The trauma of an examination *per se* is gradually being deprived of its ritual importance and the ordeal by examination paper is becoming increasingly less credible.

2.60 The need, as well as the demand, for quality in education has probably never been greater than it is today. The achievement of high quality in whatever field demands on-going evaluation. A key facet of evaluation in education has always been, and will always continue to be, student assessment. Such assessment must remain constantly dynamic and hence responsive to the changing needs of individuals and society as a whole. Much still needs to be done to ensure that this flexibility is achieved in practice and that those who use assessment are sufficiently knowledgeable to appreciate its potential and sufficiently humble to realise its limitations. There is always a need, therefore, to question the validity of conventional wisdom and procedures. To do this constructively, an on-going programme of research and development is absolutely essential both for large-scale public examinations and for smaller-scale classroom practice. Amongst issues under current consideration, and referred to mainly in this chapter, are the rationale behind weighting, the value of choice for students in examinations and the concept of structuring in questions. These, in their turn, all have implications for the ways in which work should be marked and in which information about performance might most usefully be presented – the latter a topic dealt with in Chapter 3 of *A Teacher's Guide to Assessment*, but worthy of a publication in its own right. Solutions to these and other related issues will not of themselves solve the overall problem, they will simply suggest different and perhaps more appropriate ways of balancing the conflicting tensions that are inevitable in assessment.

This chapter has made a very limited selection of the wealth of information available about techniques for assessment. The picture presented can, therefore, only be a partial one and cannot possibly reflect the enormous variety of approaches used in the field of assessment. It is the hope, nevertheless, of the compilers that all will find some approaches which they have not previously considered, and that this will stimulate enquiry and the exchange of information.

Self-teaching Exercises

Number	Exercise

5.13 (a) You have become dissatisfied with the assessment plan of a course you are teaching to a mixed class of varying ability. From your experience list those methods of assessment which you feel are the most suitable for pupils of:

   (i) high ability;

   (ii) average ability;

   (iii) below average ability.

5.13 (b) What would be your criteria for deciding what constituted the 'most suitable method' of assessment?

5.14 Define what you understand by an essay. Take three pieces of work which meet your definition and prepare a marking scheme for each piece of work which is designed to enable you to discriminate between, and hence grade, students. In what way would you have to change your scheme if the principal purpose was to help the students?

5.15 (a) List the advantages and disadvantages of multiple choice testing.

5.15 (b) (i) Find a willing colleague; each construct independently five multiple choice items. For every item, state for whom it was written and its purpose.

   (ii) Exchange the two sets of items, review them carefully and consider whether they meet their stated purpose and are suitable for those for whom they were intended.

   (iii) Using the same items, forecast how a group of pupils, known to both of you and for whom you both think the items would be suitable, would perform upon them. Your forecast should predict how many pupils will:
Select the key (correct alternative).
Select each of the distractors.
Not tackle the item.

5.15 (c) Administer the items to the group, mark the results and make an analysis of the results under the same three headings as in 5.15 (b) (iii).

5.15 (d) With your colleague compare your forecasts with the results and discuss the reasons for any discrepancies which may be apparent.

5.15 (e) As a supplementary exercise ask other members of the teaching team for that course to administer the test after forecasting the results, and to analyse the results; then compare their results with yours and discuss any anomalies.

Note: This type of exercise can be used with many other forms of objective items.

5.16   Indicate the types of objective items currently in use at your school, college or organisation. Describe the purpose(s) for which each type is used. What changes, if any, would you recommend?

5.17   List the advantages and disadvantages of short-answer questions as contrasted with objective items.

5.18   Select a course in which you are involved and identify two specific subject areas. State two objectives for each area and draft for each, either two essay, two structured or two short answer questions, selecting whichever type of question you think to be the most appropriate to assess the objective.

5.19   Construct a mark scheme for each question set in exercise 5.18. Indicate how you would try to ensure reliability of marking for each question when several markers were involved.

5.20   Define the term 'weighting', in relation to assessment. How would you try to ensure that your suggested weightings are achieved in practice?

5.21   List the advantages and disadvantages of analytical as opposed to impression marking.

5.22   Select any essay. Devise an analytical marking scheme for it and then mark it. Do not record the marks on the essay itself, but record them separately and in detail. Put the essay and the record of marks away, for about a month, and then mark the essay again using the original scheme. Compare the two sets of marks and account for any differences.

Note: There is no point in being dishonest in the conduct of this exercise!

5.23   Define the word 'rubric'. What is its purpose?

5.24   Take any terminal test used in your school, college or organisation for which a pass mark is imposed. How is such a pass mark decided and who is responsible for taking the decision?

5.25   In what ways might the assessment of practical work contribute to the measurement of affective outcomes?

E

5.26 (a)   Write out instructions for teachers for the conduct of an oral test in native language for students aged 16. In what respect might these instructions differ if the students were:
(a) aged 10,
(b) aged 20?

Provide as much detail as you think appropriate.

5.26 (b)   What steps would you take to reduce nervousness in students being tested orally?

5.26 (c)   Oral testing is most frequently used in the teaching of native and foreign languages; list other subject areas in which it might be used to advantage, giving reasons for your choice.

5.26 (d)   Define aural assessment. Suggest areas in which it might be used to advantage in schools.

5.27   What do your feel are the advantages and disadvantages of pupil self-assessment?

5.28   Define the terms 'process and product' in relation to the assessment of coursework. Is the distinction a relevant one?

Appendix A — Criteria of Assessment

EXAMPLE 1 – LANGUAGE AND LITERATURE

WRITTEN EXAMINATION

A.1 (a) In broad terms the criteria would appear to require candidates to demonstrate their abilities to:

    (i) Recall important concepts and generalisations.

    (ii) Handle experimentally derived data.

    (iii) Understand important concepts and generalisations.

    (iv) Infer results from concepts and deduce generalisations.

    (v) Make reasoned and logical statements.

    (vi) Apply knowledge gained to solve problems.

(b) The form of assessment which seems to have the largest following is a two-part paper.

    Part I – Objective questions, either multiple choice or short-answer questions.

    Part II – Questions which require greater depth in the answers. It may take the form of questions requiring essay type answers, or the evaluation of some statistical information, or questions which set a problem which has to be solved and for which data is provided, or which require the candidate to draw upon knowledge gained on the course.

(c) There is a growing commitment to increasing the challenge of examination papers by varying the techniques and encouraging a more whole-hearted involvement by the candidate.

(d) A considerable number of the criteria given for other and related aspects of written work will also be applicable, such as those for Composition, Comprehension, Summary and Expression and Presentation.

COMPOSITION

A.2 (a) The general criterion for the assessment of composition, Earnshaw (1974) suggests, may be stated as:

    Has the writer something interesting and relevant to say?

    Has it been said effectively?

The main components would include:

(i) Material — the breadth of ideas related to experiences or reading. Sensitivity to impression and feeling. Ample development of ideas.

(ii) Arrangement and coherence — the presentation of ideas or argument logically and coherently with well-chosen examples. Essential details skilfully brought out in description, in narrative, by changes of pace or by emphasis, for the proper development of the story.

(iii) Sentence structure — mastery of syntax, the ability to construct sentences that are correct, varied in pattern, length and rhythm. Possession of ample linguistic resources, also skill in the use of the full range of punctuation.

(iv) Language and vocabulary — appropriateness of vocabulary to its purpose. Sensitivity to the requirements of vocabulary in respect of the subject matter.

(v) Mechanical accuracy — correct spelling, punctuation, sequence of tenses, usage and idiom. Competence with some distinction in content or style.

(b) Possible Composition Marking Scales (out of 50)

15% Relevance and interest of the material.
15% Effectiveness of the arrangement.
10% Appropriateness of the language.
5% Mechanical accuracy of syntax.
5% Punctuation and spelling.

Note: Analytical marking tends to produce bunching of marks; impression marking ensures a more even distribution.

COMPREHENSION

A.3 (a) Complex process depending on reading, listening, thinking, or assimilation, and the expression of ideas in writing or in speech, viz: recognition of salient ideas; ability to see links between paragraphs; meanings of words and phrases; force of a metaphor; choice of an example; perception of similarities and differences between ideas and concepts; ability to state a generalisation; ability to identify exaggeration or understatement; ability to perceive exceptions or reservations; ability to grasp a writer's purpose; ability to note the relation of punctuation to meaning; ability to understand the explicit.

(b) Five-point Marking Scale

Although the main weight of assessment should be directed towards comprehension of what is explicit, for the higher ability pupil the ability to make inferences must also be given some attention, viz: the purpose of the writer; the conclusions which can be drawn; the beliefs of the writer; the background and experience of the writer; the audience for whom the author was writing. Precise and economical expression is required. Looseness of expression and vagueness of thought are more serious errors in comprehension; a five-point scale could be applied in a marking scheme, for example:

4 marks — Has identified the point precisely and has stated the answer clearly and relevantly.

3 marks — Has grasped the main point but has failed to state it exactly.

2 marks — Has a general understanding but expresses the idea rather vaguely.

1 mark — Has an inkling but the answer is vague and rambling.

0 marks — Has failed to express understanding of the question.

SUMMARY

A.4 It is perfectly possible to use the same passage for comprehension and for a summary but the passage must be capable of being summarised without destruction of its qualities — the passage should have a theme and the style should be readily comprehensible, although some elaborations are acceptable, for example:

Repetition of ideas for emphasis.
Copious provision of illustrative examples.
Inclusion of incidental but not directly relevant comments.

Passages should relate to a subject about which all candidates know enough in general terms, and yet which could not provide an unfair advantage to those who might have some expert knowledge.

Passages which provide unfamiliar information on a topic within the experience of the candidate are best.

The summary should present an accurate account of the original in a coherent form. The salient points must be identified, and credit given particularly for the coherency and accuracy of the ideas expressed, and marking schemes should not be too rigidly adhered to. Although generous, a word limit should be set to encourage succinctness of expression.

Finally, the summary should be reviewed and marked as to whether it:

makes sense;
is coherent;
is an accurate representation of the original.

LINGUISTIC SKILLS

A.5 These refer to vocabulary, punctuation, usage, synthesis from notes, meaning of metaphorical expression, sequence of tenses, word order in sentences, etc., which are, of course, also assessed in composition and comprehension. What is required here is to assess the candidate as regards handling of syntax and ability to synthesise. Tests should be set in which candidates are called upon to tackle the same requirement, but within set limits. Interlinear tests with a prose passage containing some errors which have to be identified or corrected and multiple choice tests can be suitable for this purpose.

COURSEWORK

A.6 Clear requirements for comment and interpretation of source material will help to combat mere plagiarism.

Allowance must be made as regards:

Whether the candidate had access to dictionaries and texts.
The time available to the candidate.
The initial preparation given by the tutor.
Whether the work was completed under supervision or not.
Whether a draft was discussed with the tutor.

Agreement trials for teachers can help to reduce differences in marking standards.

Coursework should allow all ability levels the best of opportunities to display their skills and strengths.

Higher weighting can be given to the marshalling of evidence, choice of illustrative material, orderly development of ideas, exact expression of meaning, variety of syntax and range of reading and reference.

LITERATURE

A.7 (a) Not all 16 year olds will have the background of reading or the ability to perceive relationships necessary for the study of literature. Programmes of work should therefore be well structured and should encourage wide reading both in quantity and range.

(b) Above all an understanding is required of what has been read, and in particular its significance, viz:

Ability to follow the sequence of events.
Knowledge of the characters.
Identification of the setting.
Ability to grasp the development of ideas.
Ability to perceive relationships.
Understanding of the plot.
Interplay of character and action.
Contribution of the setting.
Appropriateness of form and language to content.
Conscious and unconscious motives for action.
Relationship between characters.
How characters and events illustrate a theme.

(c) Response

A candidate of higher ability should be able to explain and communicate his response to what he has read, viz:

In what way was an incident remarkable?
Was it the situation, or the reaction of the character to the situation?
Was it the comment of the author or spectator?
What was it that made the incident of special interest?
Was it conflict — mental or physical?
Was it the possible consequences?
Did the writer build up suspense?
Was the outcome obvious?
Was there unnecessary detail and repetition in the account?
Were the emotions out of scale to the event?

Assessment under these criteria should take into account, of course, the depth and breadth of understanding shown. Response based upon the reaction of the reader, and authenticated by reference to the text, will distinguish the candidates of higher ability.

EXPRESSION AND PRESENTATION (LITERATURE)

A.8 Credit should be given primarily for accurate knowledge, clear understanding and relevant comment. As regards presentation, the criteria should be:

The line of thought should be intelligible.
Ideas should be linked.
Examples should illustrate the point.
The relevance of the answer to the question should be clear.
The answer should be coherently and lucidly expressed.
Quotations or references must illustrate or clarify the point being made by the candidate.

ORAL EXAMINATION

A.9 (a) Language is used to explain, to persuade, to tell a story, to recount an experience, to express our ideas and feelings — or to describe something that happens and our reactions to it. It is also capable of being used formally or informally, according to the audience. The key elements within such a complex of abilities are probably:

(i) Intelligibility — the ability to speak clearly allowing for regional variations in accent and intonation.

(ii) Breadth of register — the ability to adapt the form of speech to suit the occasion.

(iii) Fluency — the ability to express ideas without undue hesitation, the avoidance of garrulity or triviality.

(iv) Vocabulary — its suitability and adequacy for the content and purpose of what is being said. The avoidance of jargon, misuse of cliché and trendy verbosity.

(b) Whereas a 'pass' would require clarity, correctness and fluency, the award of a higher grade would demand well-chosen vocabulary, pleasing variety of pace, emphasis and expression and the establishment of 'rapport' with the listener.

(c) **Marking Scale**

Assessment can be made by general impression or analytically. When it is made analytically, the assessor must further define the qualities being sought. Within the requirements of intelligibility, 'clarity of pronunciation' might be considered paramount and the following scale could be applicable (assuming a weighting of 4 marks):

4 marks — Perfectly intelligible, no difficulty in following what the candidate said.

3 marks — Mostly clear, but one or two lapses.

2 marks — General drift grasped, but with some mispronunciation and stumbling.

1 mark — Difficult to follow, with frequent mispronunciations.

(d) It is more reliable to use two assessors, one to mark on impression and one analytically. They can then compare and discuss their marks, but it is perhaps more important to reach agreement on rank order, and numerical marks are more of a useful guide.

Some notes on oral testing can be found in Appendix B.

EXAMPLE 2 – SCIENCE

PRACTICALS (GENERAL SCIENCE)

A.10 (a) The AEB identifies four areas of practical ability to be assessed; each merits equal weighting and concerns the candidate's ability to:

(i) Apply experimental techniques, viz:

Setting up equipment and following instructions. Application of suitable techniques with relevant manipulative skills.
Presentation of the components of the investigation.

(ii) Plan and carry out investigations, viz:

Recognition of the problems and the formation of valid and testable hypotheses.
Choice of appropriate experimental techniques.
Selection of appropriate apparatus.
Recognition of sources of error and appreciation of the possible consequences.
Modification of methods to meet unexpected outcomes.
Production of a logical and sequential work plan.

(iii) Observe and record the results of investigation, viz:

Recording observations accurately and correctly.
Reading measuring instruments accurately.
Making accurate drawings or diagrams.
Recording unexpected aspects.

(iv) Interpret observations, viz:

Recognition of and making allowance for errors of measurement.
Interpretation of results.
Evaluation of findings.
Drawing correct conclusions.
Adoption of a critical attitude to results.
Suggestions for further and relevant areas of research.

(b) Suggested Marking Scale — Practicals

To test each of the four abilities the following scale can be applied:

5 marks — Has reached independence in effectively demonstrating competence.

4 marks — Can carry out most of the listed procedures effectively and with minimal assistance from the teacher.

3 marks — Can successfully carry out a number of procedures, but only with considerable assistance from the teacher.

2 marks — Finds difficulty in achieving any significant success, even though an attempt is made with considerable assistance from the teacher.

1 mark — Makes little attempt to undertake practical work or to follow through a series of activities.

0 marks — No acceptable work produced.

It is recommended that each ability is tested at least twice, the average for each ability is then totalled and doubled to provide a mark out of 40.

When averaging marks for work carried out at intervals during a protracted course, note can be taken of any steady improvement or deterioration and more weight can be given to the more recent assessments, for example:

4, 5, 4, 4 should be averaged as 4

3, 4, 5, 5 should be averaged as 5

(c) Marking Scale — Persistence

In A-level Physical Science, AEB suggest that persistence is a quality which some feel should be included for assessment. A marking scale which could be applied is given below:

5 marks — Rarely put off by difficulties. Tries to devise methods of overcoming them. Checks anomalous results and tries to find explanations.

4 marks — Usually tries one or two methods of overcoming a problem. Repeats experiments when anomalous results have been obtained but does *not* search for an explanation.

3 marks — Usually tries one other method of overcoming a problem, but then asks for help. May repeat results if obviously wrong, but makes little attempt to find an explanation.

2 marks — Occasionally tries method of overcoming a problem, but frequently only asks for help. Occasionally also tries to trace anomalies.

1 mark — Tends to give up and ask for immediate help when any sort of problem arises. Usually uninterested in the reasons for anomalous results.

(d) **Marking Scheme — Sketches and Drawings**

Ward (1981) suggests that points which could be included are:

Inclusion of a stated number of necessary components.
Correct relationship between components.
Correct proportions.
Labelling (if required by the question).
Choice of scale.
Clarity of presentation.

PRACTICALS (BIOLOGY)

A.11 (a) In an example quoted in *Schools Council Bulletin 19* (1969), six questions were involved. Questions 1a and 1b were reasonably easy. Question 2 was much harder and questions 3a, 3b and 3c were the most difficult. 90 marks were available and the most apparatus was required for questions 3a, 3b and 3c.

(b) **Marking Scale**

The allocation of marks is given on page 125 in a table, with explanatory notes in (c) and (d).

(c) **Notes on Marking**

Question 1a — required the identification of specimens using a key.

Question 1b — required the drawing of an appendage from each of the specimens.

Question 2 — involved the measurement of the time taken by some peas in sodium carbonate solution to decolourise phenolphthalein solution at room temperature and at a temperature of 40°C obtained by the use of a water bath.

Questions 3a and 3b — required the bisection of wheat seeds which have been treated in two different ways, the testing for starch in the seeds and the recording of its distribution.

SKILL OR ABILITY	QUESTIONS						TOTALS
	1a	1b	2	3a	3b	3c	
Use of Instructions	1	1	3	3		2	10
Heating Liquids	0	0	1	0		0	1
Use of Thermometer	0	0	1	0		0	1
Use of Indicator	0	0	1	0		0	1
Use of Scalpel/Razor Blade	0	0	0	3		0	3
Use of Stain	0	0	0		1	1	2
Use of Data, Drawing Conclusion	0	0	2	0		6	8
Accurate Observation	4	4	4	2		2	16
Use of Hand Lens	1	6	0	3		0	10
Recording Results	0	6	2	3		1	12
Use of Key	10	0	0	0		0	10
Relationship between Bodies of Knowledge	0	0	0	0		2	2
Formation of Hypothesis	0	0	14	0		0	14
	16	17	28	15		14	90

⌐ Indicates that the marks are combined for assessment purposes.

Question 3c – required the candidate to find by testing for starch, the number of wheat seeds which had been treated in the two ways used in 3a and 3b and then placed on a starch-agar plate.

(d) Marking Scheme

In Question 1a – the skills and abilities were used together; the marks are combined to give a total of 4 marks per specimen.

In Question 1b – note was taken of the relevant aspects of recording by drawing, clarity, sharpness of the lines and the size and proportion of the drawings. The marks for observation and the use of the lens are combined, note being taken of the accuracy of the drawings, the detailed structures shown and for the detail such as the separation of the appendages into segments.

In Question 2 – marks for observation, use of data, use of instructions, heating liquids and use of thermometer and chemical indicator were combined to give a total mark of 12 for the experimental work of the question and a mark of 2 being awarded according to the times recorded and the differences between them. Recording concerned the times, marks being awarded if each time was written clearly. The 14 marks for hypothesis formation were given on the basis of the following four scoring points:

3 marks — 40°C is higher than room temperature.

4 marks — 40°C is a more favourable temperature than room temperature for the respiration of peas, nearer the optimum.

4 marks — The higher temperature causes an increase in the rate of respiration.

3 marks — More carbon dioxide is produced.

In Questions 3a and 3b — a combined mark of 5 for observation using a hand lens, on the basis of the drawing produced, with a combined mark of 3 being awarded for recording. The combined mark of 7 is given for use of instructions, scalpel or razor blade and stain based on the actual distribution of starch recorded and the differences between the seeds in the two parts of the question.

In Question 3c — a combined mark from 14 is given according to the numbers involved.

COURSEWORK (GENERAL SCIENCE)

A.12 (a) The AEB considers that the general objectives to be assessed in Integrated Science at O-level are the abilities to:

> Recall important concepts and generalisations.
> Report scientific investigations accurately.
> Make accurate qualitative and quantitative observations.
> Handle experimentally derived data.
> Make deductions from observations and recordings.
> Understand and to use simple experimental procedures, also to use the apparatus correctly.
> Understand concepts and generalisations.
> Infer results from concepts and to deduce generalisations.
> Design and perform simple experiments to solve specific problems.
> Formulate, test and modify hypotheses.
> Apply knowledge to solve problems.
> Be competent in the use of a laboratory.
> Appraise and to be critical of results obtained, and be willing to search for and to test alternative ideas.
> Evaluate the relevance of studies to life in the community.

(b) It is of interest that research by Wood and Napthali (1977) has shown that the following criteria could also be applied in the classroom:

> Involvement of the pupil in the learning situation.
> Ability of the student in the subject.
> Overall ability of the pupil.

Quality of the work produced.
Behaviour of the pupil.
Interest displayed by the pupil.

SPECIAL STUDY (BIOLOGY)

A.13 (a) The AEB consider that the basic criteria for assessment of Biology A-level should be:

20% Originality.
65% Quality of understanding of the subject and insight into its study.
15% Presentation.

(b) **Weighting**

These basic criteria can be elaborated and weighting broken down as follows:

Originality (20%)
5% Originality (as far as the candidate is concerned) in the choice of subject.
5% Imagination and invention in the selection of the subject.
5% Use of initiative in seeking advice.
5% Use of an adaptation of existing techniques in solving related problems.

Quality of Understanding (65%)
5% Relationship of the study to current developments in the subject.
10% Analysis and evaluation of the study to identify specific aspects requiring investigation.
10% Method of approach in the collection of information.
10% The proper use of manipulative skills.
10% Accuracy of observation.
10% Proper and adequate recording of results.
10% Critical evaluation of the results by the candidate.

Presentation (15%)
5% Presentation of report clearly set out with terminology correctly used.
5% Choice of most appropriate media (photographs, diagrams, tables, etc.) through which to submit report.
5% Use of cross-references and presentation of sources.

(c) **Marking Scale**

Based upon a maximum of 5% the following marking scale could be used:

5 marks — Excellent.

4 marks — Good.

3 marks — Satisfactory or average.

2 marks — Below average.

1 mark — Poor.

For 10% maximum the scale could be:

10–9 marks – Excellent.

8–7 marks – Good.

6–5 marks – Satisfactory or average.

4–3 marks – Below average.

2–1 marks – Poor.

In both cases 0 should be awarded where the stated quality is entirely missing.

PROJECTS (GENERAL SCIENCE)

A.14 **Weighting (Approaches A and B)**

In their *Notes for Supervising Teachers* (1974), AEB suggest that there are two alternative suggested approaches to the criteria for assessment:

(a) **Approach A**

Projects, which should be a study in depth of some part of the whole syllabus, could be assessed under three basic criteria. A weighting of 40% is assumed:

Quantitative 10%
Based on the size and scope of the project, as well as the time, thought and effort expended.

Qualitative 15%
Recognition that the project is a proper development of the original proposal and that it is a genuine contribution to the education of the candidate.

Credit can also be given for the care and precision in the collection, classification and presentation of material.

Initiative 15%
For originality in pursuing the objectives of the project, seeking original sources, consulting authorities and records, surveys, interviewing people, etc.

(b) **Approach B**

Assessment could be made under five main criteria. A weighting of 40% is assumed:

Statement of Intent and Planning 4%
Clear statement of intention and the plan for carrying out the work.

Individual Investigation Work 10%
Extent of candidate's involvement in practical work, field study, literature searches, interviews, correspondence with possible sources, etc.

Results, Conclusions and Success of Project 10%
Results obtained or conclusions reached, their validity and the extent to which the candidate has achieved what was the original aim.

Presentation of the Project Material 10%
Quality — clear layout, clarity of style, selection of the most appropriate media.

Relevance of the Project 6%
Awareness of the links which the project has with the world around us.

(c) Both approaches are capable of considerable elaboration when relating the main criteria to the syllabus content.

(d) Some notes produced by SREB on the use of structure in the development of a project will be found in Appendix C.

Appendix B — Some Notes on Oral Testing

INTRODUCTION

B.1 (a) Most teachers have found how useful oral assessment can be as an alternative to written responses or practical exercises. It can in one operation assess the student's ability to communicate orally and at the same time probe the depth of the student's grasp of the objectives of the work under review.

(b) There are many possible scenarios for oral testing; for example formal, based upon a specific piece of work, or informal, where impressions are gained by the teacher through observation of the student during conversations. There are within each scenario several possible groupings for assessors and students. They could be on a one-to-one basis or on a group basis where any number of students could be assessed by any number of teachers.

B.2 (a) Oral testing, as with all forms of assessment, demands skills which need to be acquired and the notes in this appendix have been prepared in an attempt to help to meet such a need. For brevity it has been necessary to restrict the description to a formal situation, in which two teachers assess two students at a time. The points made will, it is hoped, be capable of generalisation to different situations.

(b) Some useful work has been done in this field of assessment and the findings of a Working Party, set up in 1978 by Bulmershe College of Higher Education, Earley, Reading, England, in conjunction with SREB have, in particular, been incorporated.

PRELIMINARIES

B.3 (a) Two assessors, each using different methods of marking can do a great deal to ensure the smooth conduct of an interview. One assessor can take up the leading role when the other flags, and it can reduce the possibility of a candidate being interviewed solely by a teacher who may be regarded as being unsympathetic.

(b) Each assessor should be provided with a list of the names of those being assessed and a list of their selected 'talking points', for example a recently completed project or an assignment. Each assessor should also be provided with an agreed list of headings against which to record their assessment.

(c) Assessors should discuss the 'talking points' and attempt to, first, identify key areas for questions and, secondly, to allocate responsibility between them for asking questions on the key areas.

(d) The arrangement of seating and provision of comfortable chairs for all taking part are important. There should be no implication that there are two factions in direct opposition to each other. Chairs should be on the same level and many teachers have found that the grouping of four chairs in a circle around a low occasional table provides a suitable set up.

(e) The faces of candidates and assessors need to be clearly visible to each other and care should be taken to avoid any of the group being blinded by direct sunlight.

(f) Candidates can be made to feel more secure if they are interviewed in pairs. It avoids any apprehension on their part about two teachers ganging up on one candidate.

(g) It will tend to silence candidates if marks are recorded during the interview, therefore marking schemes should be discreetly handled and preferably completed after the interview.

(h) Assessors must ensure that any documentary material needed as the basis of a talking point is to hand.

CONTACT

B.4 (a) Candidates should be greeted in a friendly and open fashion and any necessary introductions made. Care must be taken to prevent more extrovert candidates from assuming a leading role and this can be assisted by the use of a predetermined seating plan based on prior knowledge of those being assessed. Distances between assessors and candidates need to be equal for each candidate.

(b) The opening conversation should be lively, relevant and reassuring. Rapport needs to be established and the candidates given every encouragement to relax. It is best to avoid making reference to the test and once the candidates seem ready, to lead the conversation directly on to the candidates' talking point, for example 'I did enjoy your account of the tea party at the Old Folks Home, how did you all decide what to put in the programme?'

(c) It is sometimes helpful to involve both candidates together although the oral is particularly concerned with one. On occasion there may be flat disagreement and a lively discussion may ensue as the first candidate attempts to re-establish the point which had been challenged by the second.

(d) Eye contact should be maintained by the questioning assessor, but the 'resting' assessor must exercise care that the candidate does not feel to be a target for four seemingly hostile eyes.

THE TEST

B.5 (a) The duration of most oral tests involving 15/16 year olds should be between 5 or 6 minutes, of which up to 30 seconds should be spent on putting the candidate completely at ease. The percentage of time taken up by a candidate making a prepared statement will vary enormously and the assessor must be ready quickly to step in and initiate questioning if a candidate dries up. Delay at this juncture could demoralise the candidate.

(b) Although it is unwise to allow the candidate to seize and hold the initiative, the assessors must do their utmost to encourage pupils to talk. Great care must be taken in the phrasing of questions and the assessor must in particular avoid the pitfall of questions which invite monosyllabic answers: for example, 'Do you think sportmen should be allowed to advertise goods?' could be answered by 'yes' or 'no', whilst 'What do you think are the advantages and disadvantages of sportsmen advertising goods?' requires a longer and more revealing answer.

(c) The assessors must be ready to exploit avenues of inquiry revealed by a candidate's answers. It is often here that the second or resting assessor can intervene with a probing supplementary question.

(d) Assessors must try to provide a balance of questions, some of which can be readily and easily answered by means of factual information, and others which require argument and thought and provide opportunities for generalisation.

(e) Similarly, there is little point in asking candidates questions which they cannot understand and assessors must accept the need at times to rephrase or to refocus questions to bring them within the grasp of the candidate.

(f) Assessors should not be afraid of acknowledging answers given. At times a positive acceptance can be indicated and at other times a correlation or modification can be suggested; the aim must always be to encourage the candidates to show their ability.

(g) Time-wasting practices should be avoided, such as repeating questions or candidates' answers, and assessors should pass on to the next question rather than supply an answer or fall into the trap of giving an impromptu lesson.

(h) Interruptions which could assist the candidate to express ideas more coherently are often useful, but assessors need to be quite experienced in an oral assessment before they will be able to distinguish between 'the pause for thought' and the 'no knowledge' silence. It is a common fault in oral assessment for the assessors to provide the answers to their own questions.

(i) 'Open' questions which invite opinions rather than factual recall, analysis, synthesis or evaluation can put the candidate at ease and develop rapport.

(j) There is some evidence that if a 5 second pause is accepted after each pupil or assessor has made a contribution, the candidate's answer is likely to be longer than if the questions were asked in quick succession.

ASSESSMENT

B.6 **(a)** Assessors need time to decide on their marks after the candidates have left the room and then to compare them. In a majority of cases there is likely to be little significant difference in the two sets of marks, but when there is, the assessors must discuss the reasons for their having awarded their marks and come to a concensus decision.

(b) It is necessary to apply some form of outside moderation to the marks from time to time in order to ensure that they are comparable. This can be done through training sessions based on tapes designed to identify differences of judgement and the reasons for these. It can also involve visiting moderators undertaking spot checks upon the assessors when they are actually conducting the assessment. The problem with this is that it adds to the number of adults present at the time of the test and may in consequence adversely affect the students.

(c) When the test has been completed, an order of merit should be drawn up and carefully reviewed; grade boundaries can then be agreed.

B.7 ORAL ASSESSMENT OF A HISTORY PROJECT

		Initial Marking	*Oral Assessment*
I	Choice of Topic		(A) Involvement (B) Justification
II	Nature of Material	(A) Suitability (B) Extent (C) Evaluation	(A) Collection (B) Gaps
	Questions Asked in Planning	(A) Clarity (B) Range (C) Depth (D) Coherence	
	Extent to which Questions have been Answered	(A) Appropriate (B) Support	(A) Incompleteness (B) Possible Solutions (C) Retention/ Understanding (D) Generalisations
III	Presentation	(A) Mechanics (B) Balance (C) Coherence	Changes

Appendix C — Extract from SREB's Integrated Studies Handbook 'Project Work'

The purpose of the following 'sheets' is to show the process of selection and structuring involved in the development of a pupil's individual project. They do this by asking the pupil to make proposals within a structured framework, which are linked progressively as the samples show. It is recognised, however, that schools will wish to present such advice in a manner relevant to the needs of their own particular syllabus, hence only the general headings are laid out.

These are:

Clarifying the area of interest.
Establishing a framework for enquiry.
Finding and selecting resource material.
The content of your file.

Examples. These are suggestions as to the instructions which will be issued to each pupil.

SOCIAL STUDIES

CLARIFYING THE AREA OF INTEREST

C.1 All pupils must complete an individual project. If your are entered for the final examination this will be worth 25% of the marks.

Your project must have *an aim* of social relevance. That means it must have something to say about the way people in society behave, or about their attitudes.

Projects have to be completed by JANUARY of your 5th year, so it is important to choose your title now.

Some suggestions are set out below — but if you want to try something which is not on the list, make quite sure that your teacher approves. Think first about a broad area that you might be interested in, then think about a specific topic within the area.

Examples:

If you are interested in 'Yourself' you could study 'Teenagers', or 'The Generation Gap', or 'Sex Equality', or 'Youth Culture'.

If you are interested in 'People's Attitudes Towards Each Other' you could study 'Prejudice' or 'Attitudes towards Immigration', or 'The Elderly in Society', or 'The Unemployed'.

If you are interested in your own 'Environment' you could study 'Leisure Facilities in the Area', or 'Housing Conditions', or 'Playgrounds', or 'Shopping'.

If you are interested in 'Animals' you could study 'The Effects of the Threat of Rabies', or 'Man's Pressure on the Animal World', or 'The Inter dependence of Man and Animals'.

If you are interested in 'Transport' you could study 'People's Attitudes towards Motorbikes', or 'The Effect of the Motor Car on Society', or 'Public Transport in this Area'.

When you have chosen one of these topics or thought of one of your own, write it down in the space below, then see your teacher to see if it is a suitable project. If it is not considered suitable, think again. Write your second choice below your first and see your teacher again. Keep repeating this process, if necessary, until you have a suitable title.

Then ask for SHEET 2

ESTABLISHING A FRAMEWORK FOR ENQUIRY

C.2 Now you have a title for your project you must think very carefully about the kind of information you would like to find out about it. The easiest way to do this is to set out a series of questions. When doing your research you will then be looking for the answers to these questions.

For example:

If you choose Public Transport for your title, your questions might be:

1. What kinds of public transport are available in this area?
2. Who operates the various services?
3. Are the general public satisfied with the services offered?
4. What improvements could be made?

Each of these questions would form the title of one chapter in your project.

Most subjects will give rise to between 3 and 6 questions.

Complete the following:

Name of Pupil. . . . .

Title of Project . . . .

Questions to be answered in the project:

1.
2.
3.
4.
5.
6.

Try working out your questions so that they form the basis of a chapter. Discuss the questions with your teacher, parents and friends and then write them out roughly in note form.

Then ask for SHEET 3

FINDING AND SELECTING RESOURCE MATERIAL

C.3 Name of Pupil. . . . .
     Title of Project . . . .

Now that you have your questions you must think about finding the answers.

You will find useful information in two ways: from secondary sources, such as books, articles and newspapers, and from primary data, provided by observing and questioning people.

Now work your way through the list of resources suggested below. Make a note of any useful books, etc., and which questions you think they might help you to answer.

1. *The School Library* (always make a note of *Author* and *Title*)
2. *The School Resources Unit*
3. *Social Studies Textbooks* (ask your teacher or the Head of Department about these)
4. *The Humanities Files in the Social Studies Resources Area*
5. *Local Libraries* (names would be provided)
6. *Local and National Newspapers* (select cuttings carefully and mark the dates on them)
7. *Write away to 'Organisations' who might help you* (discuss this possibility with your teacher)

Now think about the useful information you might obtain from:

8. *Interviews* (if you need interviews to help you answer your questions, whom will you interview and what questions will you ask?)
9. *Survey* (do you need to conduct a survey? If so, what questions will you ask; how many people will you ask and what kind of people will you ask, old — young — male —female — etc.?)
10. *Observation* (what do you need to find out? How can observation help you? Who or what would you observe and how?)

Make sure that you keep all the rough notes that you take as these will have to be submitted with your project.

Before you begin writing up your project make sure that you have read Sheet 4.

Then ask for SHEET 4

THE CONTENTS OF YOUR FILE

C.4 <u>ALL</u> projects submitted for CSE assessment should include the following:

1. *A Title Page* — stating title of project, name of pupil, name of school and date of completion.
2. *A List of Chapter Headings* — these should be based on the questions you set yourself in Sheet 2.
3. *An Introduction* — which should be lively and an interesting account of why you are interested in the topic you have chosen and how you went about setting the questions.
4. Probably between three and six chapters set out separately.
5. *Illustrations and Press Cuttings* — these should be neatly displayed on plain paper. They must be labelled and should only be included if they relate to the text. Press cuttings should be dated.
6. *A Conclusion* — in which you sum up the answers to the questions you set yourself, and suggest other lines of inquiry which you would follow if you were able to do the project again.
7. *A List of References* — setting out clearly the resources you have used. The notes you keep on Sheet 2 will help you with this.
8. *Preparation and Rough Work* — the final section of your project should contain:
   the guidance sheets you have been given to work on;
   all the rough notes you have made during research;
   the diary which outlines when you work on the project and the problems you found doing so.

<u>REMEMBER</u> Your project should include all the sections 1–8 listed above.

<u>REMEMBER</u> Credit will be given for good presentation. Messy, untidy work is not acceptable in sections 1–7.

Appendix D — The New Coursework System — History 13–16

(As agreed by a group of Boards responsible for General Certificate of Education (GCE) and Certificate of Secondary Education (CSE) in the United Kingdom)

HISTORY 13–16 COURSEWORK SYSTEM 1982

D.1 Coursework marks are to be awarded by the teacher solely for assignments which conform to the following table:

UNIT	ASSIGNMENTS	LENGTH IN WORDS	MARKS	% ASSESSMENT
One Modern World Study	Either 1 or 2	1250 to 2000	20	10%
Enquiry in Depth	Either 1 or 2	1250 to 2000	20	10%
History Around Us	Either 2 or 3	2000 to 3000	40	20%
TOTAL	*Between* 4 and 7	*Maximum* 6000	80	40%

D.2 Assignments: An assignment is any piece of work which has a unity of theme or of objective, although it may have sub-sections which deal with different areas or serve different objectives. (See explanatory notes.)

D.3 At least one assignment, which can be from any unit, must be completed in class. When this work is sent for moderation, the time allowed and the amount of reference available should be briefly indicated.

D.4 All coursework must be the candidate's own work. Quotations should be properly marked and their source clearly indicated. A candidate must not be allowed to alter a piece of coursework in any way after the teacher has marked it and indicated errors or omissions.

D.5 The moderator may ask to see other assignments completed by the candidate in addition to those assessed and sent for moderation. His purpose will be to assure himself that the rest of the work is of a quality and type out of which the assessed work might reasonably have arisen.

MARKING SCHEMES

D.6 The coursework assignments must between them fulfil all of the following seven objectives and at least 5 marks and not more than 15 marks must be reserved for each objective. The total possible mark for each unit must not exceed the mark given in the table on page 138.

General Objectives

(which may be satisfied by work related to any of the three units mentioned in the table on page 138).

(a) Evaluation and interpretation of sources.

(b) Empathetic reconstruction of the ways of thinking and feeling of a people of a different time or place.

(c) Analysis of causation and motivation.

Objectives Specifically Related to Particular Units

(d) Interpretation of current situation in the context of past events (Modern World Study).

(e) Personal investigation and description of a site (History Around Us).

(f) Relation of a site to its historical context (History Around Us).

(g) Analysis of the role of the individual in history (Depth Study).

Other Objectives

The teacher may award 5-15 marks for other objectives provided these are consistent with the Project philosophy. Teachers in doubt about additional objectives should write to the Project for advice.

EXPLANATORY NOTES

D.7 The purpose of the change in the system is:

(a) To improve the quality of coursework by linking the mark scheme more clearly to the objectives, and by defining the objectives more clearly.

(b) To make moderation more effective by giving the moderator a clearer idea of the objectives served by each piece of work and the basis on which marks have been awarded.

(c) **Length**

Teachers should note that although variation in the number of words used for each unit is allowed, the total of all coursework must not exceed 6000 words, and a total of 4500 words would be quite sufficient. Maps, diagrams, or other graphic items need not be counted in the word totals, though they may, where they contribute to the appropriate objective, be included in the assessment.

(d) Assignments

An assignment may be based on a theme, as for instance a News Diary which might collect together news on a single topic and comment which might serve any of the objectives D.6 (a), (b), (c) or (d), and might, therefore, be marked under several of these headings. Alternatively, an assignment might be aimed at a single objective. In the case of objective D.6 (c) (Analysis of causation and motivation), for instance, discussion of the motives of several different characters might form one single assignment. In this case, the parts might well have been written at different times. If a submitted assignment is an extract from a larger piece of work, this must be clearly indicated.

(e) Security

The system is designed to safeguard the security and validity of this part of the examination. The assignment to be done in class need not be done under examination conditions. It is intended to give the moderator a quick first check if he feels that a candidate may have had unfair help with coursework. It is not intended that teachers should in any way refrain from advising and helping in all proper ways. If a candidate is anxious not to do bad work again, it is quite in order for him to complete another different assignment of similar type, but not to do the same assignment again incorporating the teacher's amendments. The moderator will not expect teachers to have stored the whole of a candidate's work over two years, but to produce a reasonable background sample against which to judge the work assessed.

PROCEDURES FOR THE TEACHERS

D.8 By 30th April in the year of the examination, the teacher completes and sends to the Board forms showing for each candidate the marks awarded for each of the three units of coursework and the marks awarded for each of the objectives.

Sends to the Moderator in May the work as requested together with sufficient details to enable him to assess it.

Marks and Objectives

Since only 5 marks must be awarded for each of the seven objectives, giving a total of 35 out of the 80 possible coursework marks, teachers are left with a good deal of freedom of choice. In the main, they will probably wish to use the 45 remaining marks to weight the basic objectives more heavily.

Among the other objectives which they may wish to reward are:

(i) Relation of the Modern World Study to its wider global setting.

(ii) Personal research and collection of information.

(iii) Awareness of change and development in history.

Appendix E — Analysis of Multiple Choice Items

Macintosh, in a series of handbooks (1971-74), provides a simple method of analysing multiple choice items which can be readily carried out by classroom teachers:

1. Record the scores of all candidates taking the test in rank order from highest to lowest, placing each candidate's score opposite his name or number. It is more simple with small numbers to use the actual scripts or answer books and sort them into the right order.

2. Record or select:
   (a) The 27% of the candidates who have obtained the highest scores on the test as a whole;
   (b) The 27% of the candidates who have obtained the lowest scores on the test as a whole.

   In both cases an approximation to the 27% may be made; it is not necessary to be absolutely accurate. 27% has, however, been found to provide the best compromise between, on the one hand, making the extreme groups as large as possible, and, on the other hand, making them as different as possible. In other words, 27% is the optimum value, the use of which enables it to be said with absolute confidence that the selected upper group will be superior in ability to the selected lower group, whilst at the same time providing an adequate sample on which to carry out calculations.

3. Take the scripts of the top 27% and record the number of times each option in each multiple choice item was selected. This information should be placed against the appropriate option upon an actual copy of the test.

4. Repeat the procedure for the bottom 27%. Each multiple choice item in the test will then resemble the following example:

   'The 1832 Parliamentary Reform Act was important because it

		Top 27%	Bottom 27%
A	deprived the landed gentry of their influence in Parliament	12	26
B	more than doubled the electorate	3	8
C	introduced voting by secret ballot	1	6
D	laid the foundation upon which subsequent Reform Acts were based'	38	14
	Omits	0	0

> Index of Item Facility 48%
>
> Index of Discrimination 0.44

For convenience it is assumed that 200 took the test. The figures in the first column on the right of each option give the number of responses made by the top 27% and the second column gives the number of responses made by the bottom 27%. The number of candidates who did not attempt the item (omits) are recorded for both groups.

Index of Item Facility

5. Take the figures for those in the two groups who selected the correct option D and add them together (in the example given this is 52). Divide this total by the maximum possible sum; this is to say, the number which would have been obtained if *all* candidates in both groups had answered the question correctly (108). Multiply the resulting fraction by 100. The result will be the index of item facility (48%) which, as mentioned above, can equally well be arrived at by counting the total number of candidates who answered it correctly and expressing this figure as a percentage.

6. Subtract the lower group of responses to the correct option from the upper group, in this case 14 from 38. Divide the resulting difference (24) by the maximum of the possible difference, which is the total number of candidates contained in one of the two groups of 27%, in this case 54. The result expressed as a decimal fraction is the index of discrimination, in this case 0.44.

7. Index of Discrimination

Although it is unwise to make definite statements as to what is an appropriate level for item discrimination, given the method of calculation used here we can say that in general a test item with a discrimination of 0.40 or better discriminates well, while one with an index of between 0.30 and 0.39 is reasonably good. Items with an index of between 0.20 and 0.29 are marginal and need reviewing, while items with an index of below 0.20 should be rejected. Two qualifications should, however, be made. First, the information provided by these figures relates only to one aspect of the item, namely, its ability to discriminate between candidates within the context of the test being analysed. It must, therefore, be considered in conjunction with other available information and with the item's relevance and importance in relation to its subject and to the group being tested. An item with a low discrimination index may be worth retaining on other than statistical grounds because it tests something significant. Secondly, the levels of the discrimination index considered to be appropriate for retention or rejection may vary from subject to subject.

8. Summing Up

This process of item analysis sounds much more involved than it is in practice, as a trial run will show. Many teachers find statistics and statistical procedures uncongenial, largely because they are unhappy about the amount of mathematics involved, and as a result they fail to use a valuable ally. Too many teachers regard statistics not as a means of enabling them to ask more intelligent questions about the tests they set but as a method of telling them, in a language they do not understand, how badly they have carried out their task. Statistics, if they are to be of use to the teacher, must have a simple mathematical basis and must not only be relevant but be seen to be relevant to the teacher's needs. A good book in both these respects, particularly where item analysis is concerned, is *Short Cut Statistics for the Teacher*, by Paul B. Dederich (1973).

References

Adams, R.H. and Murphy, R.J.L. (1980), *The Achieved Weights of Examination Components* (Associated Examining Board Research Unit, Aldershot)

Dederich, P.B. (1973), *Short Cut Statistics for the Teacher*, No. 5 in the Test and Measurement Kit (Educational Testing Service, Princeton, NJ)

Earnshaw, H.G. (1974), *Criteria and Assessment in English* (Associated Examining Board, Aldershot)

Ebel, R.L. (1956), *Measuring Educational Achievement* (Prentice Hall, NJ)

Educational Development Center (1970), *Man — A Course of Study* (EDC, Cambridge, Mass.)

Hamilton, J.B., Norton, R.E., Fardig, G.E., Harrington, L.G. and Quinn, K.M. (1977), *Establish Student Performance Criteria*, Module D1, Category D, Instructional Evaluation Professional Teacher Education Series (The Center for Vocational Education, American Association for Vocational Instructional Materials, University of Georgia)

Harlen, W. (1978), *Evaluation and the Teacher's Role*, Schools Council Research Studies (Macmillan Education, London)

Macintosh, H.G. (1971–74), *Handbooks on Objective Testing* (Methuen, London)

Macintosh, H.G. (1974), *Techniques and Problems of Assessment* (Edward Arnold, London)

Macintosh, H.G. and Hale, D.E. (1976), *Assessment and the Secondary School Teacher* (Routledge & Kegan Paul, London)

Macintosh, H.G. and Morrison, R.B. (1969), *Objective Testing* (University of London Press)

Murphy, R.J.L. (1979), *Mode 1 Examining for the General Certificate of Education. A General Guide to Principles and Practices* (Associated Examining Board)

Nuttall, D.L. and Willmott, A.S. (1972), *British Examinations — Techniques of Analysis* (National Foundation for Educational Research, Slough)

Perkins, P.J. (January, 1981), Data Response Question on the Use of Thermometers, *Classroom Geographer*

Pidgeon, D. and Yates, A. (1969), *An Introduction to Educational Measurement* (Routledge & Kegan Paul, London)

Raven, J. (1977), *Education, Values and Society: the Objectives of Education and the Nature and Development of Competence* (H.K. Lewis, London)

Rogers, T.J. (1978), *Course Work and Continuous Assessment Techniques and Problems of Assessment*, ed. H.G. Macintosh (Edward Arnold, London)

Rowntree, D. (1977), *Assessing Students — How Shall We Know Them?* (Harper & Row, London)

Schofield, H. (1972), *Assessment and Testing — An Introduction* (Allen & Unwin, London)

Schools Council Examination Bulletin 19 (1969), CSE Practical Work (Evans/Methuen Educational, London)

Schools Council Bulletin 21 (1971), An Experiment in the Oral Examination of Chemistry (Evans/Methuen Educational, London)

Southern Regional Examinations' Board (1978), *Objective Items and Structured Questions* (SREB, Southampton)

Southern Regional Examinations' Board (1980a), *1980 Written Examination History 13-16 CSE Examination*, Schools Council Project (SREB, Southampton)

Southern Regional Examinations' Board (1980b), *Explorations*, Internal Project (SREB, Southampton)

Thyne, J.M. (1974), *Principles of Examining* (University of London Press)

Ward, C. (1981), *Preparing and Using Constructed-Answer Questions*, (Stanley Thornes, Cheltenham)

Wood, D. and Skurnik, L.S. (1969), *Item Banking* (National Foundation for Educational Research, Slough)

Wood, R. and Napthali, W.A. (1977), *Assessment in the Classroom* (University Entrance and School Examinations Council, University of London)

3

Reporting of Information Obtained from Assessment

Chapter Contents

Reporting of Information Obtained from Assessment

APPROACHES TO REPORTING

3.1 The topic of reporting or describing information obtained about individuals from assessment can be approached in one of two main ways. One can concentrate upon the symbols or descriptors used (letters or numbers) and look at ways in which these can be treated in order to make the information they present as helpful as possible. Alternatively, one can concentrate upon the overall methods of presentation and consider how best to create frameworks which can enhance the range and quality of what is to be presented. This chapter will take the second of these two alternatives and will consider 'profiles', the name currently in vogue for such frameworks. The fact that the emphasis here, as throughout *A Teacher's Guide to Assessment*, will be upon the individual, should not cause us to neglect the use of the results of assessment for evaluating curricula, teaching strategies, course materials and the like. In choosing to take this approach the authors are well aware that the majority of those who assess students will use marks as their principal descriptive tool. The section will, therefore, conclude with a substantial appendix upon marks, with particular reference to two questions. First, what do we need to know about a single mark, say fifteen out of twenty, in order to make it useful, and, secondly, how can we combine marks derived from different sources in order to present valid overall descriptions?

CHARACTERISTICS OF PROFILES

3.2 In relation to educational measurement, the term profile is used to describe multi-dimensional methods of presenting information, usually about individuals and their achievements, attributes or performances. A profile is thus not a method of assessment, but an approach to presentation and it is in consequence only as full and as varied as the information it seeks to present. Profiles differ from one another, therefore, in two major ways: in the 'content' of what is being presented and in the ways in which that presentation takes place. Whatever its outward form, however, a profile ought to contain three basic elements:

(i) A list of items as, for example, subjects, skills, personal qualities, course descriptions.

(ii) A means of indicating the level and/or nature of performance in respect of each chosen item. The descriptors used can include such things as marks, grades, verbal reports, percentages, histograms or graphs — the list is endless, but they all make use of some combination of letters or numbers.

(iii) Some indication of the kind of evidence which has been used to arrive at the descriptions provided.

Many profiles in current use, incidentally, neglect the last of these to their disadvantage.

ADVANTAGES AND PROBLEMS OF PROFILES

3.3 The current popularity of profiles has stemmed largely from a growing concern about the inadequacy of the information provided by most present-day assessment. This concern derives from a number of different sources. For example, the move towards universal comprehensive secondary education has created pressure to broaden the focus of assessment in the interests of all students and not merely the academic minority. It has also led to a shift in emphasis, from labelling and grading to diagnosis and evaluation, and hence to a shift from norm to criterion referencing as the basis for comparison. A further major thrust has been sparked off by the growth of large-scale youth unemployment. This has led to much work being undertaken upon the identification, assessment and description of clusters of skills (preferably transferable) whose mastery will assist the transition from school to work by making young people more 'employable'. All this has led to a marked increase in the development and use of profiles.

3.4 This work has already led to a significant reappraisal of assessment techniques for use in large-scale assessment programmes by placing much greater emphasis *inter alia* upon assessment over time, upon observation and upon greater informality. It has also increased the range of those involved in the assessment process itself and drawn attention to the whole question of the audience which uses the results of assessment and its very varied needs. Most significantly of all, it has highlighted a number of issues whose resolution is critical to the future development of constructive assessment. Amongst the most significant of these are the potential discontinuities between the ongoing/internal (formative) and the terminal/external (summative) uses of assessment and their implications for the establishment of the credibility of profiles; staff development and training in the construction and use of assessment and profiles; the problems associated with the measurement and presentation of information about personal qualities; the problems associated with the measurement and presentation of information regarding progression over time and, finally, the implications of a negotiated curriculum for its evaluation and for the assessment of individuals. All these issues will be amplified by reference to a number of examples of profiles and their operation. These, it is hoped, will put a little flesh upon the bare bones of the opening paragraphs.

EXAMPLES

3.5 (a) The most crude form of profile is obtained by quoting the pupils' scores on all components of their curriculum instead of providing a single total score. The following example, quoted by Rowntree (1977), amplifies information about a student's degree by listing the titles of its constituent courses and the grades obtained in each. It would be possible to say, for example, that Mervyn Mynde of the class of 77 obtained a B in his Degree of Arts (Education). It would, however, also be possible to say that he obtained the following grades in the component parts of his Degree Course:

ES 608 Educational Concepts and Research   A
ES 611 Epistemology and Education   A
 P 612 Moral and Social Education   B
 P 641 Ethics and Political Philosophy   A
 P 653 Philosophy of Science   C
 P 654 Philosophy of Social Science   B
 P 672 Phenomenology and Existentialism   C

(b) Another example, taken from Rowntree (1977), of a profile which could replace an overall grade for an individual course is as follows:

Margaret Callaghan — Physics

Heat   75%
Light   40%
Sound   79%
Electricity   86%
Mechanics   50%

(c) This approach can be extended within a course to show how the pupil performed on various assessment methods. For example, the 75% obtained by Miss Callaghan for Heat could be broken down to provide more information:

		Weighting
Laboratory work	62%	20%
Personal project	89%	20%
Homework	82%	20%
Final examination	67%	40%

In order to interpret such scores, additional information might well be needed, for example, have the marks quoted been standardised?

(d) Ranking can also be shown by indicating the pupil's position in respect of percentiles:

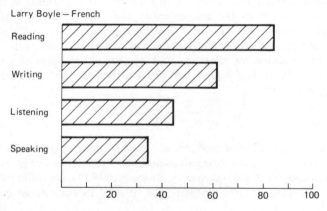

(e) Such charts may allow easier comparison of one aspect of a student's work with another, or of one student with another. The next example shows profiles of two student teachers (based on Morrison (1974)). Apart from teaching practice and history of education, in which their grades are reversed, both students have the same set of grades:

Profiles of Two Student Teachers

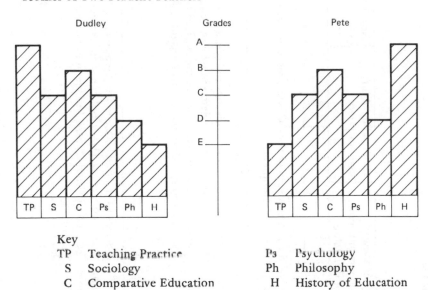

Key
TP   Teaching Practice   Ps   Psychology
S   Sociology   Ph   Philosophy
C   Comparative Education   H   History of Education

It is of interest that in this example, conflation of grades might suggest that both students were of equal merit. Inspection of the profiles, however, would suggest to someone looking for a classroom teacher that Dudley would be preferable, although Pete might excel him in some other branch of education, for example educational journalism.

3.6 (a) The five examples given in paragraph 3.5, based as they are upon a relatively limited range of marks and grades, do not provide much in the way of information about the reasons for specific student performance. A profile such as that provided for an honours graduate of Birmingham School of Architecture (see Hinton (1973)), spells out more specific talents and abilities. This is presented as a sheet with various qualities listed and ticks against those in which he has shown 'special interest' or 'above average ability'.

(b) Simpson (1976) describes a more sophisticated profile used for medical students of McMaster University in Canada, after completion of each major phase or unit in the curriculum. It consists of two sections. The first (A) allows the tutor to indicate and comment upon the extent of the student's attainment of the general goals of the medical curriculum, details of which follow in the next example. The second section (B) carries tutor comment upon how far the student has attained the goals of the particular phase or

Extract of Student Profile Form (McMaster University, Canada)

Section A

Key to Ratings

Few or none of these behaviours demonstrated	Some of these behaviours shown but definitely lacks some	Many of these behaviours but some minor difficulties	Outstanding ability demonstrated	Not Applicable

Please mark where the student was at the beginning and end of the phase in each of the following respects, according to the above key. Give an explanation for your ratings in the space provided, as appropriate.

Section A: General Goals of the MD Programme	Explanation/Comments
1. Problem-solving Ability. Able to identify and define health problems. Search for information, synthesize information into a conceptual framework. Beginning [X] NA End [X]	At first very poorly motivated and seemed to be a poor prospect. Difficult to understand why this course was undertaken. Later (after he became engaged to a third year student) a more determined effort was made with some success.
2. Understanding of Concepts and Mechanisms. Given a health problem is able to examine the underlying physical or behavioural mechanisms including a spectrum of phenomena, from molecular events to those involving the patient's family and community as appropriate. Beginning [X] NA End [X] NA	Seems to respond better to situations relating directly to pastoral matters. Has completed some useful case studies at the Local Health Centre, but seems uninterested in clinical aspects.

3. Personal Characteristics. Recognizes, maintains and develops personal characteristics and attitudes relevant to professional life. These include: (a) Awareness of personal assets, potential limitations and emotional reactions. Shows intellectual honesty/insight. Beginning [X] [/]NA End [X] [/]NA	Particularly lacking in self-awareness. Interested mainly in the plight of others, with a tendency always towards sociological aspects rather than medical.
(b) Responsibility and Dependability, e.g. Comes prepared to contribute to the tutorial, fulfils commitments. Beginning [X] [/]NA End [X] [/]NA	At first took an active part in tutorial discussion but allowed general lack of interest to make itself manifest.
4. Clinical Skills (see specific form for this phase or unit).	
5. Self-directed Learning. Is becoming a self-directed learner, recognizing personal educational needs, selecting appropriate learning resources and evaluates progress validly. Beginning [/]NA End [/]NA	
6. Group Interpersonal Skills. Is able to function as a productive member of a small group; acknowledges others' contributions; shows awareness of and ability to relate to others' feelings; identifies and copes with group problems. Beginning [/]NA End [/]NA	

unit, and his own personal objectives. His areas of exceptional ability are also remarked upon, as are the areas requiring attention. Finally, the sheet carries the overall decision as to whether the student is ready for the next phase of work.

The example on pp. 154–5 shows how a Section A might be used. Only the first four parts have been completed.

The subject emerges as a possible misfit as regards the general practice of medicine, but as one who might be better oriented towards social work.

USES OF PROFILING

3.7 The earlier examples in paragraph 3.5 illustrate varying ways in which basic information about the performance of an individual can be presented in order to facilitate its use for instructional or comparative purposes. The second of the two examples presented in paragraph 3.6 (b), however, raises some rather more significant issues.

First, it moves away from specific subjects and specific course titles and concentrates instead upon skills and concepts, although these are still set out in relation to a course of study, in this case medicine. The use of generalised cross-curricular skills such as problem-solving abilities as here, or listening and reading, as in the Scottish PPP (see paragraph 3.8), raises particular problems of assessment for teachers who are much more comfortable when dealing with skills which fit specifically within particular subject areas.

Secondly, this profile introduces the notion of rating performance against a scale. The use of scales has already been referred to in Chapter 2 in relation to the assessment of practical work in science (paragraph 2.43), and more will be found at Appendix A, paragraph A2.1(b) at the end of this chapter.

Thirdly, it attempts the assessment of personal characteristics both in an individual and a group context. This raises another whole series of issues, in particular the effect of such assessment upon the relationship between teacher and student. There are also problems of definition; what, for example, constitutes a manifestation of a particular personal characteristic such as persistence? On occasions too, the institutional environment within which a student is taught may not permit certain qualities, as, say, leadership, to develop and it may, therefore, be quite unreasonable to expect students to rate highly in relation to such characteristics or qualities.

Finally, this profile sets out to illustrate progression between the beginning of a section of the course and its conclusion. None of the examples in paragraphs 3.5 and 3.6, however, specifically draws attention to two of the most significant current issues in profiling in the United Kingdom, namely credibility and staff training, both of which were referred to in paragraph 3.4. These will now be followed through in somewhat more depth by reference to five further profiles.

FURTHER EXAMPLES OF PROFILES

3.8 (a) The first of these is the Scottish Pupil Profile Project (PPP) (1977) which laid the foundations for a national profile in Scotland, although it has yet to be implemented. The project originated from a national working party on assessment, established by the Head Teachers Association of Scotland. Its suggestions were subsequently incorporated into a research and development project supported by the Scottish Education Department and conducted by the Scottish Council for Research in Education (SCRE). The project was subsequently written up and widely publicised. The basic aim of PPP was to develop 'a procedure which would be equally applicable to all pupils; which would gather teachers' knowledge of pupils' many different skills, characteristics and achievements across the whole range of the curriculum, both formal and informal; which would with the minimum of clerical demands, provide a basis for continuing in-school guidance, culminating in a relevant and useful school-leaving report for all pupils'. The resulting record would

Figure 1.   The SCRE Profile Assessment System Class Assessment Sheet

S.C.R.E. PROFILE ASSESSMENT SYSTEM CLASS ASSESSMENT SHEET	Pupil's name	a. Quarry	T. Johnson	F. Fielding	S. Roberts	F. Drake	H. Holmes	D. Kennedy	B. McGregor	R. James	L. Fraser	M. Jackson	F. Dunn	S. Smith	O. Gordon	D. Brown	K. McIntosh	P. Anderson	F. Law
Class Group		3L	3L	3L	3L	3L	3L	3L	3I	3I	3L	3L	3L	3L	3L	3L	3L	3L	3L
Skills — Listening		2	3	2	4	2	1	4	1	2	2	1	2	3	1	3	3	4	2
Speaking		2	4	1	3	3	2	3	2	2	4	4	1	1	3	3	1	4	2
Reading		1	2	2	3	2	1	2	2	3	2	3	2	3	2	3	4	3	1
Writing		2	3	1	4	3	1	3	2	4	2	4	2	4	3	4	4	4	2
Visual understanding & expression		4	3	1	3	4	3	2			1	3	3	3		2	3		2
Use of Number																			
Physical Coordination																			
Manual Dexterity				4		2	1				4			3					1
Performance — Knowledge		1	4	3	4	3	1	4	2	3	4	3	3	4	1	3	4	4	1
Reasoning		2	3	2	3	2	1	3	1	1	2	4	3	3	2	4	4	4	1
Presentation		3	3	1	5	4	2	1	1	4	1	2	2	3	4	2	3	3	2
Imagination		2	4	1	1	3	2	2	1	1	3	4	2	1	3	3	3	4	3
Critical Awareness		2	3	2	2	4	1	3	2	1	2	4	2	2	2	4	4	4	2
Composite Grade		2	3	2	3	3	1	3	1	2	1	4	2	3	2	3	4	4	2
Perseverence		1	3	2	4	4	1	4	2	4	4	1	3	4	1	3	3	1	1
Enterprise		3	4	1	1	3	1	3	2	1	3	3	2	1	3	3	2	4	3
Subject/Activity		Hist.	Hist.	Hist.	Hist.	Hist.	Hist.	Hist.	Hist.	Hist.	Hist.	Hist.	Hist.	Hist.	Hist.	Hist.	Hist.	Hist.	Hist.
Teacher		J.R. McG	J.R. McG	J.R. McG	J.R. McG	J.R. McG	J.R. McG	J.R. McG	J.R. McG	J.R. McG	J.R. McG	J.R. McG	J.R. McG	J.R. McG	J.R. McG	J.R. McG	J.R. McG	J.R. McG	J.R. McG
Date		March 1976	3/76	3/76	3/76	3/76	3/76	3/76	3/76	3/76	3/76	3/76	3/76	3/76	3/76	3/76	3/76	3/76	3/76

Figure 2. An Example of a Completed School Leaving Report Using the Form Developed by the Working Party for the SCRE Profile Assessment System

SCHOOL LEAVING REPORT

This is a brief report on   Queenie Quarry

Date of Birth 13/7/60

who completed class S4

in   Tanochbrae High   School

and left on 3rd July 1976

This report is the result of continuous assessment by all the teachers of this pupil and has the authority of:-

E. P. Smith   Head Teacher

J. McGregor   Director

SKILLS

LISTENING

Acts independently and intelligently on complex verbal instructions ☐

Can interpret and act on most complex instructions ☐ TH

Can interpret and act on straightforward instructions ☐

Can carry out simple instructions with supervision ☐

READING

Understands all appropriate written material ☐ TH

Understands the content and implications of most writing if simply expressed ☐

Understands uncomplicated ideas expressed in simple language ☐

Can read most everyday information such as notices or simple instructions ☐

VISUAL UNDERSTANDING AND EXPRESSION

Can communicate complex visual concepts readily and appropriately ☐

Can give a clear explanation by sketches and diagrams ☐

Can interpret a variety of visual displays such as graphs or train timetables ☐ TH

Can interpret single visual displays such as roadsigns or outline maps ☐

PHYSICAL CO-ORDINATION

A natural flair for complex tasks ☐

Mastery of a wide variety of movements ☐

Can perform satisfactorily most everyday movements ☐ TH

Can perform single physical skills such as lifting or climbing ☐

SPEAKING

Can debate a point or view ☐

Can make a clear and accurate oral report ☐ TH

Can describe events orally ☐

Can communicate adequately at conversation level. ☐

WRITING

Can argue a point of view in writing ☐

Can write a clear and accurate report ☐ TH

Can write a simple account or letter ☐

Can write simple messages and instructions ☐

USE OF NUMBER

Quick and accurate in complicated or unfamiliar calculations ☐

Can do familiar or straightforward calculations, more slowly if complex ☐

Can handle routine calculations with practice ☐ TH

Can do simple whole number calculations such as giving change ☐

MANUAL DEXTERITY

Has fine control of complex tools and equipment ☐

Satisfactory use of most tools and equipment ☐ TH

Can achieve simple tasks such as wiring a plug ☐

Can use simple tools, instruments and machines such as a screwdriver or typewriter ☐

OTHER OBSERVATIONS

(includes other school activities, other awards and comments on positive personal qualities).

Royal Life-Saving Society - Bronze Medallion
Member School Photographic Club, School Debating Society
Member of School Skiing trip to Austria Jan 1976
She has been resourceful in finding costumes for the school play.
She has recently shown an appreciation and enjoyment of literature and has read widely outside the syllabus.
Works well on group activities; gets on well with both pupils and teachers. Readily accepts responsibility, particularly in school activities.

Notes

The grades A–D represent approximately 25% of the year group in each case.

The skill gradings represent a consensus derived from the individual ratings of each teacher's knowledge and reflect the standard obtained by the pupil with reasonable consistency.

All the information contained in this report is based on profile assessments contributed by each teacher on a continuous and cumulative basis, including observations of personal qualities and informal activities.

SUBJECT/ACTIVITY ASSESSMENT

Curriculum Area	Subjects Studied (includes final year level where relevant)	Years of Study	Achievement	Enterprise (includes flair, creativity)	Perseverance (includes reliability, carefulness)
Aesthetic Subjects	Drawing	1-4	2	2	1
	Music	1-4	2	3	3
Business Studies					
Community/Leisure Activities	Social Education	1-4	3	2	3
Crafts	Pottery	3-4	2	1	3
English	English	1-4	2	1	3
Mathematics	Arithmetic	1-4	1	1	2
Other Languages	German	2-4	2	2	3
Outdoor Studies	Outdoor Pursuits	3-4	2	2	3
Physical Education	General	1-4	3	1	3
Science	Biology	3-4	1	2	2
Social Subjects	History	1-4	2	1	3

include a whole variety of abilities and qualities that were not normally formally recorded at all, as well as those which appeared on more traditional certificates.

(b) The recording and reporting system that was eventually adopted, after a five-year trial, in some forty Scottish comprehensive schools involved three stages:

1. The collection of the assessments made by the teachers.

2. The collation of these assessments and their transfer from class group sheets to individual pupil profiles.

3. The production of a school-leaving certificate based on the information contained in the profiles.

The teacher's assessment form for a class group in History and the completed school-leaving report or profile in respect of a single pupil from that class, are shown in Figures 1 and 2.

The teacher's form allows for the assessment of eight basic skills where these seem relevant to a particular subject. A four-point scale, based upon nationally agreed criteria of achievement, is used for this purpose. The form also allows for the assessment of performance in two parts. The first part, as well as providing for an overall composite grade, gives a series of blank optional categories which teachers can fill with those components of achievement which they deem appropriate to their subject. In the case of History, the five choices were Knowledge, Reasoning, Presentation, Imagination and Critical Awareness. Again a four-point scale is used for their assessment, this time devised by the relevant department within the school making use of the guidelines provided in the project's handbook. The second part provides for the grading of the two work-related characteristics summarised as Enterprise and Perseverence, which research has shown to have the highest predictive validity with occupational success in later life.

(c) Another interesting example of a similar approach is that by Rentzulli and Hartman, produced for the Council for Exceptional Children (1971). The scales are designed to obtain teachers' estimates of a student's characteristics in the area of learning, motiviation, creativity and leadership, and use four scales of observed behaviour.

(d) Quite apart from the extensive use of assessment based on scales, a number of important considerations arise from the PPP which, it should be stressed, was subject to a very thorough-going evaluation. First, there is the question of practicality. There is no doubt that the scheme worked during the trial period and that it proved to be as valid and as reliable as current alternatives, as well as being a good deal more informative. On the other hand, its operation undoubtedly placed severe strains upon both staff and resources. These strains were, incidentally, even more severe for the small number of schools which took part in the subsequent Assessment in the Affective Domain Project (Dockrell and Black (1978)). In general, neither resources (the implications for computer-assisted storage, retrieval and display have not, for example, been really exploited to date) nor training were made available by either central or local government in Scotland after the project ended in 1977. This has had a markedly adverse effect on the continued use of the profile, although this situation may well change dramatically when the Munn and Dunning proposals are implemented in the mid 1980s.

(e) More significantly still, the PPP highlights the problem of reconciling within a single profile the formative and summative uses of assessment, and the implications of this for establishing the credibility of profiles. This problem becomes particularly acute when, as in the PPP, the assessment forms part of a school-leaving certificate, in this case the Scottish O Grade. As Patricia Broadfoot pertinently points out (Burgess and Adams (ed.) (1980), Chapter 6), such certificates in the United Kingdom have three principal functions which are not easily reconciled, namely, selection, motivation and control of standards and hence accountability. The form taken by any certification process will depend to a large extent upon which of these three functions is considered to be the most important at any given time. If motivation is the main concern, then it would be possible to do without formal certificates and operate pupil-completed records. If selection or the maintenance of national standards is the top priority, then formal certification based upon some external monitor, such as GCE examinations, is likely to be the order of the day. Profiles offer a measure of compromise between these conflicting demands, but like all compromises they may end up by failing to satisfy anyone.

Clearly, on the evidence of the overall current usage and acceptability of PPP, in *practice* there is a need for much more centrally supported work to be undertaken on the development of teacher-compiled profiles. These can be based upon generally agreed criteria and hence fulfil public expectations regarding comparability. This, in turn, can lead into work upon what might be termed 'negotiated records compiled jointly by teacher and pupil'. Only if this is done are we likely to begin to approach a genuinely comprehensive method of providing worthwhile information about all pupils.

3.9 (a) There are, of course, a number of illustrations of negotiated records in current use, some involving groups of schools working together and others involving a single school. Probably the best known group scheme is the Swindon Record of Personal Achievement Scheme (RPA), which originated in 1970 for all secondary school children in the County Borough of Swindon between the ages of 14 and 16.

(b) Of particular significance in the RPA scheme was the direct involvement of the student in the preparation of his own record. It was the student who, within fairly flexible guidelines, decided what constituted an achievement. It was the student who looked after the record, and the way this was maintained would, incidentally, tell a would-be user something of importance about its owner. A second important feature was the approach to validation. When an entry was made in the record it had to be verified by an adult who knew it to be factually correct. The original reason for this, as Don Stansbury points out (Burgess and Adams (ed.) (1980), Chapter 4), was to ensure that students did not falsify their records — a precaution which in the event proved totally unnecessary. It turned out, however, to be important for quite different reasons, since it involved people other than teachers, including potential employers, directly in the processes of school assessment. It also undermined, indeed rendered impossible, the practice of comparison between students which is such a prominent feature of most assessment. A third issue which arose was that of credibility. Sadly, as the evaluator's report shows (Swales (1979)), the RPA was not particularly successful in gaining the support of employers, who in the main continued to see the profile as supplementary to more traditional methods of selection, such as interviews and public examination results. An unfortunate result of this attitude was a tendency within participating institutions to confine the record to students of lower ability for whom public examinations were not thought appropriate.

(c) One of the original authors of the RPA, Don Stansbury, developed an extension of the scheme in 1974, when he moved to Totneş in Devon. This was called the Record of Personal Experience, Qualities and Qualifications — a much more revealing description of its intentions. He concentrated at Totnes on making the scheme manageable for class units of between twenty and thirty and on involving the whole ability range. He also became convinced from his experience with both schemes, that unless a record of this kind became an underwritten part of a national system then it would be impossible to establish the necessary credibility. This reinforces the points made by Patricia Broadfoot in relation to the PPP which were referred to in paragraph 3.8 (e).

3.10 (a) The problem of establishing credibility for a profile becomes even more acute when it is devised and used by a single institution, although there are compensating possibilities in such a situation at the local level. A good example of such a profile is that introduced in 1973 by the Sutton Centre Community School in Nottinghamshire. This has been described in some detail in Fletcher and Thompson (ed.) (1979). Like many similar documents, the Sutton profile is a substantial one. The staff prospectus, for example, contains the following guidelines.

'Profile sheets should be organised into the correct order as follows:

1. (a) Sutton Centre Information Sheet
   (b) Personal Section
       (i) Personal information sheet — this sheet is prepared in the Communications and Resources Department.
       (ii) Attendance — a record of attendance kept by the student.
       (iii) Centre activities — these sheets record activities of special interest which although based at or involving the Centre have usually taken place outside the 9.00 a.m. to 4.00 p.m.

session times, e.g. clubs, camps, outings and work done in 11 sessions.

    (iv) Other interests and activities.

2. General commentary by the tutor.

3. Subject section in alphabetical order but with Basic Skills at the end. There should be three types of sheets in each subject:

    (i) Departmental subject summary.

    (ii) Teacher's comment sheet — every sheet should have the correct title and date, and each comment should be initialised and dated.

    (iii) Record of activities sheets. These sheets are completed by the student when actually working in the department concerned. They are, therefore, kept for the most part by the appropriate Course Director.

Subject sheets should be in the following order:

1. Communications and Resources.
2. Creative Arts.
3. Environmental.
4. European Studies.
5. Home Management.
6. Literature and Drama.
7. Maths.
8. Personal Relationships.
9. Science.
10. Sports and Leisure.
11. Technical Studies.
12. Basic Skills.

There should be a sheet of coloured card separating sections 1/2, 2/3, 3/4, and between Technical Studies and Basic Skills.'

(b) These guidelines raise, yet again, the crucial question of the logistics of actually operating profiles within institutions and draw attention in particular to problems of time, resources and training. How can busy staff find, or be given, time to undertake such work? Are there any particular difficulties created by the range of assessment techniques needed in order to meet the requirements of the profile, particularly when personal characteristics are included? What form or forms should staff development take? These are the kinds of question that an extended use of profiles are bound to raise. Staff development has been particularly significant, for example, in the current use of profiles describing skills relevant to vocational preparation. Work on the Sutton Centre profile has also raised the question of how to prevent a profile from becoming simply another form of school report handed down by teacher to student and parent. It has tried to overcome this by providing opportunities, as part of the profile itself, for both student and parent to comment upon the teacher's initial comments, as for example:

Girl D — Literature and Drama

Teacher's Comments
D's work is spoilt by her spelling and her inability to give work in to be marked when it is finished. She is imaginative but must organise herself to finish work and take pride in it. It has taken her a long time to settle down at the Centre and I am sure will soon be forging ahead!
Signed

Pupil's Comments
15th July
I agree with this coment. my spelling is bad I will try and improve it. This term in lit and drama has been quite interesting
Signed

Parent's Comments
D has been given a dictionary to help improve her spelling, she will be encouraged to use it and to be prompt in handing in finished work
Signed

In addition, there is opportunity, also as an integral part of the profile, for students to describe their other interests and activities, as for example:

Boy P

Date	Other Interests and Activities
July	Myself and some of my friends are now making a film, which will be sent to the Screen Test competition. We are working on an idea set in Sherwood Forest. (It is also a part-time school activity as well.)
25.9.77	On Sunday John and myself went a bike ride to Selston and all round that district. On the way back it rained very hard and we both got wet through. We both had the misfortune of our front brake cable snapping!
1978	During the Whit holidays, John, Jack, Steve and myself spent some days camping in Bagthorpe. During our time camping there, we made a couple of films. One of them is an entry for the Screen Test Young film makers comp. The other film was one made just for our enjoyment and entertainment.

Both these illustrations appear in Burgess and Adams (ed.) (1980), Chapter 5.

(c) These features draw attention to the possibility of negotiation between teacher and student, both about the nature and content of what might be learnt and about the methods to be used for learning, although the Centre did not fully carry through this concept in practice. In the last resort, however, the key question for students in relation to profiles must be, will anyone read it? The evidence here from the Sutton Centre is not particularly encouraging. It appears that local employers, at least in 1976 and 1977 when a study was undertaken, devoted a maximum of fifteen minutes to each applicant for a job and regarded the interview as more important than any written material. Moreover, the more academically able the student, the lower was the value attached to the profile. The attitudes of users, however, constitute the outward-looking side of the coin. Within an institution there may well be, as there undoubtedly was at the Sutton Centre, important motivational effects and significant social developments arising from the use of profiles, which affect all students, although they themselves may not always appreciate their value.

3.11 (a) An attempt to resolve the problem of credibility, whilst retaining maximum flexibility for individuals and institutions, was proposed by Burgess and Adams (ed.) (1980). Their aim was to provide every young person at the end of compulsory schooling with something substantial to show for their years at school. The 'something' in their scheme took the form of a folder of evidence built up by every student during his last two years of compulsory schooling. The folder, which the students would retain, was to serve as the basis for an agreed school statement summarising their capacities, achievements, interests and ambitions. Their proposals for implementation, which have been subsequently developed by work undertaken at the North East London Polytechnic (1981), are in two parts. The first is the preparation of the statement itself, whilst the second is concerned with devising a framework which would give national recognition to what each institution and hence each student was doing.

The programme for the production of the statements involves three stages. The first would begin at about age fourteen (the end of the third year) when the critical plans would be drawn up; reconsideration and revision would then take place a year later and the third stage of the programme would culminate at the end of the fifth year, at about age sixteen, with the final statement. The following were deemed by the authors to be the essential features of the programme for the production of these final statements: student initiative, a formal planning period, a commitment to individual work, the blocking of the school timetable for tutorial and special content study, personal tutorship, the folder of evidence and the final summarising statement.

(b) The two key elements of the second part — the framework needed to achieve national recognition — are, first, external validation of the arrangements made by institutions for the planning of the programmes of work and the preparation of the statements, and, second, external accreditation of the statements themselves by an outside professional body. The functions of validation and accreditation are thus clearly separated.

The Burgess/Adams proposals envisaged that the institutional arrangements would be validated by a team established by and including the school governors. In addition to the governors, it would include people of standing in the local community with relevant interests and experience, particularly councillors and employers. Accreditation was to be in the hands of a different group, largely chosen from outside the local area, to include such people as HMIs, academics and teachers from other schools. Finally, the whole process of accreditation would be underwritten by a national body. At the time of writing, Burgess and Adams saw the Schools Council in this role, but its subsequent demise has ruled this out — a possible alternative would be the local authorities, either individually or working through the Association of County Councils (ACC) and the Association of Metropolitan Authorities (AMA). It was Burgess' and Adams' intention that the national body would approve the membership of the accrediting boards and would nominate representatives to them. They also considered it desirable that representatives from the accrediting boards should be appointed to each validating board. Although the whole scheme was envisaged as an alternative to public examinations, it was sufficiently flexible to include them for those who wished to do so.

Burgess and Adams, whilst not underestimating the work involved in establishing such a scheme (not least in changing attitudes), believed that the work of the Council for National Academic Awards (CNAA) and of external examiners in universities, provided working models for accreditation which could be satisfactorily adapted to meet the school situation. These claims have not, as yet, been justified in practice, although growing disenchantment with the present reforms of the examination system at 16+ could lead to the whole scheme being given more detailed consideration. Initiatives by local education authorities might prove particularly fruitful here. On the other hand, the current vogue for pre-vocational education and the associated development of grid style profiles based upon criteria may turn out to be the more significant in their impact upon future practice. Schemes like the Swindon RPA and the Burgess/Adams proposals are practitioner models with an emphasis upon general education, whereas most of the current grid style profiles are dominated by administrative and managerial prescriptions designed to improve young people's employability. This latter style has already attracted substantial criticism, as will be seen in the next paragraph, but whether it will be sufficient to give any impetus to the Burgess/Adams proposals with their potential proliferation of local and national boards must remain doubtful.

GRID STYLE PROFILES — ADVANTAGES AND DISADVANTAGES

3.12 (a) It was suggested in paragraph 3.3 that one of the two main driving forces behind the development and increased use of profiles was youth unemployment. This has led to increased national concern with the whole question of vocational preparation or how best to equip the young school leaver for the world of work taken as a whole. Central to the promotion of this concept of 'voc prep' has been the identification, development and assessment of basic skills. This in turn has focused attention upon informative and helpful ways of providing information about performance in respect of those skills, and hence led to profiles and in particular to grid style profiles. These last are simply profiles which record information through the use of a grid or grids. The content of these grids consists of designated levels of performance in

City and Guilds 365 Pilot Scheme – Profile Report – Four Weekly Review

This profile shows the levels which have been reached during the last four weeks and the learning activities which have taken place.

ATTAINMENTS IN BASIC ABILITIES

			4 (Basic Level)	3	2	1 (High Level)
SOCIAL ABILITIES	WORKING WITH COLLEAGUES	1	Can cooperate with others when led	Can work with other members of group to achieve common aims	Understands own position and results of own actions within a group	Is an active, decisive members of group. Helps and encourages others
	WORKING WITH THOSE IN AUTHORITY	2	Can follow verbal instructions for simple tasks and can perform them under supervision	Can follow a series of verbal instructions and carry them out independently	Can carry out a series of tasks effectively, given minimum instructions	Inspires confidence in those in authority and communicates well with them
	SELF-AWARENESS	3	Is aware of own personality and situation	Can determine own strengths, weaknesses and preferences with some guidance	Has good basic understanding of own situation, personality and motivation	Has a thorough understanding of own personality and abilities and their implications
COMMUNICATION	TALKING AND LISTENING	4	Can hold conversations with workmates, face-to-face or by 'phone. Can take messages	Can follow and give simple descriptions and explanations	Can communicate effectively with a range of people in a variety of situations	Can present a logical and effective argument. Can analyse others' arguments
	READING AND WRITING	5	Can understand and write simple notices, labels and short notes	Can follow and give straightforward written instructions and explanations	Can use instruction manuals and can write reports describing work done	Can select and criticise written data and use it to produce own written work
	VISUAL UNDERSTANDING	6	Can interpret simple signs and indicators	Can, after guidance, make use of basic graphs, charts, tables, drawings, etc.	Can interpret and use basic graphs, charts, tables and drawings unaided	Can construct graphs etc, and extract information to support arguments

	Level 1	Level 2	Level 3	Level 4
PRACTICAL & NUMERICAL ABILITIES				
USING EQUIPMENT — 7	After demonstration, can use equipment safely to perform simple tasks	With guidance, can use equipment safely to perform multi-step tasks	Can select and use suitable equipment and materials for the job, without help	Can set up and maintain equipment. Can identify/remedy common faults
DEXTERITY AND COORDINATION — 8	Can use everyday implements; can lift, carry and set down objects as directed	Can reliably perform basic manipulative tasks	Can perform complex tasks requiring accuracy and dexterity	Can perform tasks requiring a high degree of manipulative control
MEASURING — 9	Can read graduated linear scales and dials	Can measure out specified quantities of material by length, weight, etc.	Can set up and use simple precision instruments	Can set up and use complex precision instruments
CALCULATING — 10	N/O Can identify size, shape, order etc. Can add and subtract whole numbers	Can use $+/-/\times/\div$ to solve single-step, whole number problems. Can estimate	Can use $+/-/\times/\div$ to solve two-step problems. Can add and subtract decimals	Can use $+/-/\times/\div$ to solve multi-step problems. Can multiply and divide decimals
DECISION-MAKING ABILITIES				
PLANNING — 11	After demonstration, can identify the sequence of steps in a routine task	Can choose from given alternatives the best way of tackling a task	Can modify/extend given plans/routines to meet changed circumstances	Can create new plans/routines from scratch, using all sources of help
INFORMATION SEEKING — 12	Can find information with guidance from supervisor	Can use standard sources of information	Can assemble information from several sources	Shows initiative in seeking and gathering information from a wide variety of sources
COPING WITH PROBLEMS — 13	With guidance, can cope with simple, everyday problems	Can cope with complex but routine problems. Seeks help if needed	Can cope with unusual problems by adapting familiar routines independently	Can offer sensitive and effective help to other people facing problems
EVALUATING RESULTS — 14	Can assess own results with guidance. Asks for advice	Can assess own output for routine tasks independently	Can assess own performance and identify possible improvements	Can identify others' difficulties and so help to improve group performance

N/O – No opportunity to assess.

relation to defined skills, thus permitting the student to be graded against agreed criteria. There is nothing particularly new about this. As already indicated, grids formed part of the Scottish PPP Scheme and have been used in public examinations for the assessment of practical work. Grid style profiles have considerable merits: they are easy to fill in, compact, cover wide areas of skills and are, on the face of it, much more informative to both employer and student than other forms of certification and grading. The City and Guilds 365 Pilot Scheme provides a typical example (see pages 168-9).

Other profiles, using the same model but with different skills, have been produced by the Royal Society of Arts (RSA), the Technician Educational Council (TEC) and the Business Education Council (BEC) and the Further Education Curriculum Review and Development Unit (FEU) for the core in its report *A Basis for Choice* (Second Edition 1982).

(b) Grid profiles also have marked disadvantages, some of which raise funda-mental issues about the nature and purpose of profiling. Many of these issues have been put forcibly by the Scottish Vocational Preparation Unit (1982) and can be illustrated by reference to the extract from the CGLI profile given in paragraph 3.12 (a). Probably the most fundamental criticism is their potential lack of congruence with the needs of the students. The grid model is essentially outward looking, designed first and foremost to serve the needs of the user and not those of the student. The Scottish Vocational Preparation Unit (1982) makes this point in another way when it draws a distinction between a record, which it defines as evidence upon which outsiders can make judgements, and a report, which it regards as judgement which outsiders can take as evidence. Given that this distinction is a valid one, and to be fair there is probably an element of both record and report in most profiles, then grid style profiles; like PPP and City and Guilds 365, are primarily reports and the Swindon Scheme and the Sutton Centre profile are primarily records. It is the summative/formative distinction once again. Other points of potential weakness are:

   (i) The use of imprecise descriptions. How 'simple' is simple? What is a 'routine task'? How does one define 'from scratch'? (All these words or phrases appear in the CGLI pilot scheme.)

   (ii) The uniform nature of the progression between grades. Often the steps required of the student are extremely large and it is in conse-quence difficult to define or measure progression, particularly if the course involved is a short one. The section on Visual Understanding provides a good illustration of this point.

   (iii) The existence of overlapping categories; the tendency to confuse skills with attitudes and the use of narrow and non-functional skills.

(c) The overall thrust of the points made in paragraph 3.12 (b) is to suggest that unless grid style profiles are extremely carefully designed and flexibly used they will hinder negotiation between learner and teacher and will neither encourage nor adequately assess student development and hence progression. Having been critical by implication of the CGLI pilot scheme as an example of a grid style profile, it is only fair to draw attention to ways in which through trialling and evaluation the CGLI has tried to meet the criticisms levelled against this particular model. Stratton (1982).

First of all, great care has been taken with the wording used to describe the various grade levels and, whilst not entirely successful, a great deal of the vagueness which plagues such grade descriptions has been eliminated.

Secondly, the profile report has tried to deal realistically with the measurement of progression. This has been done in three main ways. It has not attempted to suggest that the gaps between the four grades on the grid are equal in size, but has instead indicated an overall progression from a basic level to a high level. It has also required those completing it to provide examples of the relevant abilities as demonstrated in a practical work context. Finally, the report itself covers a relatively short four-week period so that progression can be shown over a series of relatively short time spans.

Thirdly, the design of the report has endeavoured to resolve the summative/formative clash by linking the abilities to be measured, thus permitting a helpful summative judgement to be made without eliminating valuable formative data.

Fourthly, the students themselves have been significantly involved, although this involvement stops short of actual negotiation about the nature and content of the course itself. This involvement has been stimulated in three ways: by providing opportunities for the students to discuss and disagree with the judgements made on the record; by requiring students, as an integral part of their course, to keep a daily record of experience; and by a weekly review of progress between student and teacher, which results in an agreed and signed statement from both parties about areas of progress and areas which need improvement. The overall documentation is contained in a Trainee Log Book which remains the property of the student. Further developments will undoubtedly take place as the scheme becomes operational and practical experience is gained.

VISUAL PRESENTATION OF PROFILES

3.13 (a) It is, of course, perfectly possible to use a visual or diagrammatic presentation for a profile, and indeed such formats can be particularly helpful for formative use. An interesting example of diagrammatic presentation is provided by the assessment profiles devised by Overson (1980) for use in science in his school, although they are equally applicable to any subject or any course of study which is regularly assessed. These assessment profiles have two principal purposes: to provide information about how individual pupils are performing within a group and to indicate the function and performance of one group relative to other groups in the same year and following the same course. By the use of a device which he called a Polargram, Overson was able to display all the information relating to these two purposes for immediate analysis without reference to rows or columns of figures. Using the Polargram, it is possible to produce Group Assessment Profiles (GAPs) and Pupil Assessment Profiles (PAPs) which are independent of methods of grouping such as sets or mixed ability.

(b)

Figure 1   Group assessment profile — Top set physics group: Test 1

Centre 0% Outer circle 100%

Pupils

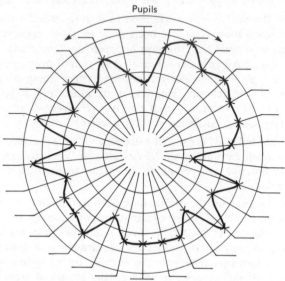

Figure 2   Pupil assessment profile — Top set physics pupil

Centre 0% Outer circle 100%   ● Group average

Topics tested

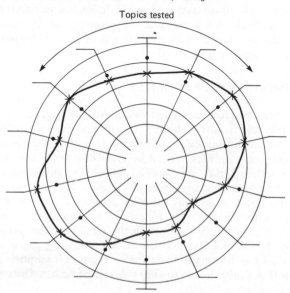

Figure 3   Group assessment profile – Mixed ability group

Inner profile: pre-test results
Outer profile: post-test results

Pupils

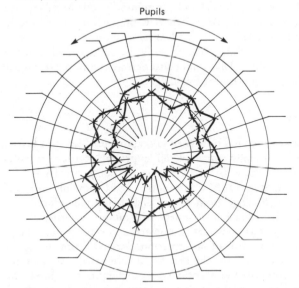

After marking a test the teacher will first of all construct a group profile for his class (see Figure 1). At the same time he inserts the individual student's marks on the PAP sheets, from which PAPs for each student in the group can be constructed (see Figure 2). PAPs can be developed for coursework as well as for examinations. As pupils move through the school, the PAPs from previous years, now overlaid with a whole range of assessment data, would be added to their files. In this way the students' academic history is readily available to new teachers – indeed the new teacher could derive great benefit from studying all the PAPs of his new class. An accurate assessment of a pupil's progress from year to year can be made by observing any expansion or contraction of the profile. Such information is of particular value in mixed ability groupings and is not easy to extract from mark books.

Overson would argue strongly that GAPs can be a most helpful aid to modern management in that:

(i) they give a perspective view of all teaching groups;

(ii) the spread of ability within each group is immediately apparent;

(iii) the effect of curriculum modification can be monitored;

(iv) the effect of a change in teaching methods can be monitored;

(v) they can be used for diagnostic purposes.

As a diagnostic instrument they could well encourage some teachers to steer their teaching more towards a set of recognised objectives. Figure 3, for example, is a GAP of a mixed ability group, which on this occasion had taken a pre-test prior to specific instruction and then taken a post-test after instruction had been completed. The data in this Polargram shows that the least able children had made more headway than the brighter students. The questions for the teachers and the school to ask here, are whether this is a satisfactory state of affairs; what might be the causes and how might the situation be improved? Great advantages in terms of exchange of information about students within a school would be gained if all departments used the GAP and the PAP. This would also permit computer storage of information as a welcome replacement for filing.

CONCLUSION

3.14 (a) More than enough has now been said about profiles, and sufficient examples provided, to permit some overall appraisal of their potential and of the problems that have to be overcome if that potential is to be realised in practice. Stanton (1982) lists some eight possible major functions for profiles, which range from acting as a structured reference through to the provision of feedback to learners and quality control of courses. Profiles and profiling thus constitute a powerful tool for promoting and facilitating the constructive use of information derived from assessment in a wide variety of ways and for the benefit of individuals, courses and institutions. This last sentence, and Stanton's list, highlights the 'Janus' face of profiles and raises yet again the most significant problem facing their development, namely, can a single profile serve several major uses at once? Any analysis of the possible uses of profiles (this could usefully be undertaken by reference to those described in this chapter) will reveal that while different profiles can look either outwards to the user or inwards to the learner, it is extremely difficult for the same profile to face both inwards and outwards and satisfy both learner and user. It is the record/report, formative/summative issue, which has been referred to so frequently in this chapter, yet again.

On the evidence available to date, this problem has yet to be satisfactorily resolved, although reference to the CGLI profile will show that improvements can be and have been made. Part of the problem lies in the retention within so many profiles of norm referencing and a desire to compare students with one another, rather than criterion referencing where the basis for comparison is stated levels of performance or mastery. Another part of the problem lies in our inadequate knowledge of how young people think and hence learn, and, in particular, how they acquire and use skills. This often means that the hypothesised stages of progression which appear in profiles bear little relationship to the actual stages of learning. We may well be in the business of making a difference and not simply of measuring it, but unless and until we can identify and then communicate these differences, without in the process disturbing the learning and teaching that has brought them about, then we will achieve little.

(b) The second major problem is a practical one and shows itself in two ways. The first of these is the question of handling profiles as an organisational problem, the second relates to assessment. The Scottish Vocational Preparation Unit (1982) emphasises four principles for assessment which it regards as essential for the successful development of profiles.

(i) Assessment should play an intrinsic role in individual learning.

(ii) Assessment should reflect a genuine balance between the values of 'reliability' and those of 'self-reliance'.

(iii) Course grids and assessment methods should match one another.

(iv) Assessment should actively involve learners in the determination and evaluation of course activities (negotiation).

Their implementation will demand an understanding of a range of assessment techniques well beyond those with which most teachers are familiar. It also requires assessment methods to be matched to course goals, an exercise which is all too rarely carried out in either classroom or school and is, moreover, one which many teachers find extremely difficult (see *Exercise 5.42*).

The answers to both these problems lie in staff development and in-service training, both for individuals and for institutions. We now know enough about profiles to be able to design them, particularly if their intended usage is relatively limited. The quantum leap lies in being able to operate them in practice in the reasonable certainty that they are doing what we want them to do.

(c) Ironically, the reader might argue, with a degree of truth, that this chapter, which has stressed training as the essential glue in the practical development of profiles, has itself made less use of training than any other chapter in *A Teacher's Guide to Assessment*. It has been largely descriptive and has so far provided no practical exercises for the reader to undertake. This is deliberate, although whether it is justified only time will tell. In a new and rapidly developing area such as profiling, the authors took the view that the most pressing need was to provide background information and a wide range of illustrations. The issues raised will be taken a stage further in the case study in Chapter 4. Here, the kind of limited profile which is typical of many schools' initial entry into this area, is considered in some detail as a practical working model. The next stage after considering the case study is to use all the information contained in *A Teacher's Guide to Assessment* as a platform upon which to develop profiles for actual use. A useful starting point for such a development would be to consider present practices in one's own school, college or organisation and then, in the light of this scrutiny and with reference to relevant good practice, to design and implement one's own profile. *Exercise 5.29 (a), (b), (c)* and *(d)* is designed to facilitate this process and to lead into the case study; *Exercises 5.38* and *5.39 (a)* and *(b)* provide longer exercises on the same topic and should be undertaken at a time convenient to the reader.

(Exercises 5.29 a to d)

Appendix A should be read before attempting Exercises 5.30 and 5.31.

Self-teaching Exercises

Number   *Exercise*

5.29 (a)   For your own school, college or organisation, list those who receive the information gained from the results of assessment, and indicate how this information is collated.

5.29 (b)   Indicate in what form these results are passed on to:

    (i) parents;

    (ii) other educational establishments;

    (iii) would-be employers.

5.29 (c)   In what respects are the groups listed in exercise 5.29 (b) likely to require different information? Should this affect the ways in which the information is presented, and, if so, how?

5.29 (d)   In what ways do you feel the system in your school, college or organisation could be improved?

5.30 (a)   Construct a distribution graph based on some results recently obtained from a test you have used and marked. Is the shape of the curve what you anticipated it would be? Comment on any unexpected differences.

5.30 (b)   Take the marks from any recent test which is available to you and construct a distribution graph. What can you learn from this graph?

5.31   Collect in respect of one particular teaching group, the results they obtained for a single test in different subjects. How would you set about combining these marks in order to provide an overall order of merit such that you could award a prize to the 'first' student.

Appendix A — Marks and Marking

THE TREATMENT OF MARKS

A1 Methods of marking have already been discussed in Chapter 2 (paragraphs 2.28 to 2.36). This appendix is concerned with the interpretation of marks. If you are told that Anne or John has gained a mark of 60 then you will eventually ask questions or make inferences, for example, does this mark indicate a good or bad performance? Before any real meaning can be attached to numerical information it must be supplemented by a number of numerical facts. These facts are known as statistics and are used as references against which the quality of a particular mark can be judged. It may also be necessary to make comparisons between sets of marks which have been derived from different sources, for example from different tests or from different markers. Unless these marks are placed upon a common scale, valid comparisons cannot be made. This appendix, therefore, aims to do two things. First, to describe the information that is necessary in order to be able to gain information from marks and hence to answer questions about them and, secondly, to describe the process known as standardisation, whereby different sets of marks can be placed upon a common scale thus permitting them to be added and/or compared.

THE TREATMENT OF INDIVIDUAL MARKS

A2.1 **(a)** A numerical score, which theoretically can fall anywhere within the available range of marks, has no absolute value. It is simply the score obtained by a particular person, in a particular test, on a particular day, and marked according to a particular marking scheme by a particular individual.

(b) Raw numerical scores can be misleading and their intended use must be fully understood beforehand. Questions need to be asked, for example, how many other pupils obtained a particular mark, and what was the average for the group? For the relationship of 'observed' to true scores see paragraph 2.28 (c).

(c) The Center for the Study of Evaluation, USA (1978), points out that raw scores out of context are hard to interpret, but they are directly interpretable in tests where you can clearly describe what the test measures. Raw scores, because they are most directly derived from tests, are the most appropriate raw material for calculating statistics. Analyses of Variance (T Tests), computed to determine whether there is a difference in the average score between a programme and control group, should be based on average raw scores not on converted scores.

(d) Pidgeon and Yates (1969) utter a word of caution about percentages, which although generally favoured as a method of reporting for parents, have disadvantages which are perhaps most obvious when used to express a pupil's performance in a number of subjects. For example, if parents are told that their child has 60% for English and 75% for Mathematics, they are liable to conclude that their child is a better performer at Mathematics than in English. This conclusion should not be made unless the scales used for both have common bases. Similarly, they might think that both performances were good (or bad) without justification. It would be more meaningful if the parents were informed of the mean of the group, or that the percentages quoted were related to the total mark which the teacher was prepared to award in that particular examination.

(e) Results can normally only be compared when a ratio scale is used, i.e. a scale with equal intervals and an absolute zero. Most examinations where the zero is not absolute do not satisfy these conditions, and we are compelled to look for some alternative reference point. It is unlikely that the maximum or minimum can be defined, but the average can be determined, both empirically and objectively. It is perfectly possible to ascertain the average performance in any group, and to relate any individual performance to that figure.

To learn that a child has so many marks more or less than the average for some group, reveals their relative status within that group. So many marks more than some undefined zero level tells nothing about performance.

SCALES

(f) On the subject of scales, Stephens (1951) provides a useful definition of a scale as a means of assigning numerals to objects according to rules. He identifies four levels:

   (i) Nominal scales – Assigning numerals to objects and events as labels by which they can be identified, for example vintage years in wines.

   (ii) Ordinal scales – Arranging objects or individuals in order according to the degree that they display a particular characteristic, for example rank order in the results of a test or examination.

   (iii) Interval scales – Ordinal scales within which the intervals have been made equal, for example a thermometer.

   (iv) Ratio scales – Interval scales with an absolute zero, for example units of length or weight.

(g) It is, of course, theoretically possible to devise educational tests with an absolute zero, for example French vocabulary – French into English equivalents could produce a scale in which a zero mark indicated a complete ignorance of the language, but the practical difficulties of producing a true ratio scale would be considerable. We must be content for the most part with interval scales, and in many cases we shall have to be content with ordinal scales since the problems in creating scales of measuring with greater flexibility are not practicable for everyday usage.

It is important that the kind of scale which is being employed can be recognised, and that the results are not submitted to inappropriate treatment and interpretation.

ERROR OF MEASUREMENT

A2.2 (a) When considering individual scores the relationship between the observed score and the true score, known as the error of measurement, needs to be taken into account.

(b) The term error of measurement does not imply that a mistake has been made, but simply that the actual mark of grade awarded to candidates can vary, bracketing the mark of grade which they ought to obtain (the true score). This can result from a number of causes, such as the length of the test or its content, variations of the marker, state of the candidate's health, and so on.

(c) This variance is expressed by the classical test theory model. In this theory, the reliability coefficient is defined as the square of the correlation between the score and the observed score:

$$\text{Observed Score (O)} = \text{True Score (T)} \pm \text{Error Score (E)}$$

The reliability coefficient ($r\hat{t}t$) can be shown to equal the ratio of the variance of the true scores VAR(T) to the variance of the observed scores VAR(O) thus:

$$r\hat{t}t = \frac{\text{VAR(T)}}{\text{VAR(O)}}$$

or alternatively, as T and E are assumed to be independent (Variance of the Error Scores is denoted as VAR(E)):

$$r\hat{t}t = \frac{1 - \text{VAR(E)}}{\text{VAR(O)}}$$

(d) The variance of the observed scores can be calculated from the data, but neither the true score variance nor the error score variance is directly observable. If it is desired to calculate the reliability of an examination, the use of grades is particularly unhelpful since the data is insufficiently precise.

DEFINITION OF TERMS

A2.3 Statistics, like any other professional activity, has its own language and technical terms. It is important that the meaning of these terms is clearly understood by all who use them. The following definitions may prove helpful in this regard.

(a) **Mean**

A set of marks is added up and divided by the number of individual scores to produce the mean (what most people would describe as the 'average'), for example:

The marks: 73, 70, 68, 63, 60, 56, 53, 50, 48, 43, 40 and 36

Total of marks 660   *Number of scores* 12

$$\text{Mean} = \frac{660}{12} = 55$$

As a formula the mean is sometimes expressed thus:

$$\bar{æ} = \frac{\Sigma æ}{n}$$

Where $\bar{æ}$ = the mean, Σ = the sum of, $æ$ = a mark and n = the number of marks.

(b) **Median**

The middle value of another set of marks, which has been arranged in numerical order, for example:

The set: 27, 23, 23, 23, 23, 22, 20, 19, 18, 17 and 8

The median would be the sixth of eleven numbers, i.e. 22.

(c) **Mode**

The mode is the score which occurs most often in a set of marks, for example:

Using the set given at A2.3 (b), the mode would be 23, which occurs four times.

(d) **Scatter or Distribution**

A mark has meaning only when its relationship with other marks is known. Reference must be made to the scale of marking for which the mean is an appropriate measure. Two sets of marks, even when having the same mean, are not necessarily comparable. A difference in distribution gives different values to the marks in each set, for example:

Consider the position of a pupil scoring 15 in these two sets of scores with the same mean (10):

(i) 2   3   5   5   7   12   14   15   18   19

(ii) 2   6   7   8   10   11   13   14   14   15

(e) Range

One measure of the distribution of the marks is the difference between the largest and the smallest values of the set of marks. This is known as the range and takes into account only the extremes. It is unreliable when frequent or large gaps occur in the list of marks, and when the distribution tails in either direction, for example, the range for the two scores above would be:

(d) (i) = 16

(d) (ii) = 13

(f) Mean and Standard Deviation

(i) To obtain a more accurate measure of the distribution, the amount by which each individual score varies from the mean must be taken into consideration. In the example below the mean is 60:

Individual Score	Deviation from the Mean
80	+20
70	+10
65	+5
60	0
55	−5
50	−10
40	−20
420	70

$$\Sigma æ = 420; \quad \overline{æ} = \frac{420}{7} = 60$$

(ii) In subsequent calculations, and in order to avoid the zero sum of the positive and negative deviations, there are two procedures which can be adopted. The first is to ignore the signs of the negative deviations and to obtain the mean deviation by dividing the sum (ignoring the signs) by the number of scores. So using the same example:

$$\begin{array}{c} \text{(The sum)} \\ \text{(The scores)} \end{array} \quad \frac{70}{7} = 10 \text{ (mean deviation)}$$

Another method is to average the squares of the deviations. This average is known as the variance. Since the average of the squares (the variance) is used, the square root is taken in order to yield a value comparable with the mean deviation, thus the square root of the variance is called *the standard deviation*, often abbreviated to SD or σ (sigma).

Using the same scores as those used in A2.3 (f) (i), the calculation of SD would be as follows (based on a mean of 60 for the seven scores):

Individual Scores ($æ$)	Deviation (d) from the mean ($æ - \bar{æ}$)	(d^2)
80	20	400
70	10	100
65	5	25
60	0	0
55	−5	25
50	−10	100
40	−20	400
420		1050

Mean $(\bar{æ}) = \dfrac{420 \,(\Sigma æ)}{7} = 60$

Number of scores $= 7$

Sum of the squares of the deviation $= 1050$ $(\Sigma d^2 = 1050)$

Variance $= \dfrac{1050}{7} = 150$

SD or $\sigma = \sqrt{150} = 12.247\,448$

STANDARDISATION

A2.4 (a) When two or more sets of marks are considered alongside one another the principal features which distinguish them are their means (their mean deviations). This spread can normally be expected to follow a consistent pattern.

(b) In a randomly selected sample of reasonable size, the marks obtained by the pupils would be distributed symmetrically about the mean, which when portrayed graphically would produce a bell-shaped curve known as the Normal Curve of Distribution:

Spread of Marks Around the Mean

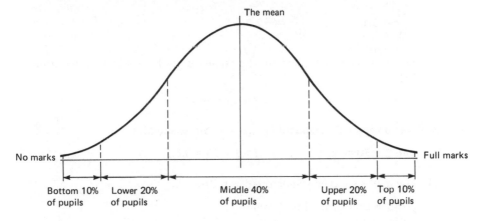

Taken from *Assessment and the Secondary School Teacher*, Macintosh and Hale (1976) page 100.

As will be seen from the graph, the largest number of marks is to be found at the peak or fattest part of the curve.

A2.5 Tile Hill Wood School supply an example of the use of simple statistical techniques for standardising marks by the use of a straight line graph, given at A2.5 (g), the object being to produce a graphical representation of the relationship between raw and standardised marks. The example relates to identical scripts being marked by two teachers, known as the standard marker and the assistant marker, and the process by which the graph has been produced is as follows:

(a) After a preliminary experiment, it is found that the mean scores and SD of the standard marker and an assistant marker are as follows:

	Mean	Standard Deviation (SD)
Standard marker	50	15
Assistant marker	45	10

(b) The assistant marker then marks his own scripts. Of these, the top and bottom marks are taken, for example:

Top 76

Bottom 20

(c) The assistant's mean (i.e. 45) is subtracted from both top and bottom marks:

$76 - 45 = 31$

$20 - 45 = -25$

(Consistency in marking across the range is assumed.)

(d) The results are now divided by the assistant's standard deviation (i.e. 10):

$$\frac{31}{10} = 3.1 \qquad\qquad \frac{-25}{10} = -2.5$$

(e) The result is then multiplied by the standard marker's standard deviation (i.e. 15):

$$3.1 \times 15 = 46.5 \qquad\qquad -2.5 \times 15 = -37.5$$

(f) Now the mean of the standard marker (i.e. 50) is added:

$$46.5 + 50 = \underline{96.5} \qquad\qquad -37.5 + 50 = \underline{12.5}$$

(g) The raw marks are then standardised as follows:

76% is standardised to 96.5%

20% is standardised to 12.5%

These pairs are now plotted on a graph:

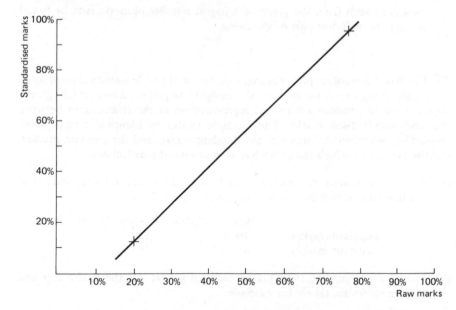

Other marks can then be standardised from the graph.

A2.6 Another useful example of standardisation of marks is supplied by Macintosh and Hale (1976).

(a) For this example, the following extract from the records of English and Mathematics marks of five pupils (A to E) is used.

Pupil	English Mark	Mathematics Mark	Total
A	58	4	62
B	54	10	64
C	50	18	68
D	46	32	78
E	44	42	86
	Total 252	Total 106	
	Scores 5	Scores 5	
	Mean = 50.4	Mean = 21.2	

(b) The two sets of marks have been scaled to the same mean and standard deviation. In other words, a set of marks for English having a mean of 50.4 and a standard deviation of 5.1 is now to be standardised to a mean of 21.2 and a standard deviation of 14.0 (Mathematics). (Note: The scale used does not allow for plotting to more than one decimal place, hence 5.12 becomes 5.1, and 14.01 becomes 14.0.)

(c) The procedure would be as follows (see graph on page 186):

    (i) Use one of the two axes of the graph for the English marks and the other for the Mathematics marks. It is helpful in labelling the axes to include in each case the values of the mean and standard deviation.

    (ii) Plot three points (X, Y and Z).

        X – Opposite the English mean (50.4) and the Mathematics mean (21.2).

        Y – Opposite the English mean plus one standard deviation (55.5) and the Mathematics mean plus one standard deviation (35.2), i.e. English 50.4 plus 5.1 = 55.5, Mathematics 21.2 plus 14.0 = 35.2.

        Z – Opposite the English mean minus one standard deviation (45.3) and the Mathematics mean minus one standard deviation (7.2), i.e. English 50.4 minus 5.1 = 45.3, Mathematics 21.2 minus 14.0 = 7.2.

    (iii) Join the plots with a straight line.

(d) It will then be found that by reading vertically to the line you have plotted, it is possible to convert English scores with an original mean of 50.4 and a standard deviation of 5.1, to a mean of 21.2 and a standard deviation of 14.0. The illustration of the conversion of the original English mark of 58 is shown with a broken line on the graph. The graph can be used to check the converted English marks given in the table on page 186, which have been worked out by use of this formula.

Pupil	Converted English Marks	Mathematics Marks	Total Marks	Rank Order
A	42.0	4	46.0	1
B	31.1	10	41.1	4
C	20.1	18	38.1	5
D	9.2	32	41.2	3
E	3.7	42	45.7	2

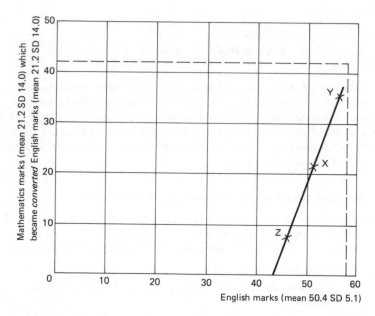

(e) It must be emphasised that the scale of the graph makes some approximation necessary. It is unlikely to occur in practice that teachers would wish to work with other than whole marks.

The graph can also be used to convert a set of marks having a mean of 21.2 and a standard deviation of 14.0, to one with a mean of 50.4 and a standard deviation of 5.1. Often, however, it is useful to convert a set of marks which have the same mean and standard deviation, for example a mean of 50 and a standard deviation of 15. From the example already given on the graph it is easy to see how this can be done. Use one axis for the set of marks to be scaled and the other axis to show marks with a mean of 50 and having a standard deviation of 15. The task is exactly the same as that already illustrated in paragraphs (ii) and (iii). It is only the values that differ.

APPLICATION OF STANDARDISATION

A2.7 (a) The principle of standardisation, as outlined at A2.5, is seen to be an essential element in the use of Standardised Tests. These are norm referenced tests which are usually concerned with the measurement of aptitude, intelligence or personality rather than attainment, although there are many standardised tests in current use for reading, for example, those devised by the National Foundation for Educational Research (UK) and the New Zealand Council for Educational Research Progressive Achievement Tests, Series 3, Reading Study Skills.

(b) According to Shipman (1979), in such tests under controlled conditions, the raw scores of any pupils are related to a table of predetermined norms and converted to a score which takes account of age and sometimes sex. Two characteristics of such scores can be readily seen, the mean (arithmetical average) and the spread of marks around the mean. Because all scores on the test have these same known characteristics they can be compared one with another and with scores on other tests having the same characteristics. Most standardised tests are designed to have common characteristics and can provide a useful way of comparing performance in different areas of attainment. The usual mean is taken as 100 and the spread of marks around the mean (the standard deviation) is 15 out of a total of 200.

(c) In a conventionally standardised test, the design ensures that in a large sample some two-thirds of the scores would fall between 85 and 115, and all but one-twentieth fall between 60 and 130. Designing tests with these characteristics means that the results of each can be compared. (Jackson (1974) provides useful guidance.)

STANDARD SCORES

A2.8 (a) In the construction and standardisation of objective tests, a set procedure has been developed, involving the use of standard scores. Standard scores are expressed in terms of standard deviations or fractions of a standard deviation above or below the mean, which is used as a reference point. The normal curve (see paragraph A2.8 (c)) plays a prominent part in these arrangements and it is necessary to consider why.

(b) A normal curve of distribution tends to be found when a variable is subjected to a number of randomly operating influences.

A number of human attributes have been found to be normally distributed, presumably because they are determined by random genetic influences. In educational measurement we frequently encounter this type of distribution because we have discovered that abilities, aptitudes and attainments are necessarily distributed in this way. Because of our familiarity with the properties of the normal curve, we can take steps to ensure that marks and scores can be similarly distributed, and scales produced with approximately equal units.

(c) The diagram overleaf shows a normal curve divided up by units of standard deviation. The advantages of using this form of distribution are readily recognisable. When scores are distributed in this form we can calculate the proportion of cases that are to be found between any two points of the scale.

Normal Curve (In units of Standard Deviation)

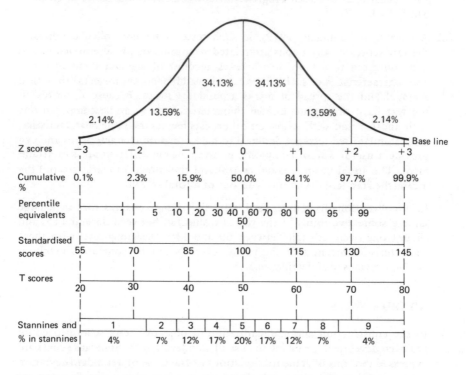

(d) Thus, between the mean and one standard deviation above the mean, we can expect to find 34.1% of the pupils concerned, a further 13.6% between 1 and 2 standard deviations above the mean, and so on. In interpreting scores expressed in this form, it is useful to remember that approximately two-thirds lie between plus and minus 2 standard deviations and virtually all (99.9%) between plus and minus 3 standard deviations.

(e) The diagram also illustrates the relationship between some of the varieties of standard scores that are in common use. Clearly, if we are expressing scores in terms of standard deviations, or fractions thereof, from the mean, the quantities which we assign to these measures are purley a matter of convenience.

(f) Below the base line is shown the 'cumulative percentage of scores falling beneath each part of the curve'. Thus 15.9% of the scores have been accounted for between the lower end of the scale and the point where minus one standard deviation has been reached, and 50% by the time the mean is reached.

(g) The 'percentile equivalents' are shown in relation to the curve, and, as has been intimated earlier, the intervals between the ranks are not equal.

(h) The lines below indicate their relationship to the curve in expressing 'standard scores'. Thus it can be said of any pupil who scores 115 or above on such a test, that he belongs to approximately the top 16% of the age group on which the test has been standardised. There are other forms of expressing test scores through the use of different means and different standard deviations. Three such forms (Z Scores, T Scores and Stannines) are shown in the example.

(i) Along the base line of the normal curve the mean is indicated as 0 and the standard deviations as units of plus 1, plus 2, minus 1, minus 2, etc. Such scores are referred to as 'Z scores'.

(j) Some tests with a mean of 50 and an SD of 10 are expressed as 'T scores'. Thus a child scoring 115 in a standardised score will be accorded a score of 60 on a T Score test.

(k) Finally, there are 'stannines'. These have a mean of 5 and an SD of just under 2, dividing the range into nine divisions as shown. The area under the curve within each division (expressed as a percentage) is referred to as an 'in stannine'.

CONFLATION OR COMBINATION OF MARKS

A3.1 (a) Rowntree (1977) points out that having obtained marks relating to a pupil's attainment in several subjects, a problem arises which grows larger and larger as the span of assessment is increased. How can we bring together the results of assessments and report them in some coherent way? As an example, for each component of an assessment, a pupil is given a mark, a percentage of a grade. These will have been produced by the combining of the results of each part of that assessment. This process is known as conflation. A grade for coursework, for example, could include conflated marks for essays, lecture notes, maps and so on. This grade would then have to be conflated with that awarded perhaps for a terminal examination and an oral test in order to arrive at a grade for overall performance.

(b) This cannot be done, however, without distorting the final result, owing to the variations in the values of marks awarded, as was touched upon earlier in paragraph A2.1 (d). An overall award of 60% or 75% is not meaningful without some common reference point.

(c) The simple, obvious, but very misleading procedure, would be to report on the whole by adding up the parts, for example, five courses producing percentages of 85, 70, 80, 45, 40 = 320%, which could be averaged as $\frac{320}{5} = 64\%$, but the average does not take into account the meaning of such scores in relation to the whole distribution, The 70% may, in fact, be relatively more meaningful that the 85%, or the 45% more meaningful than the 70%. It is very much dependent on the spread of the marks and the weighting of that component relative to the overall assessment.

A3.2 (a) The following example from Rowntree (1977) illustrates this point and concerns four students (A, B, C and D) who take two papers meant to have equal weight. Their scores and rank order for each paper were as follows:

STUDENT		A	B	C	D
Paper I	Score	10	21	38	50 (out of 100)
	Rank	4	3	2	1
Paper II	Score	90	85	75	70 (out of 100)
	Rank	1	2	3	4

(b) The 'obvious' method of adding the two scores would give the following totals and rank orders:

STUDENT	A	B	C	D
Total Score	100	106	113	120 (out of 200)
Rank	4	3	2	1

(c) Note that the overall ranking is the same as for Paper I, and although Paper II had no effect on the students' relative positions it is supposed to have equal weight. This has not happened because the range of marks on Paper I is twice that on Paper II, i.e.:

Paper I   Top 50 Bottom 10 *Range* 40
Paper II   Top 90 Bottom 70 *Range* 20

Consequently, the students would have done themselves the most good by scoring highly on the paper with the greatest range of marks.

(d) There are several possible methods of correcting the situation by scaling the marks (Lacey (1960); Vesselo (1962), page 133; Thyne (1974), page 131; Forrest (1974)). Essentially these methods involve 'stretching' the least scattered distribution so that its range of scores (or, for greater rigour, its SD) matches that of the other. The 'nomogram' method based on the idea of similar triangles is one method, and is reproduced on page 191. It is related to the examples in A3.2 above.

A3.3 NOMOGRAM METHOD OF SCALING

(a) The diagram consists of two parallel lines of equal length, subdivided into convenient intervals within the spread of scores, i.e. intervals of 5 marks for Paper II and 10 marks for Paper I. Two lines are drawn connecting the maxima on the two scales, and the minima. A line, if drawn from a score on one scale, through the point of intersection of the two lines connecting the maxima and the minima, will lead to the corresponding score on the other scale. The scaled mark on the line opposite this score can now be read

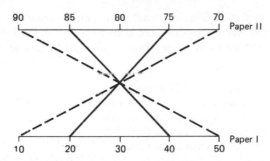

off, for example if a line from 70 on Paper II is drawn through the inter-section it will cut the Paper I line at 10. This figure of 10 is the scaled score for Paper II.

The method is crude and more rigorous scaling can be done by standardising all marks to a common mean and standard deviation (as in Macintosh and Hale (1976), see paragraph 3.A2.6).

(b) Having been scaled, the two sets of scores now have comparable range and can be added in the knowledge that both papers carry equal weight. When this is done the rank order is transformed:

STUDENT	A	B	C	D
Paper I Score	10	21	38	50
Paper II Score after scaling	50	40	20	10
Totals	60	61	58	60
Rank	3 =	1	4	3 =

The student in third place (B) is now first, the student previously first is now equal third, and the student who came second is now fourth.

Scores derived by the Macintosh and Hale method for Paper II would be:

A	B	C	D
48	38	19	9

(c) Real life distributions are not likely to show such large differences of score as well as this perfect negative correlation between the high rank of one and the low rank of the other. But in real life, however undramatic the changes brought about by scaling, any difference brought about in rank order may have a very telling effect on the grade awarded.

PERCENTILES

A3.4 (a) Rowntree (1977) suggests that percentiles are designed to show approxi-mately what percentage of pupils scored lower than a given raw score. The need arises from a weakness in the rank order system, which tends to infer that the intervals between ranks are equal, whereas the first student in rank order may have scored 80% while the second scored 59% and third 57%. To avoid giving such an impression, it may be necessary to provide information about the score distribution as well as the performance of a particular pupil. Alternatively, reference points could be provided in the form of percentiles – or the scores that divide the class into slices of particular percentages.

(b) An example could be:

90% of the pupils scored less than 60%
75% of the pupils scored less than 48%
50% of the pupils scored less than 33%
25% of the pupils scored less than 20%
10% of the pupils scored less than 9%

If Student X had scored 57%, it can be seen that at least 10% of the group had exceeded that score, but that at least 75% had scored less.

(c) David (1979) provides some useful definitions:

   (i) The 'fiftieth percentile' is also called the median, i.e. half of the scores in the distribution lie above it and half below. 'Quartiles' refer to the 25% at the upper or lower extremities of a class. The 'lower quartile' is the mark below which 25% of the class lies, and the 'upper quartile' the mark below which 75% of the class lies, and the pupils who fall between the upper and lower quartiles are said to be in the 'interquartile range'. Half the interquartile range is known as the 'quartile deviation'. The 'sextile' in a similar way corresponds to one-sixth of the pupils and in any ranked set of marks there will be an upper and lower sextile. The 'intersextile' range is the range of marks between the upper and lower sextiles, and further divisions are possible.

   (ii) Lyons Morris and Taylor Fitzgibbon (1978) provide a great deal of useful information upon the processing of scores.

Z AND T SCORES

A3.5 (a) Z scores, T scores and other linear standard scores will provide information about how many standard deviations above or below the mean a given raw score has fallen.

(b) T scores, stannines and other normalised standard scores which record how many standard deviations above or below the mean a given raw score has fallen, are actually based on percentiles. An explanation of all these scores will be found in paragraph A2.8.

CUMULATIVE FREQUENCY

A3.6 (a) Macintosh and Hale (1976) point out that useful information regarding a test, and the pupils who took it, can be gained by the use of a cumulative frequency table (opposite) or histogram (see paragraph A3.6 (b)). In this example the following twenty test scores are used (in reverse rank order):

1, 2, 3, 5, 5, 6, 7, 7, 7, 8, 12, 13, 13, 14, 14, 14, 15, 17, 18, 19

Cumulative Frequency Table

MARK	Frequency of Occurrence in Test Scores	Cumulative Frequency
0	0	0
1	1	1
2	1	2
3	1	3
4	0	3
5	2	5
6	1	6
7	3	9
8	1	10
9	0	10
10	0	10
11	0	10
12	1	11
13	2	13
14	3	16
15	1	17
16	0	17
17	1	18
18	1	19
19	1	20
20	0	20

(b) **Histogram Showing Cumulative Frequency of Scores**

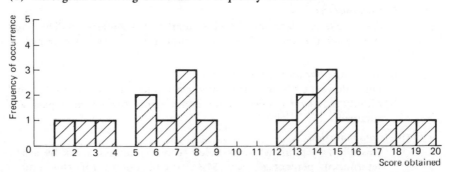

This sort of representation is more likely to be useful with larger numbers, and for this purpose it would not be practicable to show individual scores, and would be more likely to show frequency within groups of marks, for example:

0-4, 5-9, 10-14, or 0-9, 10-19, etc.

(c) The advantages of the presentation of cumulative frequency data are mainly for the teacher in that it can highlight the degrees of difficulty experienced by the pupils in any assessment. In the example (b) on the previous page, it could be said that the test seems to divide the pupils into two distinct groups and should lead the teacher into an examination of the reasons for such an uncharacteristic distribution compared to the bell-shaped curve discussed in paragraph A2.4 and in paragraph A2.8 of Appendix 3.

DETERMINATION OF OVERALL RESULTS

A4.1 (a) Ward (1980) warns us that however much pupils and their teachers seem to relish numerical marks, marks can be very misleading. Even if they are standardised, they can only reflect how the pupil responded to questions on the day of the examination, and how a particular marker marked that pupil's responses. A difference of one mark between two pupils conveys an implication that pupil A is better at the subject than pupil B, which in fact may be totally untrue. There is a great deal to be said for a simple pass/fail system and many examining bodies limit their awards to three classes: merit, pass or fail; or four classes: distinction, credit, pass or fail. In the United Kingdom, traditionally, there are grades for both 'pass' and 'fail', although recently 'ungraded' has superseded 'fail'.

(b) The main problem lies in arriving at a fair overall result when there are several components in an assessment scheme. The ideal would be to indicate the grade of pass or fail for each component and the reader could then make a subjective judgement as to the overall result. Nevertheless, there is a demand for overall results and there are a number of methods by which they can be calculated.

(i) *No Compensation*
Pass marks are determined and all marks are standardised. The pupil must reach the pass mark for *all* components to be awarded an overall pass.

(ii) *No Compensation with Referment*
This allows pupils to retake any component in which they failed without having to retake other components for which a pass was obtained.

(iii) *Compensation*
This allows a pupil who has failed to reach the pass mark by a pre-determined percentage, say 5%, to compensate for this under-achievement by some over-achievement in another component.

A system of compensation has disadvantages. The rules are likely to become complicated when applied to individuals and injustices could arise. It could be thought unfair to fail a pupil because the mark is just outside the compensation limit, but how could any adjustment be applied fairly? Compensation could mask the fact that there is a lack of parity in the facility or relevance of components.

(iv) *Adding or Averaging*

Addition merely combines the results of a series of tests, such as a series of coursework assignments. If, however, it is required to average two or more sets of marks, then the marks must be scaled. If raw marks are used, the component with the highest standard deviation (SD) will exert undue influence on the result.

Averaging, which is simply the addition of the marks obtained from each component and then dividing the total by the number of components, can have the effect of reducing the reliability of the overall result if the components are of mixed reliability, for example an objective test, an essay and a project. In such a case, where different knowledge and abilities were being assessed, the no compensation method would be more logical. The following example illustrates the effects of SD on the addition of marks.

Eleven students have each taken two papers. In the example their marks have been added; they are not highly correlated:

STUDENT	Paper 1 Marks	Rank Order	Paper 2 Marks	Rank Order	TOTAL MARKS	OVERALL RANK ORDER
A	38	1	38	2	76	2
B	37		30	6	67	6
C	37	= 2	34	4	71	3
D	37		44	1	81	1
E	36		32	5	68	5
F	36	= 5	20	11	56	11
G	36		22	10	58	10
H	35		24	9	59	9
I	35	= 8	26	8	61	8
J	35		28	7	63	7
K	34	11	36	3	70	4
MEAN	36		30.4		66.4	
SD (σ)	1.1		7.0		7.5	

Inspection of the overall rank order will show how closely it relates to the rank order of Paper 2 with its higher SD. Some notable contrasts have emerged:

Student A who came top on Paper 1 and second on Paper 2, reverts to second place in the overall rank order through Student D benefitting from the higher SD of Paper 2.

Student B similarly was ranked second in Paper 1, but only sixth in the overall rank order by the negative effect of the high SD for Paper 2.

Student K was ranked eleventh on Paper 1, but fourth overall by virtue of his third place for Paper 2.

(v) *Weighted Addition or Averaging*

Scaled marks are essential for this method, the marks being multiplied by the weighting factor. For example, an assessment plan consists of three components whose weighting is 20%, 50% and 30%. As before, it is only appropriate as a method if the components test the same abilities and knowledge. The product of the weighted marks is totalled and can be divided to bring the figure down to a more manageable percentage. In the example below, a pass of 50% and a pass with merit of 65% have been applied.

Ward (1980) points out that there would not normally be any justification in practice for a scheme as complicated and apparently unjust as this:

STUDENT	COMPONENT 1		COMPONENT 2		COMPONENT 3		TOTALS		RESULT
	Marks	*Weighted at 2*	*Marks*	*Weighted at 5*	*Marks*	*Weighted at 3*	*Out of 1000*	*Out of 100*	
A	52	104	58	290	65	195	589	58.9	Pass
B	45	90	60	300	55	165	555	55.5	Pass
C	45	90	40	200	70	210	500	50	Pass
D	65	130	70	350	65	195	675	67.5	Merit
E	65	130	60	300	80	240	670	67	Merit
F	30	60	70	350	50	150	560	56	Pass

(c) **Borderline Students**

There is a degree of unreliability in all assessments, and it cannot be assumed that a pupil whose marks just fail to reach a pass mark should in fact be failed. A reasonable policy would be to review results which lie up to half a standard deviation below the pass mark, but this would depend upon the reliability of the component; it could be less for an objective test and more for a less reliable component.

A student's overall performance could be reviewed and a decision taken as to whether it merited a pass of referment for the failed component.

(d) It is necessary to reiterate that the score actually obtained by an individual in a test is only one of a large number of possible scores that could be obtained if the test were repeated many times without memory or practice having any effect. In these circumstances it can be assumed that these possible scores, being subject to errors of various kinds, would be normally distributed and that the 'standard error' is in fact an 'estimate of the standard deviation' of this distribution of marks.

(Exercises 5.30 (a), (b) and 5.31)

References

A Basis for Choice (1982), (Further Education Curriculum Review and Development Unit, Department of Education and Science, London)

Balogh, J. (1982), *Profile Reports for School Leavers*, Schools Council Programme 5 (Longman Group, for Schools Council)

Burgess, T. and Adams, E. (Ed.), (1980), *Outcomes of Education* (Macmillan Education, London)

David, C. (1979), The Simple Treatment of Raw Marks, *Secondary Education*, **9**, No 13

Dockrell, W.B. and Black, H.B. (1978) *Assessment in the Affective Domain*. Scottish Council for Research in Education, (Edinburgh)

Fletcher, C and Thompson, N.T. (Ed.), (1979), *Issues in Community Education* (Falmer Press, Brighton)

Forrest, G.M. (1974), *The Presentation of Results in Techniques and Problems of Assessment*, ed. H.G. Macintosh (Edward Arnold, London)

Garrett, H.E. (1965), *Statistics in Psychology and Education* (Longman Group, London)

Goacher, B. (1983), *Recording Achievement at 16+*, Schools Council Programme (Longman Group, for Schools Council)

Harrison, A. (1982), Review of Graded Tests, *Schools Council Examinations Bulletin 41* (Methuen Educational)

Harrison, A. (1983), Profile Reporting of Examination Results, *Schools Council Examinations Bulletin 43* (Methuen Educational)

Hinton, D. (1973), A Teamwork Graduate Profile to Replace the Graduate Sieve, *The Times Higher Education Supplement*, 20th April

Lacey, O.L. (1960), How Fair are your Grades? *Bulletin*, Vol. **46**, pp. 281–6 (American Association of University Professors, Washington, D.C.)

Macintosh, H.G. and Hale, D.E. (1976), *Assessment and the Secondary School Teacher* (Routledge & Kegan Paul, London).

Morris, L.L. and Fitzgibbon, C.T. (1978), *How to Measure Achievement* and *How to Calculate Statistics*, Program Evaluation Kit (Center for the Study of Evaluation, Sage Publications, University of California)

Morrison, R.B. (1974), The Application of Statistics to Assessment, in *Techniques and Problems of Assessment*, ed. H.G. Macintosh (Edward Arnold, London)

North East London Polytechnic (1981), *Statements at 16+, An Example Working Paper on Institutions No. 29*

Nuttall, D.L. (Ed.), (1982), *Educational Analysis*, Vol. **IV**, No. 3 (Falmer Press, Lewes)

Overson, K. (1980), Pupil Assessment Profiles, *Secondary Education*, **10**, No. 1

Pidgeon, D. and Yates, A. (1969), *An Introduction to Educational Measurement* (Routledge & Kegan Paul, London)

Profiles (1982), (Further Education Curriculum Review and Development Unit, Department of Education and Science, London)

Rentzulli, J.S. and Hartman, R.K. (1971), Scale for Rating Behavioural Characteristics of Superior Students, *Exceptional Children*, **38**, No. 3 (NZCER, Wellington)

Rowntree, D. (1977), *Assessing Students — How Shall we Know Them?* (Harper & Row, London)

Scottish Pupil Profile Project (1977), *Making the Most of Teachers' Knowledge of Pupils*, Scottish Council for Research in Education (Hodder & Stoughton, London)

The Scottish Vocational Preparation Unit (1982), *Assessment in Youth Training — Made to Measure* (Jordanhill College of Education, Glasgow)

Shipman, M. (1979), *In-School Evaluation* (Heinemann Educational, London)

Simpson, M.A. (1976), Medical Student Evaluation in the Absence of Examinations, *Medical Education*, **10**, pp. 22–6

Stansburry, D. (1974), *Record of Personal Experience, Qualities, Qualifications, Tutors Handbook* (RPE Publications, South Brent, Devon)

Stephens, S.S., (ed.) 1951, Mathematics, Measurement, and Psychophysics, *Handbook of Experimental Psychology* (Wiley, New York)

Stratton, N. (1982), *An Evaluation of a Basic Abilities Profiling System Across a Range of Education and Training Provision* (City and Guilds of London Institute, London)

Stanton, G. (1982), Profiles and Profile Reporting, *Coombe Lodge Report*, **14**, No 13 (Further Education Staff College, Blagdon)

Swales, T. (1979), *Record of Personal Achievement*, Schools Council Pamphlet 16 (Schools Council, London)

Tattershall, K. (1983), *Differentiated Examinations — A Strategy for Assessment at 16+*, SCEB 42 (Methuen Educational, London)

Tile Hill Wood School, *Assessment — A Case Study* (Curriculum Development Committee, Coventry)

Vesselo, J.R. (1962), *How to Read Statistics* (Further Education Curriculum Review and Development Unit)

Index to Self-teaching Exercises

Index to Self-teaching Exercises

4

Imaginary Case Study — Assessment of an Individual Pupil

Chapter Contents

Imaginary Case Study — Assessment of an Individual Pupil

INTRODUCTION TO THE CASE STUDY

4.1 This case study, which follows an individual student through a four-year period of secondary education, is designed to illustrate how some of the material and information contained in the first three chapters might be applied to meet a practical need in a particular school.

Despite the inherent disadvantages for overseas readers of taking as an example a specifically English comprehensive school for 12 to 16 year olds, it was felt on balance that this would be offset by the greater degree of realism which would result.

A case study is, in any case, only a model, readers can derive considerable benefit from creating their own case studies which take account of different structures and organisational patterns, and which make use of their own experiences. These structures and patterns, incidentally, vary greatly within the United Kingdom as well as outside it.

PLOWDEN COMPREHENSIVE SCHOOL

4.2 (a) Plowden Comprehensive School is a mixed eight form entry 12–16 comprehensive school, situated in the New Town of Hadowton, which has a population of around 50 000. Hadowton was one of a number of New Towns established in the 1950s and 1960s to relieve urban congestion.

The school is administered by the Education Department of Camshot County Council; at the time that Student X enrolled it had approximately 600 students although this number was destined to fall to around 500 by the mid 1980s.

(b) The organisational pattern of educational provision in Hadowton is as follows:

Primary	5–8 years	(The numbers in each case refer
Middle	8–12 years	to age on arrival and at departure)
Secondary	12–16 years	
Sixth Form College	16–19 years	

There are two secondary schools of which Plowden is one, the other being Carlyle Comprehensive. These two schools are both fed by six middle schools. Although currently there is some provision for parental choice of secondary school — a provision which is likely to increase — each of the two schools draws the bulk of its students from three specific middle schools. Since Plowden is situated on the eastern edge of Hadowton, its main catchment area includes two middle schools located on a large housing estate, built by the local authority, in the suburbs astride the eastern approaches.

The sixth form college serves both secondary schools, but caters mainly for students intending to go on to higher education or to undergo training to enter a profession — a policy which does not satisfy everyone. Students with a more practical bent can attend a technical college in Old Tufton, an industrial town about fifteen miles from Hadowton.

(c) Plowden has a good reputation, although recently it has tended to rely perhaps too much upon past successes. It has a strong Parent Teacher Association (PTA) and maintains good relations with the community through regular Open Days and Parent Evenings.

THE STAFF AT PLOWDEN

4.3 (a) The Headmistress, Serena Williams, M.A., is dedicated to her belief in all-ability schools as the only answer to the needs of a modern industrialised society. Prior to her becoming a teacher, she spent several years in industry (in personnel management). In the nicest possible way she rules her staff with a rod of iron, while appearing to observe all the democratic niceties that the staff, quite properly, expect. Mrs Williams is particularly sensitive about the reputation of the school and secretly regards Carlyle Comprehensive as a rival. Her staff treat her with respect, but secretly resent her insistence upon efficiency in all things.

(b) There are two Deputy Heads:

    (i) David Hackett, B.Sc., M.Ed., as First Deputy, carries a heavy load of mixed responsibilities, including discipline and the in-service training of teachers.

    (ii) Diana Hope, B.Sc., is mainly responsible for timetabling and staff problems. She also acts as Director of Studies and is the Secretary of the PTA.

(c) Background information about members of staff involved in the case study is given below:

    (i) Bruce Bennett, B.A. — History graduate with earlier experience of personnel management in industry. He has taught in a middle school.

He caught the eye of the Headmistress and was given special responsibility for Pupil Profiles, something which is very dear to her heart. Popular in the Staff Room, he is regarded as something of an educational expert.

(ii) Greta Glover, B.Ed. — Recently appointed assistant teacher in the History Department. Highly intelligent and very outspoken for a newcomer.

(iii) George Rafferty, B.A. — Geography graduate, who became particularly interested in educational measurement during his teacher training.

(iv) Harry Davenport, M.A. — Head of History Department. History graduate. Very senior but unlikely to move higher. Patient and diplomatic.

(v) Claude Chippendale, B.A. — History graduate, recently appointed and much involved in school youth work.

(vi) Dick Henderson, B.A. — Very popular and senior History teacher of considerable experience.

(vii) Matthew Corby, B.Sc. — Head of Mathematics. Old school friend of Bruce Bennett, Ambitious and well thought of. Has recently published his second book on curriculum development.

(d) For pastoral care Plowden has a horizontal year structure with each year having a head of year. These members of staff are permanently in charge of a designated year and have no specific forms in their care. Form teachers, who of course play a sympathetic role in pastoral care, move up each year with their forms into a new year group. After four years they start again, taking charge of a form from a new intake.

THE BACKGROUND OF STUDENT X

4.4 Student X is the eldest child of a reasonably well-to-do doctor in general practice at a local medical centre. Student X is a lively, healthy young person who mixes well in adult circles and with other young people. Student X has particularly strong and rather individual interests in tennis and motor racing. The family are close knit, all three children and parents taking part together in community events. They are well liked and respected.

At the age of 12+ Student X enters Plowden Comprehensive School.

4.5 The final report on Student X from the middle school includes the following results of assessment:

'Ivydale Middle School

Report: Summer Term 1979   Name: Student X
                             Date of Birth: 20 June 1967

English Excellent. Imaginative, orderly and
         promising written work. Very good
         vocabulary.   Place 1/30

Mathematics 71% Very Good.   Place 2/30

Local Environment Very Interested. Has produced an
                   excellent project on the Town
                   Centre. Very good graphic work.   Place 3/30

Workshop 69% A neat and thorough worker.   Place 4/30

Religious Education · A good listener, but shows little
                   enthusiasm for the subject.   No places given

Physical Education A thoroughly reliable team player.
                    Energetic and has leadership
                    potential.   Place 3/30

Absences: 2 days
Positions held: Form Captain 1978-79
Position in Form: 2/30

Headmaster's Comments:

         Student X has been a hard-working and reliable
         member of the school community. A rare
         combination of academic promise and athletic
         ability.

(Exercise 5.32)

THE PLOWDEN SYSTEM IN OUTLINE

4.6 (a) Student X was assigned to the form in the charge of Claude Chippendale. Being newly appointed, Claude asked Bruce Bennett for information and advice upon the system of pupil records in use at Plowden.

Bruce explained that two years earlier, following discussions initiated by the Headmistress in which he had played a major part, proposals had been put to the Local Education Authority (Education Department of Camshot County Council), for the introduction on a trial basis of a system of pupil profiles.

The profile was intended to provide information which could be used, on the one hand, to identify individual learning difficulties, and, on the other, to evaluate progress on a broader front in relation to classroom practice, course design and the use of teaching materials.

The proposal had been approved for a trial period of three years to start in September 1978 and was, therefore, in September 1980, in its second year of operation. If successful, it might be adopted by the authority for use in all its secondary schools and some financial support had therefore been given for the pilot scheme.

(b) At present, the profile was concerned purely with the cognitive aspects of pupil progress. Personal characteristics were already covered in the half-yearly reports of the Form Teachers and Heads of Year. These latter reports were held by the Head of the relevant year and were passed on each year as the student moved up the school. The reports were available to the form teacher of the pupil concerned and, of course, to the Headmistress and the Deputy Heads.

The academic records, on the other hand, were held centrally under Bruce's care and were available for inspection by a wider audience, which included all members of staff, parents and the pupils themselves. Bruce had hoped to extend the scope of the profile coverage to include the affective domain, and had indeed worked out something which would involve the assessment of some purely personal characteristics. The Headmistress was not, however, anxious to proceed with this until the final period had successfully been completed. On balance he had to agree that the Headmistress was probably right in this, not least because of the sensitive issues, such as confidentiality, which could be raised by the assessment of personal characteristics.

4.7 (a) At Claude's request Bruce then described the scheme as it currently operated and he suggested that Claude should raise queries as he went along.

On entry into Plowden, all relevant information available about the students (and in particular the reports from the Middle School) was used in assigning them to subject groups. In their first year, mixed ability teaching applied to all subjects. In their second year, 'setting' was used for French and Science, and setting in most subjects was standard for the third and fourth years, with particular reference to entry for public examination. It was, therefore, the intention that the first year's subject groupings should all have a comparable spread of ability.

(b) At the end of the first term's work, an initial profile was prepared for each student, making use of the assessment of work over the three-month period September–December. This was then compared with the report from the Middle School, or elsewhere if the student had come in from outside the area of the Local Education Authority (LEA).

The information generated as a result of this comparison was then discussed early in January at a meeting of the relevant form and year staff. As a result of this meeting, adjustments could be made to the teaching groups in order to ensure a balance of ability.

The process of comparison could draw attention to areas of apparent under-achievement and/or significant improvement by individual students. Assessment of the first term's work could also identify aptitude which needed exploitation in future work programmes or deficiencies which perhaps needed remedial consideration.

The main purpose of this initial profile was thus diagnostic.

(c) At the end of the first year, an assessment, based upon an examination in all subjects, took place. The results of this were used to prepare a second profile, which could then be compared with the first.

The information was intended for general purposes but was particularly concerned to assess the extent to which all students had benefitted from instruction over the year. It was thus concerned with evaluation as much as diagnosis.

(d) Subsequently pupil profiles were prepared twice a year, once in early January and again at the end of June. These were based upon work undertaken in the relevant periods June to December and January to June. In general, the January profile placed more emphasis upon coursework than that of June, which took more account of the results of the end of year examination, but this system of coverage varied a little between different subjects. This tendency, however, grew more marked in the third and fourth years when the influence of external examinations became more pressing and where decisions relating to entry requirements as, for example, between GCE O-Level and CSE, had to be taken on a subject by subject basis.

Form teachers and the Heads of Years were expected to compare each new profile with the previous profiles, and, on the basis of this comparison, enter into appropriate discussions with the relevant staff and initiate any action which might be necessary.

THE PUPIL PROFILE FORMS

4.8 At this point Claude, who had been looking increasingly gloomy, interrupted and suggested that it could be a great deal easier if Bruce could actually show him the profile forms and clarify the system, particularly the allocation of responsibility for their completion. Clearly the work involved would be considerable and this aspect worried him. Bruce agreed at once and showed Claude a copy of the two Pupil Profile Forms (PPF1 and PPF2). (These are reproduced in paragraphs 4.9 and 4.10 respectively.)

Bruce added that if the extension of the system to the affective domain ever got off the ground, there could be a PPF3 designed for this purpose.

4.9 Example of Pupil Profile Form 1

NO CARBON REQUIRED   PLOWDEN COMPREHENSIVE SCHOOL   FORM PPF1

Form: . . . .   Date of Report: . . . .   Reporting Teacher: . . . .

Course Code No.

COURSE SUBJECT

NAMES OF PUPILS

01 English Language
02 English Literature
03 Mathematics
04
05
06 Science (General)
07 Physics
08 Chemistry
09 Biology
10
11 Language 1
12
13 History
14
15 Geography
16
17 Integrated Study
18 Home Economics
19 Technical Drawing
20
21 Woodwork
22 Metalwork
23 Art
24 Music
25 Drama
26
27 Physical Education
28 Rural Science
29 Religious Education
30
31
32
DAYS ABSENT since last Report

Number in Group
Highest Score
Lowest Score
Mean

H

4.10 Example of Pupil Profile Form 2

PLOWDEN COMPREHENSIVE SCHOOL		FORM PPF2

Name of Pupil: . . . .   Form: . . . .

Date of Profile: . . . .

Total days Absent since last Profile: LESS than/MORE than 7 days . . . . .

SUBJECTS		SCORES								
Code Number	Name of Course	10	20	30	40	50	60	70	80	90

10   20   30   40   50   60   70   80   90

Instructions

1. This is your half-yearly Profile – Complete it carefully.

2. Copy down on a piece of paper the following data from the PPF1 (the summary of your reports):
   Code Number of the Course
   Name of the Course
   Your Score
   The Mean Score for your particular group studying that subject. (This you will find at the bottom of the form.)
   Example: '07 Science (General)   53   47.2'

3. Write in the *code numbers* and names of courses *in numerical order*.

4. Plot *in pencil* against each subject *your score*.

5. Connect up the horizontal plot of your score on the base line to the right of the name of the course by forming bars.

6. Plot with a *dashed line* the Mean Score for each subject.

7. Write in figures at the base of each bar your score for each subject and shade remainder of bar.

   Example:

07	Science (General)	53% //////////////

4.11 Prior to the introduction of the pilot scheme, consultations had taken place with the Teacher Unions on the whole question of the workload involved. It had been agreed that the form teacher would be responsible for the completion of the PPF1 which summarised the results of all the pupils in the form. The financial support from the LEA had enabled the PPF1s to be printed on NCR (no carbon required) paper, thus providing two copies without extra work. Claude asked why two copies were needed and Bruce explained that the duplicate could be retained by the form teacher and the original would be passed via himself to Matthew Corby, the Head of Mathematics, who was responsible for the completion of the PPF2 for each pupil.

The completion of the individual PPF2s was undertaken by the students themselves during a normal Mathematics period, the details being obtained from the PPF1. Each student was responsible, therefore, for the preparation of his own profile.

Claude expressed some concern about the capacity of all students to complete their PPF2s with the necessary care and accuracy, but he was assured by Bruce that mistakes were very few and far between — indeed, the Mathematics Department regarded it as a worthwhile practical exercise in the use of mathematical skills.

4.12 (a) Claude also raised the whole question of comparability of the scores reported in the profile (PPF1), bearing in mind that the teachers might use grades, percentages, letters or raw marks. Bruce agreed that this had posed problems initially, but these had been overcome by the Headmistress, who had laid down some rather arbitrary criteria, namely, that only marks out of a possible total of one hundred were to be used and that there was to be an upper ceiling of 85% and a lower ceiling of 15% on all marks awarded.

About a year earlier Bruce had met a number of teachers at a conference on assessment, organised by the Department of Education and Science, and had learnt of the simple technique for standardising marks used by Tile Hill Wood School (see Chapter 3, Appendix A2.5). This had been adapted for use with the pupil profiles, but Bruce was very conscious of the rough and ready nature of the marking system in use at Plowden, and had quite serious reservations about the whole aspect of these procedures. He had decided, however, that this was not the moment to express them to Claude.

(b) Thanks again to the financial assistance from the LEA, it had been possible to print the PPF2s on transparent sheets, punched at intervals along the left hand edge so that each form could be inserted in a stiff covered loose-leaf folder. The profiles could thus be easily and accurately overlaid and comparison made without difficulty. Bruce further explained that Matthew Corby passed all the completed PPF2s to him after a spot check for mathematical accuracy.

Bruce then filed the forms in the individual folders grouped in classes. In this he was assisted by a number of parents recruited from within the PTA.

Claude seemed rather dazed by the complexity of the whole process, but, even at this stage, could see the theoretical advantages of the scheme. He felt that he should reserve judgement on the practical application until he had seen it in operation with an individual student. Bruce agreed with him that it did involve extra work, but the time and effort expended in this new system more than paid off at parents' evenings and at staff meetings when the progress of individual students was under review.

(Exercise 5.33)

STUDENT X – FIRST TERM PROFILE (JANUARY 1980)

4.13 (a) The first term profile in respect of Student X was as follows:

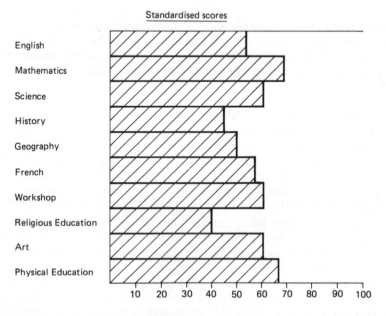

(See Chapter 3, paragraphs 3.1–3.11.)

(b) At a meeting between Claude Chippendale and the subject teachers concerned, this profile, as well as many others, was compared with the reports from the previous school. The anomalies which were commented upon by the subject teachers in respect of Student X, were:

English 56% — Student X was in a group of high-spirited but average ability children who tended to look down on 'swots'.

History 47% — A very similar situation to the English group (hardly surprising since they were the same students).

(c) Anomalies in the profiles of other students were also discovered, and the Heads of English and History agreed to make adjustments to a number of their subject groups within the year in order to create groups in which the ability levels were better balanced. These changes involved Student X in both subjects.

(d) The Science and Mathematics teachers reported favourably on the attitude and general performance of Student X who had been placed initially in different groupings from those for English and History.

4.14 This first, essentially diagnostic, assessment thus provided information whereby:

(a) An initial profile could be produced.

(b) Strengths and weaknesses in new subjects could be seen.

(c) Anomalies could be detected and remedied.

(d) Placements could be made more accurately within learning groups.

(e) Teachers could be alerted to the special needs of particular pupils, for example:

Student X appeared to be under-achieving in English and History, which might be due to placement in an inappropriate peer group. The information, moreover, ought to alert the Science and Mathematics teachers that they were dealing with a potentially able pupil who might need to be stimulated.

STUDENT X — END OF FIRST YEAR ASSESSMENT (JUNE 1980)

4.15 (a) As a result of this end of term examination the following profile was prepared and compared with that of January 1980:

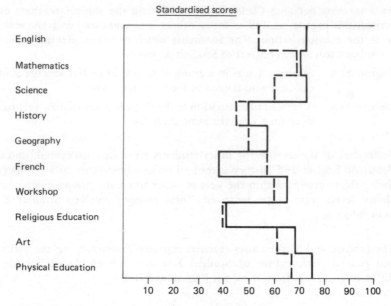

The dashed line gives the Profile at January 1980.

(b) This profile reveals reasonable improvement in all subjects with the exception of French. In four subjects, Student X is up to and above the 70% level, and three of these are major subjects. Progress in History is only slight and not so good as that in Geography.

(c) At a discussion between Claude Chippendale and the subject teachers, the following points of interest emerged about Student X.

    (i) The History syllabus included ten studies of famous men and women and this seemed to evoke little interest either orally or in written work.

   (ii) Student X showed particular interest in Geography although progress did not apparently reflect this interest.

  (iii) French was thought, initially, to be fun by Student X, but the oral exercises seemed to present increasing difficulties, and Student X, when interviewed, admitted that every lesson had become torture.

  (iv) The Technical Studies teacher spoke well of the progress made by Student X in the workshop. Great interest was shown and in handling tools Student X was above average ability, particularly in metal.

   (v) The Games Mistress reported very favourably on Student X, who was not only a good performer but showed considerable knowledge of competitive sports, particularly athletics and tennis.

(d) Similar profiles prepared for Student X during the second year at Plowden, in January 1981 and June 1981, drew attention to a significant difference in performance as between Geography coursework and the end of year examination in Geography. Apart from this, the profiles added little to the information already available about Student X.

STUDENT X'S CHOICE OF OPTIONS FOR THIRD AND FOURTH YEAR COURSES

4.16 (a) Claude Chippendale, in June 1981, circulated to all pupils the schedule of courses leading up to public examinations at both GCE Ordinary Level and CSE. Student X, who was considered suitable for GCE O-Level in all subjects, selected the following:

*English

*Mathematics

*Physics

*Chemistry

Geography

Metalwork

Technical Drawing

Home Economics

*Art

*Physical Education (not examined)

*Core Subjects (*not* optional)

(b) At a prediction conference attended by the year tutor, Claude Chippendale, and representatives of Heads of Departments, the following points were agreed about the options selected by Student X:

(i) History could be dropped.

(ii) Social Studies should be substituted for Home Economics, since it was felt that there was too much emphasis upon practical subjects.

4.17 (a) Having dealt with internal course choice, the staff then considered Student X and others as regards possibilities for higher education and hence their suitability for GCE A-Level courses at the sixth form college. To do this, the staff applied a predetermined criterion of a minimum qualifying percentage of 70% in any four or more major subjects, i.e. English, Mathematics, Physics, Chemistry, Biology, History, Geography, Foreign Language, Art.

Student X satisfied this criterion as regards English, Mathematics, Science and Art, but was considered a borderline case. Subject teachers, however, felt that the potential was there, and, after discussion, the name of Student X was included in the list of prospective A-Level candidates for subsequent entry to the sixth form college, and the relevant Heads of Department took note.

(b) Claude Chippendale, after discussions with the Vocational Guidance Counsellor and the parents, then finalised the third and fourth year time-table of Student X as follows:

English

Mathematics

Physics

Chemistry

Geography

Technical Drawing

Metalwork

Social Studies

Physical Education

Art

(Exercise 5.35)

THE PROBLEM OF STUDENT X'S GEOGRAPHY (AUGUST 1981)

4.18 (a) During the summer holidays George Rafferty decided to follow through the evidence of the 1981 profiles of Student X, in order to try and discover why there was this marked difference between coursework and examination performance. There seemed to be no obvious reason – Student X was always keen and alert in class and seemed to enjoy the subject. Moreover, he had learnt from his colleagues that Student X had performed well in four other subjects. Perhaps there was something wrong with his teaching or the material he used.

(b) He decided, therefore, to analyse the results of the assessment of both the coursework and the written examination of Student X in an effort to identify the problem area of study or perhaps some difficulty experienced with specific types of assessment.

AIMS AND OBJECTIVES OF COURSE

(c) The aims and objectives of the Plowden second year Geography syllabus were:

(i) *Aims*

To introduce the pupil to the study of Geography as a subject in its own right and to teach the basic skills of a Geographer.

(ii) *Objectives*

The pupil must be able to:

1. read conventional signs,

2. interpret contour lines,

3. measure distances from the map and read the compass.

The pupil must be able to show a basic understanding of:

4. the hydrological cycle, and the work of rivers,

5. volcanoes and earthquakes,

6. the positions of the continents and oceans,

7. the distribution of the peoples of the world,

8. the importance of farming, fishing and industry,

9. the principal characteristics of physical, human, world and regional Geography,

10. local Geography through field study.

CONVERSION OF GRADES TO MARKS

4.19 In George's mark book there were twenty sets of grades recorded during the year. He preferred grades to marks because he felt that they were not as destructive of students' self-respect. A was good, B not quite so good, C a bit below par and D not good. He was able to introduce a greater degree of discrimination by the use of pluses and minuses, although he was not sure whether these subtleties really meant anything to his students. These grades referred to coursework and included elements which had been completed as homework. Pupils' work was graded from A through to D—. George Rafferty made an extract in respect of Student X, incorporating references to the objective being assessed. In brackets he showed the numerical mark equivalent for each grade given. This was derived from a simple conversion scale and needed to be done since the examination results were recorded as marks. The equivalences were as follows:

A = 10	B = 7	C = 4	D = 1
A— = 9	B— = 6	C— = 3	D— = 0
B+ = 8	C+ = 5	D+ = 2	

MARKING OF COURSEWORK

4.20 The extract from the mark book was as follows:

Objective	Grade	(Converted Marks)	Subject	Type of Assessment
1	B	(7)	Conventional Signs	CWK
1	B—	(6)	Map Work Problems	Test
3	C+	(5)	Route Description	CWK
2	B	(7)	Imaginary Island	Test
3	B—	(6)	Map of School	CWK
2	B—	(6)	Description – Map Area	Test
4	B	(7)	Hydrological Cycle	CWK
4	C+	(5)	Three ages of a river	CWK
4	B+	(8)	'I like my river'	Essay
5	B—	(6)	Volcano	CWK
5	B+	(8)	'The Eruption'	Essay
6	B	(7)	Continents and Oceans	CWK
7	C	(4)	An Indian Village	CWK
7	C	(4)	An Eskimo Family	CWK
8	C+	(5)	The Mixed Farm	CWK
8	B—	(6)	Intensive Farming	CWK
9	C+	(5)	Northern Fishing Port	CWK
9	B	(7)	'Where is my Herring?'	Essay
10	B—	(6)	Map of Local Area	CWK
10	B+	(8)	Our Local Environment	Project

Total marks $\frac{123}{200}$ or 61.5%

This total mark was higher than that obtained in the written examination.

For the remainder of the group: Mean 51.4%

SD   5.8

MARKING THE EXAMINATION

4.21 (a) The written examination consisted of three parts, with a maximum of 80 marks being available. The breakdown, and the objectives which were being assessed, was as follows:

Part I   – 20 multiple choice items. 20 marks. Two questions based upon each objective (all to be attempted).

Part II – 10 short-answer questions. 20 marks. Two questions based upon upon objectives 4, 5, 6, 8 and 9 (all to be attempted).

Part III – 2 open-ended questions from a choice of six. 40 marks. Testing objective 10 only.

(b) (i) The marks of Student X were as follows:

Part I — 11 marks

Part II — 8 marks

Part III — 22 marks

Total — 41 marks

i.e. $\dfrac{41}{80} \times 100 = 51.25\%$

(ii) For the remainder of the group:

Mean 49.6%

SD 7.2

PREPARATION OF RAW SCORES FOR THE PROFILE

4.22 (a) From an initial survey of both these results, George Rafferty was only able to observe that Student X had performed better when called upon to respond in descriptive prose. He therefore decided to adjust the marks for both coursework and the examination so that each would be out of 50, and to prepare a profile showing the response of Student X to each objective in an attempt to identify any one objective giving trouble. The raw scores and the derived scores (from which the profile was prepared) were as follows:

OBJECTIVE NUMBER	SCORES					
	Coursework Scores		*Written Examination Scores*			
	Raw	*Derived*	*Part I*	*Part II*	*Part III*	*Derived*
1	13/20	65%	1/2			50%
2	13/20	65%	1/2			50%
3	11/20	55%	1/2			50%
4	20/30	66.6%	1/2	2/4		50%
5	14/20	70%	2/2	4/4		100%
6	7/10	70%	1/2	1/4		33%
7	8/20	40%	0/2			0%
8	11/20	55%	1/2	0/4		16%
9	12/20	60%	2/2	1/4		50%
10	14/20	70%	1/2		22/40	52%

Totals $\dfrac{123}{200}$ marks 61.5% $\underbrace{11 \qquad 8 \qquad 22}$

$\qquad\qquad\qquad\qquad\qquad\quad$ 20 $\qquad$ 20 $\qquad$ 40

$$= \frac{41}{80} = 51.25\%$$

(b) George Rafferty of course realised that the reliability of the derived scores obtained in the written examination was of a very rough and ready nature. No account had been taken of either the number of questions set for each objective or of the relative facility of each question. For example, objective 1 was assessed by only two multiple choice items for a total of two marks, but objective 10 was assessed, in addition to two multiple choice items for two marks, by two essay-type questions for a total of 40 marks. This lack of reliability did not, however, significantly affect his particular object, which was to identify specific objectives which might have caused trouble for Student X. A profile showing the component scores for each objective was then produced.

COMPARISON OF RESULTS BY THE USE OF A PROFILE

4.23 (a) Although it was possible to read the scores by direct comparison, George Rafferty preferred to use a profile, which, when completed, provided the following information:

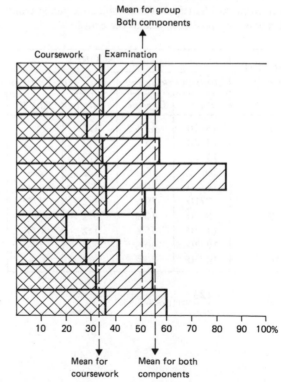

(b) From a careful study of this profile, George Rafferty could obtain some insight into the strengths and weaknesses of Student X. He therefore resolved to discuss the results of this analysis with Student X and to recommend that he paid greater attention to:

    (i) the human aspects of Geography (see the low scores for People of the World and Farming). Distance measurement from maps and use of the compass also needed more work, as did the study of continents and oceans;

    (ii) the multiple choice items and short-answer questions. Although these did not usually carry anything like the same weight as the essay questions, they covered important aspects of the syllabus and if neglected could easily lead to substantial gaps in understanding.

(c) It had been a lot of work, but George felt that this method highlighted problem areas in a very compelling fashion, and was well worth the trouble he had taken.

(Exercise 5.36)

STUDENT X – END OF THIRD YEAR EXAMINATION (JUNE 1982)

4.24 (a) The January 1982 profile did not reveal anything significant but the end of year examination, and the resulting profile, showed that Student X had achieved a slight but perceptible improvement in all subjects except Social Studies and Art.

(b) George Rafferty was delighted to see a definite improvement in Student X's Geography marks, although human Geography was still not in line with the other aspects of the subject.

(c) Claude Chippendale, when discussing the results with George Rafferty, was very interested in the apparent lack of response by Student X to human aspects of Geography. This would seem to connect with a similar difficulty noted in the case of Social Studies, and further back still to Religious Education. Student X seemed to be happier with the Sciences and other more abstract subjects.

Nevertheless, he resolved to point out to Student X that neglect of such subjects as Social Studies and Art could lead to an unbalanced curriculum. Moreover, both could be taken for public examinations and could provide useful qualifications when seeking employment.

STUDENT X – FINAL ASSESSMENT (DECEMBER 1982)

4.25 (a) This was the final assessment prior to the public examinations in the Summer of 1983. Student X had already applied for entry into the sixth form college in September 1983. The following profile of the results of the latest examination had been prepared:

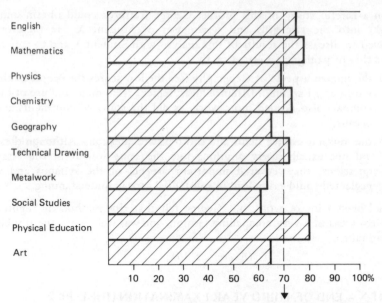

Minimum qualifying criterion for entry for higher education
(set by Plowden School)

(b) At a parents' evening, Claude Chippendale confirmed with the parents that Student X had their approval to apply for the sixth form college. There were favourable predictions of good GCE O-Level passes in four major subjects, as well as in Technical Drawing, with a possibility of two more (Geography and Art). Physical Education was also a strong asset, although it was not formally examined.

Claude was told by the parents that Student X had no particular career in mind (which confirmed his own impression), but that they hoped that Student X would go on to University, probably to read Science.

He pointed out that acceptance for the relevant GCE A-Level courses at the sixth form college would be conditional on the requisite level of passes in the O-Level examinations to be taken in 1983, and the parents agreed to review the situation in the summer of that year.

(c) The Vocational Guidance Counsellor, on learning of these results, and the predictions of subject teachers regarding the passes likely to be obtained, endorsed the decision of Student X to apply for a place in the sixth form college to take GCE A-Level examinations. In view of a technical bias, he had looked carefully at the possibility of apprenticeship, but this seemed to him not to be desirable in view of Student X's aspirations.

PLACEMENT CONFERENCE (JANUARY 1983)

4.26 (a) A placement conference was held in January 1983 to consider the possible courses to be taken by those likely to enter the sixth form college in September 1983 in order to take GCE A-Level courses. Those attending were:

David Hackett, Deputy Head, in the Chair
Heads of all Departments
Head of the Fifth Year
Vocational Guidance Counsellor
Bruce Bennett (with the PPFs of the candidates)

(b) There was little disagreement over the three major subjects which Student X could take at A-Level, these were:

English Literature,
Mathematics,
Physics.

(c) (i) The Chairman suggested that Latin should be included at GCE O-Level since at least one University which could be chosen by Student X required this qualification.

(ii) An eloquent plea by the Languages Department for the inclusion of French was rejected, largely on the strength of Bruce Bennett's pointing out the record on the PPF of the student's rejection of the subject at the end of the third year.

(d) The Head of Humanities urged the inclusion of Geography, but his colleagues politely pointed out from the PPF that the performance of Student X was consistently under par here and that it was not wise to include what could be a troublesome subject. Geology might be considered as a possible subsidiary.

(e) The Head of the Fifth Year passed on the recommendation to Student X and his parents. Student X firmly rejected Physics as boring and favoured Chemistry as being more interesting. The Counsellor and the Head of Science both attempted to persuade Student X to accept Physics, since it had more relevance to a wider band of career opportunities, but they were unsuccessful. The final recommendation for Student X was therefore:

(i) GCE A-Level: English Literature, Mathematics (syllabus to be decided later) and Chemistry.

(ii) GCE O-Level: Latin.

STUDENT X — PUBLIC EXAMINATION RESULTS (AUGUST 1983)

4.27 The public examination results were published, and those in respect of Student X were as follows:

GRADE	A	B	C	D	E	Ungraded
English	*					
Mathematics	*					
Physics		*				
Chemistry	*					
Geography		*				
Technical Drawing	*					
Metalwork			*			
Social Studies						*
Art	*					

EPILOGUE (SEPTEMBER 1983–DECEMBER 1984)

4.28 Student X entered the sixth form college and was given the following timetable in the 35–period school week:

Subject	Periods	Type of Examination
English Literature	6	⎫
Mathematics	6	⎬ GCE A-Level
Chemistry	6	⎭
Latin	4	⎫ GCE O-Level
Geology	4	⎭
Special Project	4	
Private Study	5	

Note
Special Project: This was a community project involving the reclamation of waste metals from a municipal rubbish dump, and the design and production of metal objects, either artistic or of a practical nature, for sale in aid of a local charity.

4.29 Summer 1984

(a) An assessment of Student X satisfied the 70% criterion in all except Latin and Geology. The profile produced by the college was as follows:

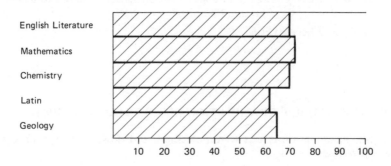

(b) At a discussion between the Tutor for the Lower Sixth and the parents, it was agreed that Student X should be entered for University, to enter in October 1985.

SUMMARY

4.30 (a) As has already been stated, the devotion of so much attention by so many teachers to one student may seem unreal, but in fact teaching staffs throughout the world attempt to provide such levels of service.

The large numbers of pupils, the widening of the curriculum and the ever-shortening amount of time which can be devoted to making the best use of the results of assessment, all too often bring feelings of frustration and disappointment to teachers; they realise that opportunities have been missed and that perhaps more could have been done by them for particular pupils.

(b) The intention of this part of *A Teacher's Guide to Assessment* is to provide a (possibly too ideal) picture of how a pupil's abilities and aptitudes can be investigated through diagnostic assessment, and developing strengths or weaknesses detected. These can then either be encouraged or remedied and progress in general monitored throughout the period of schooling.

(c) The essential connecting threads throughout this whole process are, first, that there should be a properly organised and maintained system of academic records, and, secondly, frequent, if not regular, consultation between members of staff. At Plowden Comprehensive School the records were held centrally, and there are, of course, as many arguments in favour of this solution as there are against it. The important point to note, however, is that the system should be agreed by all using it, particularly where, as here, pupil profiles were to be used for a variety of purposes.

(d) In Chapter 1, it was urged that teachers should be able to discuss details of assessment with their colleagues at all stages. They would also be well advised to be aware of the objectives of other teachers for their pupils. In the case of Student X, if it had not been noted by the staff, at the time of the initial diagnostic assessment, that a much better performance in English and History could have been expected, immediate remedial action would probably not have been taken. Action was taken, however, thus possibly preventing decline and even ultimate failure by Student X in two major subjects.

(e) The profiles of Student X for the summer of 1980 and winter of 1982 provide good illustrations of the facility with which a well-designed profile can detect either improvements or deterioration of performance in particular subjects. Nothing positive would have been gained from such information if there had not been adequate provision built into the system for staff consultation, and these are well illustrated in the case study, with particular reference to the choice of third and fourth year options, and in the January 1983 placement conference.

(f) The holiday task undertaken by George Rafferty in an attempt to understand the apparent failure of Student X to reach anticipated levels of
achievement in Geography is included as an example of diagnostic assessment in depth.

(Exercises 5.34 and 5.37)

Self-teaching Exercises

Number	Exercise

Number   *Exercise*

5.32   Look at the report from the local feeder school on Student X (paragraph 4.5) and suggest ways in which the report could be improved. Do you think Plowden used it to the best advantage?

5.33   In paragraph 4.12 the range of marks to be awarded by teachers had been set by the Headmistress. Discuss the advisability of predetermining a range of marks in this fashion. What would you consider to be an acceptable alternative system?

5.34   Approval has been given by the Headmistress to assess the personal characteristics of pupils at Plowden. Design a PPF3 for this purpose. How would it be completed?

5.35   Paragraph 4.17 (a) explains that a percentage mark had been applied as a minimum qualification for a pupil to be considered for higher education. How justified is such a process? What decisions ought to be taken in determining such a criterion?

5.36   George Rafferty attempted to discover why Student X had achieved disappointing results in Geography (paragraphs 4.18–4.23). Was this an isolated incident? How could the system at Plowden detect these instances of under-achievement in the pupils? Do you think that George Rafferty took all the relevant factors into account in his investigation? If not, what did he omit?

5.37   Having regard to the detail provided on profiles in Chapter 3, what alterations would you make to the Plowden system? Give reasons for any changes you would propose.

5

Longer Duration Self-teaching Exercises

Longer Duration Self-teaching Exercises

These exercises relate to the whole of *A Teacher's Guide to Assessment*.

Number *Exercise*

5.38   This exercise needs to be considered as a long-term project. It will require that you should be teaching a particular course to a particular group and that you produce profiles of a sample of your students. The suggested procedure would be as follows:

   (i) Select five objectives of the course which you feel need to be reviewed, for example those which you suspect are not being adequately achieved by some of the teaching group.

   (ii) Based on the assessment scheme, select a number of points in the course at which the assessment of these objectives is to be carried out. Their number and frequency will depend on many factors, but four or five assessments would be suitable.

   (iii) Select the pupils for whom profiles will be prepared. It is suggested that they should span the full ability range and that the distribution of ability should conform to a normal curve. The number in the sample will depend on the availability of your time.

   (iv) Record the results of each assessment (using standardised marks) and prepare profile forms for each pupil.

5.39 (a) List the conclusions you can draw from the profiles when exercise 5.38 has been completed? Give reasons for these.

5.39 (b) How would you suggest the preparation of pupil profiles could be made worthwhile for the:

   (i) Teaching staff of that subject?

   (ii) Pupils?

   (iii) Parents?

   (iv) Staff responsible for monitoring academic progress in the school or college?

5.40 (a)   You are to imagine that you are the head of a busy subject department or faculty which has recently decided to adopt a different syllabus for a two-year course. You have three months before the first lesson has to be given by yourself and the four members of your subject teaching staff.

5.40 (b)   Draft an assessment plan for such a course. You would find it more interesting to create a new syllabus yourself, but if pressed for time make use of a syllabus which is known to you, but not taught by you.

5.40 (c)   Write a plan of action, which sets out in stages how you would finalise details of syllabus content and the assessment plan, with the members of your department. Include a breakdown of tasks which you would delegate to your teaching colleagues, for example timetable for coverage of syllabus, construction of tests and marking schemes, drafting criteria of assessment, co-ordinating of marking, review of question papers and recording of results, etc.

5.41 (a)   Collect a batch of completed and marked examination papers and analyse the results with a view to allocating weightings to the questions or part questions (see paragraph 2.36).

5.41 (b)   Compare these 'post hoc' weightings with the weightings allocated in the course syllabus. What conclusions can you draw from the information?

5.42   Coursework Exercises Matching Criteria to Actual Work

1. *Background*
   (a) This exercise involves a comparative analysis of two documents, pertaining to the Sian Mutiny.
   (b) It was originally completed as a homework assignment by children in an inner-city comprehensive late in the first term of their fourth year.
   (c) Pupils were 'well prepared' for the exercise:
      (i) it was not their first attempt at this sort of thing;
      (ii) they had a 'good grasp' of events leading up to the Civil War;
      (iii) the teacher explained his aims to the children.
   (d) Pupils were instructed, first, to analyse the two documents, and, secondly, to produce an 'unbiased account'.
   (e) Samples A and B were, respectively, the weakest and the best assignments produced.

2. *Relation to Project Criteria*

(a) The exercise was designed to fulfil two criteria for Modern World Studies coursework for the Histry 13–16 project:

    (i) 'Pupils have studied some primary as well as secondary source materials and tried to understand, evaluate and analyse them as evidence.'

    (ii) 'Pupils have attempted some exercises which demand ability to produce a simple written synthesis or account of themes or "ideas or events".'

3. *Suggested Exercises*

You should attempt some, or all, of the following:

(a) Evaluate and moderate Sample C.

(b) Discuss whether or not the exercise fulfils the two Project criteria.

(c) Criticise the suggested moderating criteria. Suggest alternatives.

(d) Evaluate the application of the suggested moderating criteria to Samples A and B.

(e) Evaluate the suggested grades (bearing in mind that this work was produced by fourth year pupils).

(f) Discuss the merits of the exercise as an exercise.

4. *Suggested Moderating Criteria*

The following list of criteria was composed in the light of discussions held with two groups of Project teachers:

		Samples	
		A B C	

(a) (i) Place documents in a context. — A ✓ B ✓

    (ii) Reference to sources other than those indicated (where appropriate). — —

    (iii) Establish points of dispute, and what is, therefore, open to doubt, ✓ ✓

    (iv) Establish points of agreement and what, all other things being equal, can be accepted as true. — —

(b) (i) Analysis of accounts in terms of interests and perspectives of writers. (Guard against *one* account being used as a standard against which to establish the 'bias' of the other!). ✓ ✓

    (ii) Analysis of accounts (and points of disagreement) in terms of provenance of sources and likely information at writer's disposal.   −   ✓

    (iii) Analysis of accounts (and points of disagreement) in terms of their consistency with events preceding and succeeding those they purport to describe.   −   ✓

    (iv) Analysis of accounts in terms of their internal consistency and plausibility.   −   ✓

(c) Synthesis of an 'historical account' from original source.

    (i) Use of more than one source.   ✓   ✓

    (ii) Production of an account which 'goes beyond the information given' in the sense of being something *more* than a paraphrase of original sources.   −   ✓

    (iii) Explicit reference to and quotation from original sources.   −   −

    (iv) Synthesis using data *inferred* from the sources.   −   −

    (v) Judgement as to what can be said with confidence, what is probable and what must remain uncertain in the final analysis.   −   −

5. *Assessment of Grades Originally Awarded for Samples A and B by Teachers, Examiners and Moderators*

Samples

	A		B		C
	Exam System	Grade	Exam System	Grade	
Teachers Group I	CSE	2	GCE	A	
Teachers Group II	CSE	3	GCE	A	
O-Level Chief Examiner	CSE	2	GCE	A	
O-Level Chief Moderator	CSE	2/3	GCE	A	
CSE Chief Examiner	CSE	1/2	GCE	A	

Notes

In the British examination system there are five numbered grades of Certificate of Secondary Education (CSE 1 to 5) and the same number of lettered grades for the General Certificate of Education (GCE A to E) O-Level.

SAMPLE A (Candidate's own words)

9th November, 1977 — The Sian Incident — A Document Study

By 1936 there were signs that Japan was planning a full-scale invasion of China. Chiang Kai-Shek however was afraid that if he fought the Japanese first his army would be weakened and that the way be clear for the communists to secure power so he wanted to defeat the communists first. He sent a force to attack the Red Army in Shensi province but soon after he received reports that his troops were refusing to fight. The troops commander had been persuaded by the communists to join forces with them to fight against the Japanese in order to restore his army Chiang Kai-Shek flew to Sian. When he arrived however he was kidnapped by some of his own officers to regain his freedom he was forced to agree to the communists demand that the kuomintang should fight alongside the Red Army to defeat the Japanese invaders.

Chiang Kai-Sheks whole account itself was evidence in him being bias. The way he describes it makes him look, and his side, in the right, and the other side lying. He states that he was caught in civilian dress but in Shen Po Chuns account it is said that he fled with pyjamas on and hid behind a rock where as he meaning Chiang Kai-Shek said he fell into a cave. Chiang said that he was heavily guarded but Shen Po Chun said that they broke into Chiang Kai-Sheks room with no fighting but there must have been a fight if Chiang was heavily guarded.

An Unbias Account

Chiang Kai-Shek awoke at 5.30 a.m. and after exercising got dressed. Minutes after he heard gun firing. He sent one of his body guards to see what was happening when he didn't return he sent two more. He left from the back of the house up the mountains. *Shen Po Chuns* men searched the house, realised that Chiang Kai-Shek wasn't there so they searched behind the building. Behind a rock they found Chiang Kai-Shek. They then drove him to General Yang's residence where they held him captive for three days.

SAMPLE B (Candidate's own words)

9th November, 1977 — The Sian Incident — A Document Study

Chiang Kai-Shek was worked with the Nanking government and the K.M.T. (of which he was the leader) to try and organise China. They had earlier joined forces with the Chinese Communist Party but after the collapse of this force Chiang Kai-Shek decided that K.M.T.'s first priority was to rid China of the Communists rather than rid her of the Japanese. Mao Tse-tung, one of the main leaders of the Chinese Communist Party, was against this, he wanted the two organisations to join forces and fight the worst enemy, Japan, rather than each other. Chiang was, however, afraid that if the Japanese were attacked before the Communists, the K.M.T. forces would be too weakened to stop the Communists taking over. Chiang sent a body of men to attack the Red Army in the Shensi province but when they arrived there they were persuaded to join forces with the communists against the Japanese. Perhaps the commander of the body of men didn't need much persuading as most people (including those of the K.M.T.) thought it was madness to fight the communists when the Japanese were the enemy of China. When the K.M.T. refused to attack the Shensi province, Chiang decided to go to restore order himself. When he arrived he was kidnapped and forced to agree to eight proposals (demands) made by the Communist Party in favour of the K.M.T. fighting alongside them. Chiang eventually agreed to this and rules such as the Red Army being put under the rule of the K.M.T. government and being called the Eighth Rowe Army were enforced. These new rules only worked in theory, in practice the communists carried on, almost oblivious of the K.M.T. rule, as before.

In Chiang Kai-Shek's account of his kidnapping there are several pieces of guidance which show how biast he is against the *communists* and their kidnapping of him. This may be because he needed to 'keep his face' after he had tried, if indeed he had, to escape his kidnappers. Perhaps we should believe Chiang Kai-Shek's account more than Shen Po-Chun's as the former is a primary source whereas the latter is a secondary source of information.

The first bias we can read is at the beginning of the account where Chiang says that he could hear guns firing whereas Shen Po-Chun's account describes it as 'a short tussel'. When Chiang and some of his bodyguards were climbing up the mountain and had then reached the mountain top he claims, 'Bullets whizzed quite close to my body. Some of my guards were hit and dropped dead.' If the communists wanted to make a truce with the K.M.T. would they really endanger the truce by putting his life so close to death?

He continues his biased account with, 'I then realised that I was surrounded, that the mutiny was not local', was it really a mutiny? The soldiers were only turning against Chiang Kai-Shek because he refused to acknowledge the fact that the K.M.T. needed the communists to help fight against the Japanese, if they were to have any hope of defeating them. This fact is also illustrated by the word 'rebels' in the following quotation from his account, 'I knew that my faithful bodyguards at the headquarters continued their resistance and that the rebels were using artillary to attack them'. The only way the K.M.T. could persuade Chiang Kai-Shek to join forces with the communists could be described in his words as becoming 'mutinous soldiers and rebels'.

Eight proposals were put forward to Chiang Kai-Shek, among others who were hoping for the two parties to join forces against the K.M.T. Chiang Kai-Shek calls these 'the so-called eight proposals', which, to me, insinuates that he does not classify them as proposals at all. Chiang Kai-Sheks account finished, 'I said I had determined to sacrifice my life rather than signy any document under duress'. Although this tells us that Chiang felt strongly about joining forces with the communists, did he really feel strong enough to sacrifice his life for it? Later, we find, that he did agree to these proposals.

The evidence of bias in Shen Po-Chun's account of the capture of Chiang Kai-Shek at Sian is entirely different to Chiang's own account. This may be because this account is a secondary source of information (therefore the author may have added or deducted small amounts and have distored the truth) or it may be because this is a communist account and they do not have to put on an act in order to 'save Chiang's face'.

The first obvious sign of bias is in the opening of the second paragraph, 'Generals Chang and Yang had been impressed by the Communist Party's front against the Japanese and had signed a secret friendly agreement to refrain from attacking each other and to resist Japan'. This implies that all the idea of joining forces against Japan was the communist's idea, which is probably untrue because Chiang Kai-Shek's account states, '. . . since many people had participated in the matter, he said everything had to be decided by them jointly'. I can find no reason why Chiang should lie in this part of his account, although I can for Shen Po-Chun's account. The second piece of bias in Shen's account describes much of the account, 'After a short tussel with the sentries, they broke into his (Chiang's) room, It was empty, but the bedding was still warm. His clothes were strewn about . . . . The men searched the hill behind the building. There, cowering behind a rock, they found Chiang, barefoot and shivering, clad only in a silk robe and undertrousers'. This part of the account implies that Chiang had run away when he heard the soldiers outside and that he was hiding, frightened, behind a rock. Perhaps Chiang's own account of falling is more truthful here. The fact that they describe Chiang as 'barefoot and shivering' and 'cowering behind a rock', degrades him as a leader which is what, I believe, this account aims to do. This is a stark contrast to Chiang's description of himself as in 'civilian dress'.

Shen Po-Chun's account also includes some description of the event from Mao Tse-tung, 'The K.M.T. were forced to abandon their civil war policy and yield to the demands of the people. With the settlement, an internal co-operation under new circumstances took shape and a nationwide war against Japan started.' Mao Tse-tung implies that the K.M.T. did not do what the majority of the Chinese wanted or what was best for them.

This is my account of the Sian incident, with as much bias removed as possible.

Chiang Kai-Shek had just risen from bed and was in the process of dressing when he heard a commotion outside his bedroom door. Guessging something was wrong, he sent a bodyguard to find out what, the bodyguard didn't return. Chiang and two men (officers) decided to climb up the mountain, Chiang injured his ankle when falling into the moat. They eventually made their way up the mountain and Chiang decided to retreat a little way to a cave because of the shooting of his bodyguards and because of his ankle. He knew the soldiers were coming nearer and that he had to hide from them because they may shoot him like they did his bodyguards. He realised that most of his own soldiers (members of the K.M.T.) were on the opposite side to him and wanted him captured so that he would agree to fight against the Japanese before the communists.

The soldiers found him, half dressed and shivering, due to his fall in the lake. They established the fact that he was Chiang Kai-Shek, the generalissimo, and called to some others. He was taken to General Yang's residence. Soon General Chang came to see him. He told him of eight proposals that had been worked out between the K.M.T. and the communists. He said Chiang would have to agree to some of these proposals because most other people did. The proposals included such rules as stopping all civil wars and pardoning all political offenders. Eventually, Chiang agreed to the proposals and a nation-wide war against Japan began.

SAMPLE C (Candidate's own words)

9th November, 1977 — A Document Study — The Sian Incident

1. In 1936 there were signs of a Japanese invasion and Mao Tse-tung urged the Kuomintang to join up with the communists and fight the invaders.

   But Chiang knew that after, if the Kuomintang army fought the Japanese first, his army would be weaker to fight against the communists so he wanted the red army destroyed first. He sent forces to the Shensi province to do exactly that, but heard later that his army refused to attack. This was because the General Chang Hoveh-liang was persuaded by the communists to fight Japan. Chiang Kai-Shek fled to Sian and on his arrival to restore his army he was kidnapped by his own officers.

2. The evidence of bias in Chiang Kai-Sheks account is all too clear. He has written it as a galent and brave affair. He scaled a walls of which was easy to get over. He was hurt after falling, but his brave and loyal bodyguards helped him scramble up a mountain. At the top his men were shot and realising he was surrounded he was returning to his base but fell down into a cave. Here he did

painfully express the agony he was going through with the pains he had to bear and by doing this winning the heart of many people for sympathy.

In the end he called to the nearby men surrounding him, and told them to kill him rather subject him to indignities and even after the eight 'so-called' proposals that he was to obey he still would rather give up his life than to go against his will. This to me is a very glorified account.

3. This account was written by a communist for the communists to read in 1962. This man, Shen Po-Chun was not present at the Sian incident and the article was taken from supposed eye witness accounts.

    The article was made rather to show up the Kuomintangs leader by saying he was found cowering behind a rock in only his under-trousers and a silk robe and he was bare footed (in his account the men were looking for a man dressed in civilian dress). This is a good biased and anti-Kuomintang account and there is certainly no mention of Chiang Kai-Sheks bravery.

4. At 5.30 a.m. whilst changing Chiang heard the sound of gun shots and panicked, leaving the room and hotel only half dressed. He headed for the hills accompanied by Tso Peio an officer and Chiang Hsiao Chung.

    After finding all the doors locked they scaled the walls and waded through the moat surrounding the place, leaving their clothes damp and cold, but none of the men were hurt. When passing the mountain temple his bodyguards on duty there were afraid for their lives and so they joined Chiang. As they reached the top of the mountain the men surrounding them opened fire and the bodyguards fell to the ground. Chiang was forced to leave them and continued on his way.

    The headquarters were surrounded and so Chiang had no choice but to hide. He hid in a cave in the mountain side, but by dawn he was suffering from the cold and so weary and exhausted that he called to nearby men, one of them being Chiang Hsiao-Chung, one of his fellow officers and he was taken and held prisoner.

    But he wouldn't agree to the eight proposals given to him and told them he would rather die than agree to them.

Suggested Further Reading

Suggested Further Reading

Angus, E. (1974), Evaluating Experimental Education, *New Directions*, No. 6, 77–84

Ball, C. and Ball, M. (1973), *Education for a Change* (Penguin, London)

Beck, B. and Becker, H. (1969), Modest Proposals for Graduate Programs in Sociology, *American Sociologist*, **4**, 227–34

Black, H.D. and Dockrell, W.B. (1977), *The School Based Assessment in the Affective Domain Project* (Scottish Council for Research in Education, Edinburgh)

Black, P.J., Eggleston, J.F. and Mathews, J.C. (1970), *Examining in Advanced Level Science Subjects of the GCE* (Joint Matriculation Board Occasional Publications, Manchester)

Bloom, T.K. (1974), Peer Evaluation — A Strategy for Student Involvement, *Man, Society and Technology*, **33**, 137–8

Broadfoot, P. (1979), *Assessment, Schools and Society* (Methuen, London)

Burke, R.J. (1978), Some Preliminary Data on the Use of Self-evaluation and Peer Ratings in Assigning University Courses Grades, *Journal of Educational Research*, **62**, 444–8

Deale, R.N. (1975), Assessment and Testing in the Secondary School, *Schools Council Examinations Bulletin 22* (Evans/Methuen Educational, London)

Dean, J. (1972), *Recording Children's Progress* (Macmillan Education, London)

Duckworth, D. and Hoste, R. (1976), Question Banking — An Approach Through Biology, *Schools Council Examinations Bulletin 35* (Evans/Methuen Educational, London)

Dunn, S,S, (ed.) (1974), *Public Examinations — The Changing Scene* (Rigby, Adelaide)

Eggleston, J.F. and Kerr, S.F. (1969), *Studies in Assessment* (English Universities Press)

Eisner, E. (1972), *Educating Artistic Vision* (Macmillan, New York)

Ferguson, S. (1967), *Projects in History* (Batsworth, London)

Flanagan, J.C. (1950), Units, Scores and Norms, in *First Course in Statistics*, ed. E.F. Lindquist (Houghton Miflin, New York)

Foster, J. (1971), *Recording Individual Progress* (Macmillan Education, London)

Fred Learns Basic Statistics (1979), (Continua Publications)

Furst, E.J. (1958), *Constructing Evaluation Instruments* (Longman Group, London)

Garrett, H.E. (1965), *Statistics in Psychology and Education* (Longman Group, London)

Hamilton, J.B., Norton, R.E., Fardig, G.E., Harrington, L.G. and Quinn, K.M. (1977), *Determine Student Grades*, Module D5, Professional Teacher Education Module Series (The Center for Vocational Education, American Association for Vocational Instructional Materials, University of Georgia)

Hanson, J.J. (1975), *The Use of Resources* (Allen & Unwin, London)

Hitchman, P.J. (1966), *Examining Oral English in Schools* (Methuen, London)

Hoffman, B. (1962), *The Tyranny of Testing* (Collier Macmillan, New York)

Hopkinson, D. (ed.) (1978), *Standards and the School Curriculum* (Ward Lock Educational, London)

Hudson, L. (1966), *Contrary Imaginations* (Methuen, London)

Hudson, B. (ed.) (1973), *Techniques of Assessment* (Methuen, London)

Jackson, S. (1974), *A Teacher's Guide to Tests and Testing* (Longman Group, London)

James, W. (1902), *The Varieties of Religious Experience* (Modern Library, New York)

Jones, R.T. (1969), Multi-form Assessment, a York Experiment, *Cambridge Review* (15th November)

Kibler, R.J., Barker, L.L. and Miles, D.T. (1970), *Behavioural Objectives and Instruction* (Allyn & Bacon, Rockleigh, NJ)

Klug, B. (1977), *The Grading Game* (NUS Publications, London)

Krathwohl, D.R. (1975), Stating Objectives appropriate for Program for Curriculum and for Institutional Material Development, *Journal of Teacher Education*, **XVI**, No. 1, 83–92

Lewis, D.G. (1965), Objectives in the Teaching of Science, *Educational Research*, **VII**, 186–99

Lewis, D.G. (1967), *Statistical Methods in Education* (University of London Press)

Lewis, D.G. (1974), *Assessment in Education* (University of London Press)

Lindvall, C.M. (1964), *Defining Educational Objectives* (University of Pittsburgh)

Lopez, F.M. (1966), *Evaluating Executive Decision Making* (American Management Association, New York)

MacDonald, B.M. (1976), *Education and the Control of Education in Curriculum and Evaluation Today, Trends and Implications*, Schools Council Research Studies (Macmillan Education, London)

Macintosh, H.G. (1976), *Assessing Attainment in the Classroom* (Hodder & Stoughton, London)

Macintosh, H.G. (1983), The Structuring of Questions, *History News* (Journal Natal History Teachers Association, Vol 19, March 1983)

Mager, R.F. (1962), *Preparing Instructional Objectives* (Fearon, Palo Alto)

Marcus, D. (1973), *Reports and Reporting*, The Bosworth Papers (Bosworth College Bookshop, Desford, Leicestershire)

Morris, L.L. and Fitzgibbon, C.T. (1978), *How to Deal with Goals and Objectives* (Center for Vocational Education, Sage Publications, University of California)

Mullis, I.V.S. (1974), The Primary Trait System for Scoring Writing Tasks, *National Assessment of Educational Progress* (E.G.S., Denver, Colorado)

Murray, H. (1938), *Explorations in Personality* (Oxford University Press, New York)

Nuttall, D.L. and Willmott, A.S. (1972), *British Examinations – Techniques of Analysis* (National Foundation for Educational Research, Slough)

Otter, H.S. (1968), *A Functional Language Examination* (Oxford University Press, London)

Peters, R.S. (1967), What is an Education Process? *Concept of Education* (Routledge & Kegan Paul, London)

Petter, G.S.V. (1978), *Standards and the School Curriculum* (Ward Lock Educational, London)

Reid, N.A., Croft, A.C. and Jackson, P.F. (1977), *Progressive Achievement Test: Study Skills Tests* (New Zealand Council for Educational Research, Wellington)

Report of a Study Group on 16+ Pre-Employment Courses (1979), *A Basis for Choice* (Further Education Curriculum Review and Development Unit, Department of Education and Science, London)

Schwab, J (1969), *College Curriculum and Student Relations* (University of Chicago Press)

Shipman, M. (1979), *In-School Evaluation* (Heinemann Educational, London)

Shocksmith, G. (1968), *Assessing through Interviewing* (Pergamon Press)

Simpson, E.F. (1966), *Classification of Educational Objectives — Psychomotor Domain* (University of Illinois)

Stones, E. and Anderson, D. (1972), *Educational Objectives and the Teaching of Psychology* (Methuen, London)

Straughan, R. and Wrigley, J. (ed.) (1980), *Values and Evaluation in Education* (Harper & Row, London)

Taylor, J.L. and Walford, R. (1973), *Simulations in the Class Room* (Penguin, London)

The Second National Assessment of Writing (1978), National Assessment of Educational Progress (Education Commission of the States, Denver, Colorado)

Turney, C., Cairns, L.G., Williams, G., Hatton, N. and Owens, L.C. (1973), *'Microteaching'* and *'Sydney Microskills'* (Sydney University Press)

Valette, R.M. (1960), *Modern Language Testing* (Harcourt Brace Jovanovich, New York)

Warburg, J. (1961), *The Best Chosen English* (University College, London)

Ward, C. (1980), *Designing a Scheme of Assessment* (Stanley Thornes, Cheltenham)

Willmott, A.S. and Hall, C.G.W. (1975), *O Level Examined. The Effect of Question Choice*, Schools Council Research Studies (Macmillan Education, London)

Willmott, A.S. and Nuttall, D.L. (1975), *The Reliability of Examinations at 16+*, Schools Council Research Studies (Macmillan Education, London)

Wood, R. (1968), Objectives in the Teaching of Maths, *Educational Research*, **X**, 83–98

Index and Glossary

Notes

1. For the purposes of easier identification the five chapters are numbered as follows:

   1 Purposes and Objectives
   2 Techniques of Assessment
   3 Reporting of Information Obtained from Assessment
   4 Imaginary Case Study — Assessment of an Individual Student
   5 Longer Duration Self-teaching Exercises

2. The material is cross-indexed, and an explanation or a definition of some of the terms is included where the meaning could be uncertain.

3. The key to the system of indexing is as follows;

   Example '1.30 (a) (iii)' refers to:

   Chapter 1 — Purposes and Objectives
   Paragraph 1.30 — When to Assess — Timing
   Sub-paragraph (a) — Stages in a Course of Study
   Sub-paragraph (iii) — Terminal Assessment

Index and Glossary

Key Factors (Curriculum Evaluation)
*Aspects of activity within a school
which are capable of identification
and evaluation, for example remedial
provision within the area of academic
standards.*

Knowledge
necessity to organise and explain
1.37 (a)
principles (Saupe)   1.Appendix B
(B.7 (a)–(h))
taxonomy (Bloom)   1.14 (a)
testing of   2.19 (c)

Language
advantages of, higher ability   2.23 (b)
assessment of, oral tests   2.45 (c)
continuous assessment of   1.30 (b)
(iv)
criteria of assessment   2.Appendix A
(A.1–A.9)
objectives   1.Appendix B (B.2)

Latin
university entrance requirement
4.26 (c) (i)

Learning
Saupe's principles of   1.Appendix B
(B.7)

Levels of Measurement   *The various
devices by which the performances of
individuals can be compared one with
another.*
scales for   3.Appendix A2.1 (f)

Linear Subjects   *Subjects for which
the teaching is organised in successive
stages.*
continuous assessment of   2.4 (b)

Linguistic Skills
criteria of assessment   2.Appendix A
(A.5)

Literature   criteria of assessment
2.Appendix A (A.7)

Local Education Authority (LEA)
*The Education Department of a local
government such as Camshot County
Council.*
assistance from   4.11

Local History Syllabus
aims and objectives   1.11 (d)
alternative syllabus   1.11 (e)

Markers
inconsistencies in   2.35 (c)–(f)
standardisation of scores of
3.Appendix A2.5
variations in   1.24 (a) (iii), 1.24 (b),
2.32 (b)

Marking
analytical   2.29, 2.30
criteria related   2.29 (b), 2.33
impression   2.31
methods of   1.25 (e)
of multiple choice items   2.6 (a),
2.9 (a) (iii)
of orals   2.45–2.47, 2.Appendix A
(A.9), 2.Appendix B
of practicals (problems)   2.43 (b)
of short-answer questions   2.19 (a)
(iii)–(iv)
of structured questions   2.21 (a)
·policy regarding missing work
2.57 (a) (iv)
positive and negative   2.34
scales,   3.Appendix A2.1 (f) and (g)
scales, composition (language)
2.Appendix A (A.2 (b))
scales, comprehension (language)
2.Appendix A (A.3 (b))
scales, orals (language)   2.Appendix
A (A.9 (c))
scales, practicals (science)   2.43,
2.Appendix A (A.10 (b)–(c))
scales, projects (science)
2.Appendix A (A.14 (a)–(b))
scales, special study (science)
2.Appendix A (A.13 (c))
schemes. limitations of   2.28 (e),
2.33 (b) (i), (ii), (iii), 2.35 (a)